AF531425

SUSTAINABLE FORESTRY
People, Culture and Economics

SUSTAINABLE FORESTRY
People, Culture and Economics

Edited by
Somnath Ghosal

L.G. PUBLISHERS DISTRIBUTORS

First Published, 2013

ISBN 978-81-910382-9-3

Published by
LG PUBLISHERS DISTRIBUTORS
49, Gali No. 14, Pratap Nagar
Mayur Vihar Phase I, Delhi 110 091
Tel : 011 2279 5641 email: lgpdist@gmail.com

Printed at
Sapra Brothers, Delhi 110 092

Contents

Preface

Sustainable management of forests may play an important role for human well- being in future. New challenges related to forest cover management are becoming an important issue for environmentalists, forest scientists, social scientists as well as for planners. Forests were, till the recent past, considered for their product (timber and non-timber) value. However, for socio-economic development and to establish rights of marginal people (both within forests and fringe areas), sustainable forest governance can play a positive role.

With the rapid urbanisation and the growth of population, management of natural forest covers has become a challenging task for the government Forest Departments in the Global South. Rights of the native forest dwellers over forest area are making it necessary to reorganise the forest management policy. Giving the native forest dwellers the ownership rights over forest areas is considered one of the most useful tactics to save the natural forest covers through the vigorous involvement of local forest dwellers. For the management of existing forest covers and the inclusion of new areas under green covers, the economic status of the indigenous forest communities of that particular area and their social lives are important issues that are to be considered. More than 90 per cent of total Indian forest cover is owned either by the state or central government. These forest covers are classified as reserved forests, protected forests, unclassed state forests, sanctuaries and national parks. One of the most important criteria for the division of such forest covers is the accessibility of forest dwellers over the forest area for the harvesting of forest products for commercial as well as household needs.

Considering the number of forest villages and the number of indigenous population in Indian forest areas, decentralisation of forest management has been accepted by the central as well as state governments. Although, the theory of decentralised forest governance in India received enough attention by national and international organisations, it still needs to be assessed as to how much the target of sustainable forest management, and subsequently, the socio-economic improvement of forest dwellers has been fulfilled.

Forests are the source of different kinds of floral and faunal species. Protecting native forest biodiversity means saving different endangered species. With the increase in forest products harvesting for household and commercial purposes since World War II, the pressure on forest areas has increased a lot. However, due to the active participation of indigenous forest dwellers through Joint Forest Management (JFM), the areas under forest covers have increased in India considerably in the last three decades. Presently, the success of JFM in India has been followed by some other countries as well. The success behind JFM was the protection of forest dwellers' rights by endowing them with equal right as that of the Forest Departments owned over the forest resources. Recent research shows that more than 275 million people living close to forest covers in India depend on forest products harvesting. Only 5% of Indian forest covers are under sanctuaries and national parks which are strictly protected in terms of forest products harvesting by forest dwellers or by outsiders. The remaining forests including reserved forests, protected forests and unclassed state forests are open to forest dwellers for the collection of forest products for their survival. Therefore, all these three kinds of forest covers are under severe pressure. The JFM technique has proved to be the most useful for the protection of such forest covers.

The Forest Department through the JFM technique invites

forest fringe villagers to come forward and participate in the conservation of existing forest covers and to include new areas under green covers giving forest dwellers a sense of ownership. The JFM members, who are primarily selected from native forest villages are paid as wage labourers during plantation as well as schedule felling of timber products. This schedule plantation and felling is organised by the Forest Department or by some other Forest Department authorised bodies. A minimum of the 25 per cent of the revenue generated after selling timber products harvested from a particular forest area goes directly to the concerned JFM members. Therefore, JFM is not only an initiative to manage the native forest covers with the active participation of forest villagers, it also ensures economic improvement of marginal forest communities. Apart from the management of forest covers, several other social schemes are also adopted by JFM members with the guidance from different government departments such as the Forest Department, Department of Tribal Welfare and Department of Agriculture.

The target of the JFM programme, therefore, is not only to protect the existing forest covers, but also to empower socio-economically deprived forest fringe communities and to establish their social, economic and environmental rights through their active involvement in different government schemes. Involvement of forest dwellers can reveal their traditional knowledge for environmental and natural resources, including forest cover management. The Government of India followed the strict rules and regulations produced by the British government to control illegal timber felling for at least three decades after independence in 1947. However, it has been proved that the centralised forest protection policy is not that effective to control the illegal forest products harvesting compared to the decentralised policy which allows native forest dwellers to take a willing part in the government endeavours with a sense of ownership over the native forest.

Introduction

In the Global South, an ambiguity regarding the rights of ownership of a common property resource and the rights for using the same property is quite common, particularly for those people who are struggling for socio-economic enhancement for years. Therefore, the rights of the socio-economically deprived communities in the Global South over the common property resources, such as forests, must be discussed both from the legal (actual) and virtual (effective) perspectives.

In India, the rights that forest dwellers enjoy can also be examined through the evaluation of these two kinds of rights – a) legal (ownership rights) and b) virtual (use rights). Through the study of legal rights, we can comprehend what kind of legal rights the government has offered to the deprived forest communities regarding the access of forest resources in the adjacent forest areas; whereas, virtual rights show to what extent forest dwellers enjoy their forest rights in their everyday life in actual practice.

Forest covers in India are divided into many categories. They are mainly – Reserved Forest (RF)[1], Protected Forest (PF), Unclassed Forest (UF), Sanctuaries and National Parks. Forest covers in India have been categorised on the basis of the accessible rights over the forest areas of the native forest fringe villagers and the kind of forest management practised by the state or central Forest Departments. To clarify the status of the forest dwellers' legal and/or virtual rights over the accessibility in any particular forest area in the country, it is certainly essential to identify the category of that particular forest cover.

During the colonial period, with the nationalisation (Forest Act, 1894) of forest covers in India, the British government owned legal ownership of the forest and the practice continued even after independence till the mid 1980s of the 20th century. However, with the course of time the Forest Department realised that it is quite impossible for the Forest Department staff alone to manage the entire Indian forest covers. The conflict between forest villagers and the Forest Department staff regarding the accessibility of the forest area for the collection of forest products increased with the implementation of strict forest acts and policies in favour of the Forest Department. Therefore, to reduce the anguish of forest villagers, participatory forest management was started.

A few people-friendly forest officers like Elwin, Stebbing and Brandis initiated the strategy of participatory forest management during the colonial period itself. However, the technique was augmented by the Department of Forest and Environment, Government of India only during the 1980s. Therefore, presently, although the Forest Department has legal rights over the Indian forest covers, but we see that a virtual ownership has been offered to the forest villagers for managing the native forest covers through participation with the Forest Department. Basically, there exists an analogous situation, where the Forest Department has all the rights to manage the forest covers, but, at the same time, forest dwellers have also been given rights to some extent for assisting the Forest Department to control the forest degradation. That was the beginning of participatory forest management in the country.

Through the implementation of the National Forest Policy 1988, the Central Government gave special importance to local people regarding the conservation of the forest ecosystem. With the return of the authority of forest management to the local *panchayat* (local governing body) and the direct involvement of the forest dwellers in the preservation of the forest covers, a new era of Indian forestry started (Palit, 1993). Following the success of Arabari (in West Midnapur district of West Bengal) forest management, the Ministry of Environment and Forest, Government of India, was inspired to work together with forest dwellers for the management of native forests all over India. Henceforward, the state governments also got more power over their state-forest areas. The state Forest Departments could independently take decisions for the conservation of forest resources and forest culture within their state.

The involvement of tribal people in the harvesting of minor forest products including food, fodder and fuelwood with the cooperation of forest officers encouraged forest dwellers to protect their surrounding forests (Guha, 1989). By the end of the 1980s, the central Government of India spent around $400 million through different state governments for the improvement of forest areas (which covers about 23 per cent of its total geographical area) and the forest villages (Poffenberger et al., 1996).

From the early 1990s, Forest Departments of different states started a range of programmes to increase awareness regarding forests and forest products and in each programme the participation of local people was emphasised as a part of a broader initiative to promote greater cooperation between local people and the Forest Department regarding the forest use and the management of original forest biodiversity (Saxena, 2003). Forest officers explained to the forest dwellers that for a continuous and uninterrupted supply of forest products, native forest dwellers have to undertake sound initiatives towards afforestation. To include government waste or barren lands within the official forest area, a massive afforestation programme was started following the Draft Forest Bill, 1994.

Presently, in the National Afforestation Programme (NAP)[2] forest dwellers are paid by the Forest Department for planting trees and preserving forest areas (Regional Centre, National Afforestation and Eco-Development Board, 2005). Steps have been taken to transform barren or unused non-cultivated land into forest areas through massive plantation programmes using traditional as well as modern techniques involving local forest people. In many cases, forest villagers can collect NTFPs from these areas free of cost and when the trees mature, they are paid to assist with felling operations and may be allowed to keep a proportion of the profits (usually 25 per cent) generated from the selling of the timber. To protect the forest, Forest Protection Committees (FPC) have been formed by the Forest Departments of different state governments which are often closely linked with the local *panchayats*. This communal forest policy inspired many forest dwellers to protect the old as well as newly created forest areas for the purpose of their own subsistence (Pathak, 1994).

Actually, Joint Forest Management (JFM) is a decentralised method through which native people get an opportunity to protect local forests from further degradation. The guidelines for JFM were set out in the 1988 Forest Policy (Prasad, 1999; Kumar, 2002). Observing the success of community-based forest management in West Bengal's Arabari Forest Range (in 1974), the Central Government of India gave rights to individual state governments to establish their own JFM schemes that would involve the role of the local forest communities in the management and protection of the local degraded forest areas. The main idea behind the JFM was the 'care and share' principle in which local people would be more likely to protect forests if they get a share (the exact amount of which was to be determined by individual states) of the final timber harvest (Prasad, 1999). Employment opportunities have also been developed to encourage forest-based communities to cooperate with the Forest Department. The success of the Arabari experiment even helped to secure international funding from the World Bank and the Ford Foundation to enhance the programme in other parts of the country.

As many forest-dependent communities struggle to achieve their needs for subsistence, the JFM scheme proved popular as it helped them to meet their requirements for forest products such as firewood, fodder and some other NTFPs and encouraged a long term view with regard to forest protection. According to environmentalists and NGOs (such as the Regional Centre for Development Cooperation—RCDC, Orissa), community-based forest management can be considered a social movement in eastern India. Through this system, deprived forest communities (especially tribal) regained their own age-old social and cultural lifestyles based on adjacent forest environments (Poffenberger et al., 1996). The success of JFM in India has attracted the attention of the governments of the other countries, environmentalists as well as NGOs.

Initially, the power and socio-economic differences between the local forest dwellers and the Forest Department officers created some problems in the JFM system (Bahuguna, 2000), but through prolonged discussions, these problems were solved. By January 2000, around 10.24 million hectares out of 76.5 million hectares of India's total forest came under the JFM system and about 36,075 forest protection communities were working all over India. The basic objective of the National Forest Policy, 1988 was "the maintenance of environmental stability through preservation of forest as a natural heritage". Priority was given to women's participation to increase forest cover and the productivity of the forests to meet the national demand. Presently, there are 63,618 JFM committees all over India managing 14.09 million hectares (22 per cent of India's total forest covers) of forests.

Although India has the largest professional forest service including 150,000 forest officers, only 20.6 per cent of its total geographical area is under forestry at present. About 54 million tribal and 250 to 300 million rural people still depend on forest products for their household purposes directly or indirectly (Poffenberger et al., 1996). Planned use-control and sustainable use could save Indian forest resources for future generations. In the National Afforestation Programme, steps have been taken to transform barren or unused non-cultivated land into forest areas through massive plantation programmes using traditional as well as modern techniques involving local forest people. During afforestation, however, it must be taken into consideration that those plants which are useful for the livelihood of the forest communities should be planted alongside commercially valuable timber species (Saxena, 2003). Although tribal or forest people use forests and forest products for their subsistence purposes, this usually has far less of an impact on forest ecology than the commercial collection of forest products (Fried, 1975; Gadgil and Iyer, 1989; Shvidenko et al., 2005). Therefore, the current social afforestation programmes are giving more emphasis to tribal needs and their lifestyle than commercial importance.

For the proper management of Indian forest covers, it is necessary to think carefully about the forest dwellers' socio-economic lives. Without having a thorough understanding of forest-based livelihoods, it is quite impossible to protect forest quality in India. Indigenous people have been living in or around forest covers for centuries in India, but their population has increased considerably in the last few decades. Many of these indigenous people, however, are not highly dependent on forest product collection now and are trying to find different kinds of occupations outside the forest areas. The uses of forest products for medicinal, cosmetic and household purposes have also diminished with the increasing uses of manufacturing products. Even then for the sustainable management of India forest covers, forest cultures must be considered.

It is likely, however, that as forest people broaden their livelihood portfolios, certain aspects of aboriginal forest-based culture are likely to be lost. In order to protect forests and forest culture, it is necessary to identify and promote the regeneration of those plants which have great importance in forest-based socio-economic life. This will help indigenous communities in maintaining their traditional culture without destroying the forest resource base.

Presently, it is a very difficult task for the Forest Department to improve existing Indian forest covers and, at the same time, to protect the forest-based socio-economic life of indigenous communities. A comprehensive research on forest-based indigenous socio-cultural life and its influence on the surrounding forest might be useful to calculate the use and non-use value of forest covers.

Notes

1. Reserved Forest (RF) – "An area notified under the provisions of the Indian Forest Act or State Forest Acts having full degree of protection. In Reserved Forests all activities are prohibited unless permitted.

Protected Forest (PF) – "An area notified under the provisions of the Indian Forest Act or State Forest Acts have a limited degree of protection. In Protected Forests all activities are permitted unless prohibited."

Unclassed Forest (UF) – "An area recorded as forest but not included in reserved or protected forest category. Ownership status of such forests varies from state to state."

Source: State Forest Report, West Bengal 2003-2004, p. 4.

2. "The scheme titled National Afforestation Programme (NAP) has been formulated by merger of four 9th Plan centrally sponsored afforestation schemes of the Ministry of Environment & Forests, namely, Integrated Afforestation and Eco-Development Projects Scheme (IAEPS), Area Oriented fuelwood and Fodder Projects Scheme (AOFFPS), Conservation and Development of Non-Timber Forest Produce including Medicinal Plants Scheme (NTFP) and Association of Scheduled Tribes and Rural Poor in Regeneration of Degraded Forests (ASTRP), with a view to reducing multiplicity of schemes with [the] similar objectives, ensuring uniformity in funding pattern[s] and implementation mechanism[s], avoiding delays in [the] availability of funds to the field level and institutionalising people's participation in project formulation and its implementation. The Scheme will be operated by the National Afforestation and Eco-Development Board, Ministry of Environment and Forests as a 100 per cent Central Sector/Centrally Sponsored Scheme."

(Source: http://www.envfor.nic.in/naeb/nap/NAEBwebst.html)

1

Forests, Biodiversity and Sustainable Development

Ramprasad Sengupta

Abstract: The paper intends to analyse the role of forests and bio-diversity in the sustainable development of human well-being and points to the challenges of management and valuation of the forest resources for arriving at the policies for forest land use and conservation of forest resources. We begin by situating the issue of forest resource use in the context of human economy-nature interaction to show how the scale of the human system would create pressure on the environment through competing demand for alternative land uses with impact on forests and biodiversity. As land use policy becomes a critical one for striking a balance between the equilibrium of ecosystems and meeting the developmental needs of people, one has to address the problem of evaluation of alternative land use with appropriate valuation criteria. As the government of all countries would like to know the trade off between protecting forests or biodiversity and other conflicting developmental use of land leading often to irreversible environmental losses, such evaluation of land use in turn leads us to the task of monetised valuation of ecosystem services rendered by forests among others. The forests and biodiversity represent a highly complex integrated system with intricate interdependence among its innumerable components of flora and fauna as existing in the concerned a-biotic environmental condition. The valuation or monetisation of such resources becomes therefore quite difficult and challenging requiring a variety of interdisciplinary inputs and innovative tools of analysis. While we may be able to draw upon the theory of environmental valuation of neo-classical economics in this task, the specificity of different eco-system environment and resource endowments of forests would warrant the use of case study approach to capture the ground reality and factor in the various ecological factors and generate enough results to make policy conclusion.

Introduction

The paper intends to analyse the role of forests and native bio-diversity in particular, in the sustainable development of human well-being and points to the challenges of valuation of the interdependent resources for arriving at the policies for forest land use and conservation of biodiversity. We begin by situating the issue of forest resource use in the context of human economy—nature interaction to show how the scale of the human system would create pressure on the environment through competing demand for alternative land uses with impact on forests and bio-diversity. As land use policy becomes a critical one for striking a balance between the equilibrium of ecosystems and meeting the developmental needs of people, one has to address the problem of evaluation of alternative land use with appropriate valuation criteria. As the governments of all countries would like to know the trade off between protecting forests or biodiversity and other conflicting developmental use of land leading often to irreversible environmental losses, such evaluation of land use in turn leads us to the task of monetised valuation of ecosystem services rendered by forests among others. The forests and biodiversity represent, in fact, a highly complex integrated system with intricate interdependence among its innumerable components of flora and fauna as existing in the concerned a-biotic environmental condition. The valuation or monetisation of such resources becomes therefore quite difficult and challenging, requiring a variety of interdisciplinary inputs and innovative tools of analysis. While we may be able to draw upon the theory of environmental valuation of neo-classical economics in this task, the specificity of different eco-system environments and resource endowments of forests would warrant the use of the case study approach to capture the ground reality and build in the various ecological factors into the concerned economic model of analysis. One has to however, generate enough results through a series of case studies to arrive at any generalised policy conclusion.

Ecological Footprint of Human Activities and the Criticality of Forest Land Use

Nature's ecosystems provide ecosystem services comprising both the regeneration and supply of natural resources to the human economy and the absorption of wastes arising out of their entropic use in the production and consumption of different goods and services in the economic system. Forests play an important role in providing most of these eco-services—particularly the crucial ones of providing timber and non-timber forest products for various intermediate inputs and final uses, acting as a watershed and regulating the local hydrology, controlling microclimate, conserving soil and providing the habitat of biodiversity. The eco-service rendered by bio-diversity is of crucial importance for pollination, maintenance of the resilience of the eco-system and for acting as a library of genetic and other scientific information relating to the functioning of the ecosystems. The scale of human economy in terms of the size of population and the volume of economic activities (measured in terms of Gross Domestic Product or GDP) create pressure on the ecosystem for the use of land for providing various types of such eco-services requiring different respective levels of bio-productivity for the concerned alternative land uses—like uses for crop land, grass or pasture land, forest land, water body as fishing ground, land for carbon absorption or carbon footprint, and built up land. The concept and measure of ecological footprint has evolved as an indicator of human pressure on the natural environment in terms of such land use requirement expressed in terms of land area of average global primary (photosynthetic) productivity based on an appropriate normalising rule for meaningful aggregation across various uses and various regions of the world. However, it has to be noted that bio-productivity varies both across land uses and across countries. As the primary productivity of land varies across uses and for any given use across countries, the methodology of calculation of ecological footprint involves the use of yield factors for normalising the bio-productivity of a particular land use across the countries in terms of world average for that particular use and also equivalent factors which bring in alternative land uses in terms of equivalent primary crop land requirement at global average primary productivity of crop land. Ecological footprint as thus calculated at the global or the national level represents an assessment of pressure of the scale and composition of the human economic system in terms of demand for various types of land use (including forest use) vis-à-vis their respective bio-productivity or bio-capacity.

It may be further noted that of the different components of ecological footprints the carbon uptake land in a given year represents the forest area required for the balance of CO_2 emissions not absorbed by forests, ocean and soil but accumulating in the atmosphere, in crop land equivalent units If the totality of requirement of all land uses exceeds the bio-capacity of the land and water area of a country then the gap between the two (ecological footprint minus bio-productivity) is called the ecological deficit which may be positive or negative. It would represent the measure of ecological degradation of the concerned geographic regions. However, a country can import or export commodities or resources from or to another country. The bio-capacity in terms of land use area required for the net import of a country would have to be added to obtain the ecological footprint of the total consumption of an economy (Sengupta, 2011).

The total ecological footprint per capita and the bio-capacity per capita of such different types of land as estimated shows that the world as a whole had an ecological deficit of 0.9 global hectares per capita in 2007. Besides, out of the total ecological footprint 2.7 hectares per capita in that year the share of carbon uptake footprint had been more than half, i.e. 1.41 hectares per capita. It may be noted that India had faced an ecological deficit of 0.5 global hectares per capita and out of her total ecological footprint of 0.9 hectares, the share of carbon footprint has been about one third, i.e. 0.33 hectares. Even the total carbon footprint of the world has been very unevenly distributed across the countries. The per capita carbon footprint of USA had been 6.51 global hectares while that of India and China had been 0.33 hectares and 1.13 hectares respectively. China's carbon footprint has been 3.5 times that of India (Table 1).

The total per capita ecological footprint of the world increased in global hectares from 7.0 in 1971 to 17.4 in 2005, while the bio-capacity increased from 13.0 in 1961 to only 13.4 in 2005, causing the ratio of per capita ecological footprint to bio-capacity ratio to increase from 0.54 in 1971 to 1.31 in 2005, the overshoot taking place some time around 1990.

It is highly important to notice that while the bio-capacity of the forest land would be exceeding forest land footprint at the global level and at least for some nations as for example it was in 2007, the major share of the total ecological footprint of the world has been carbon footprint which has been responsible for the experience of greenhouse gas accumulation in the atmosphere and global warming. As this is measured in terms of forest land required for absorbing the balance of CO2 emission from fossil fuel not absorbed by soil and ocean and nor captured for storage, there will be huge pressure for expanding the forest cover and curtail other land use if the climate is to be stabilised by the recycling of the entire unabsorbed carbon through afforestation.

It is therefore not unusual that there would arise an opposite pressure for deforestation arising from the growing demand for land use for the primary products of food, fodder, fibre and other agricultural products with growth of population income on the one hand and for the removal of poverty, unemployment, hunger, malnutrition and diseases on the other through policy intervaluation on welfare grounds. There is similar pressure for land use change away from forest for meeting the land demand for infrastructural development, industrialisation and urbanisation induced by high economic growth. The availability of land has now emerged as the greatest bottleneck factor for the purpose in India. While the development of science and

Table 1: Ecological Footprint and Bio-capacity, 2007

	ECOLOGICAL FOOTPRINT (global hectares per capita)							*BIO-CAPACITY (global hectares per capita)*							
	Population (million)	*Total Ecological Footprint*	*Cropland Footprint*	*Grazing Footprint*	*Forest Footprint*	*Fishing Ground Footprint*	*Carbon Footprint*	*Built-up Land*	*Total Biocapacity*	*Cropland*	*Grazing Land*	*Forest*	*Fishing Ground*	*Built Land*	*Ecological (Deficit) or Reserve*
World	6.476	2.7	0.64	0.26	0.23	0.09	1.41	0.07	2.1	0.64	0.37	0.81	0.17	0.07	(0.6)
High Income Countries	972	6.4	1.15	0.28	0.61	0.17	4.04	0.13	3.7	1.42	0.33	1.20	0.58	0.13	(2.7)
Middle Income Countries	3.098	2.2	0.62	0.22	0.16	0.09	1.00	0.08	2.2	0.62	0.40	0.83	0.23	0.08	0.0
Low Income Countries	2.371	1.0	0.44	0.09	0.15	0.02	0.26	0.05	0.9	0.35	0.28	0.13	0.07	0.05	(0.1)
China	1323.3	2.1	0.56	0.15	0.12	0.07	1.13	0.07	0.9	0.39	0.15	0.16	0.06	0.07	(1.2)
India	1103.4	0.9	0.40	0.01	0.10	0.01	0.33	0.04	0.4	0.31	0.01	0.02	0.04	0.04	(0.5)
Japan	126.1	4.9	0.58	0.04	0.24	0.28	3.58	0.08	0.6	0.16	0	0.27	0.06	0.06	4.3
North America	330.5	9.2	1.42	0.32	1.02	0.11	6.21	0.10	6.5	2.55	0.43	2.51	0.88	0.10	2.7
Canada	32.3	7.1	1.83	0.50	1.00	0.21	3.44	0.09	20	4.89	1.80	9.30	3.96	0.09	13.0
USA	298.2	9.4	1.38	0.30	1.02	0.10	6.51	0.10	5.0	2.30	0.29	1.78	0.55	0.10	(4.4)
Europe (EU)	487.3	4.7	1.17	0.19	0.48	0.11	2.58	0.17	2.3	1.00	0.21	0.64	0.29	0.17	(2.4)

Source: Global Footprint Network 2008, www.footprintnetwork.org

technology can help to ease the situation by conserving land use, the critical issue of meeting the challenge of balancing the need for removing poverty, hunger, malnutrition and infrastructural development on the one hand and that of conservation and expansion of forests for maintaining the local and global ecosystem in equilibrium on the other would call for careful formulation of the land use policy.

However, such a method of assessment of ecological stress has a built in bias. Table 1 shows apparently no deficit of bio-capacity to meet the human requirement of cropland, pasture land, fishing ground, built up area and even forest area for all purposes other than that of carbon uptake. This however does not mean that the product markets of goods and services produced out of the supplies from such land use have all been in equilibrium. As dualism exists in the development process with growing disparities between the rich and the poor in spite of the process of globalisation, it remains a fact that millions of the poor are marginalised in some of the product markets of essential commodities. It is the deficiencies in the supply of many of the life support requirements like those of food, fodder, fibre and shelter for the poor which are expressed in terms of existence of malnutrition, illiteracy, homelessness, etc. just as global warming is an expression of non-availability of bio-capacity of land for sufficient carbon uptake. Thus both the measures of ecological footprint and ecological deficit are incomplete expressions of eco-pressure and eco-scarcity when we compare the total need of support from nature for the basic needs of all the humans with earth's bio-capacity.

However the policy issues relating to forest land use and forest management involve the careful consideration of the property rights on forests and forest products and the valuation of forest products and the forest eco-services including bio-diversity. The common property nature of forests the public good character of some of its eco-service products and their non-marketability pose challenges in developing institutional arrangements for the efficient resource allocation and management. The latter would be of importance for ensuring cost effective conservation of forest resources as well as for the rental valuation for signalling the true scarcity of such resources.

While the valuation of marketable forest products may be conceived as one of private goods giving market-based assessment of the scarcity rent/royalty values of the concerned biomass products, the valuation of forest eco-services becomes quite challenging as they are not only non-marketable but also themselves arise from the functioning characteristics of the ecosystems whose various components are interdependent and represent a highly complex and integrated system. The bio-diversity which itself can be conceived as an asset and attribute of forests is also worth for separate valuation for arriving at a bio-diversity conservation policy. In view of the interdependence among the different components of the forest ecosystem which are integrated in highly subtle and complex ways, we cannot treat the forest ecosystem to be a box filled with unrelated objects that we can remove or replace any one of it at will with little or no effect on others through externality. Such resources like forest ecosystem or biodiversity are therefore not amendable to the simple marginalist principle of valuation. This requires development of appropriate models of economic valuation by duly factoring in the ecological factors involved in such problems for capturing interdependences into the basic economic model. However once output yielding some tangible benefits from a forest ecosystem has been identified, the items of costs have to be ascertained for the protection for the concerned forest ecosystem services to obtain the defensive cost-based valuation of the eco-services using a production function approach of environmental quality or benefit. The pre-existing methods of valuation of environmental economics like those of revealed preference, production function, dose-response and stated preference may have to be adopted with ingenuity on the other hand for the purpose of estimation of the value of identified benefits.

Why Biodiversity is of Special Importance

The issue of biodiversity which the forest ecosystem provides, deserves some special mention in the context of valuation as well as conservation policy. Biodiversity is a part of the forest ecosystem which needs to be properly conceptualised for understanding the deeper challenges of its valuation. Biodiversity is not just the number of variety of species that exists, but also the evenness or unevenness in the distribution of population of organism across species. It is the extent of the variability in genetic characteristics across species and organisms and not the volume of total species and organisms as such which is of importance in respect of biodiversity. Its value lies not only in the use value of the component species, but also from the options of future use of species for medicinal and other consumptive purpose and for biotechnological discoveries out of genetic resources through R & D, etc.. There is also the important indirect use value that the diversity factor provides in the form of provision of resilience to the ecosystem by reducing the probability of any species getting extinct in the case of occurrence of an external shock and therefore raising the volume of the conserved genetic resource for further use after the shock. There is a notion of distance of the characteristics of one species from another at the different taxonomic level of classification. The diversity factor is captured by the dispersion of distribution of the species/organisms in terms of such distances. It is this diversity that conditions the interactive behaviour or relationships among species and and their interaction with the surrounding a-biotic elements and provides the robustness of the eco-system in maintaining the stability of its equilibrium.

The value of biodiversity thus need not be the same as the value of conserving any endangered species as such, since the most endangered species need not be genetically the most distinct and distant in characteristics contributing highest to the diversity at the margin (Pearce, 2001). As the probability of survival of a species depends on its ability to adapt itself to the new environment emerging after the shock, there are, however, vast uncertainties in such ability of the species and in the ability of the ecosystem to reorganise itself to adapt to the changing situation so that the eco-system in its totality may stand the chance of survival with all its major characteristics. In the case of such uncertainties being vast, one has to take a precautionary approach in conservation policy as the cost benefit analysis of biodiversity conservation becomes difficult for obtaining a reliable estimate of the net present value (NPV) or internal rate of return (IRR). It is nevertheless important to understand the functioning of species interaction and the challenge of conservation of forest or biodiversity in our understanding some of the basic issues of alternative land uses, sustainable forest management and the forest and biodiversity valuation for arriving at the right policies for sustainable development.

While valuation of eco-services as well as that of biodiversity are important for deciding allocation of land among various alternative uses for sustainable development and also for the choice of strategy of bio-diversity conservation. We have just outlined in the preceding sections the sources of values of biodiversity as well as the conceptual and methodological framework of the valuation of such complex assets. In view of the role of interdisciplinary factors in determining the relationship between the growth or decline in biodiversity and the associated flows of values accruing to a society, the precise methods of valuation are often case-specific depending on the nature of interdisciplinarity involved although these would follow some common broad methodological principle of economic analysis. In view of the huge diversity within and across our various eco-system more of research in the area is needed to acquire more insight into the cause of value and reliable estimates of value of the diversity factor.

The valuation of biodiversity is often confused to be just the valuation of various biotic species individually or in their totality in an ecosystem. It is not just the volume of different species, but also that of diversity which is important for the stability of the ecosystem behaviour. This valuation would in fact be critically important in the policy context of protection of endangered species and its cost-benefit analysis.

The ecological deficit and human poverty together define the state of environmental degradation and human deprivation indicating both the pressure of scale and institutional deficit in equitable sharing of the social product. Analysis of ecological footprint focuses on the consumption need of humans. The entire discussion of the preceding section was with reference to the adequacy of the bio-productivity of land for meeting directly or indirectly the requirement of actual human final consumption. The issue of biodiversity further raises the issue adequacy of availability bio-productive land for meeting the requirements for food and habitat of all non-human species. The human appropriation of net primary production of the world is in fact a critical factor for determining ecological stress in the form of pressure on biodiversity.

Concept and Measurement of Biodiversity: Biodiversity as an Indicator of Impact of Human Intervention

In the natural environment of an ecosystem the biotic component is found to contain great diversity comprising a wide range of species of plants, animals and microorganisms in a square mile of forest or ocean. Biodiversity is defined as the variability among living organisms and the ecological complexes of which they are part. The diversity can be defined within and across species and ecosystems and is manifested at species, genetic and ecosystem levels. This diversity as observed has however the feature that a few species dominate in the distribution of the total population of all organisms of the concerned place. A few common species are associated with a large number of rare species. A hardwood forest, may for example, contain 50 species of trees of which half a dozen or less would possibly account for 90 per cent of the timber. Similarly if a sample of vegetation of a grass land is taken it may contain 30 grass species, while it will not be surprising if it is found that one grass species having a share of 25 per cent in the total standing biomass, one third of species having a share of 85 per cent and the remaining two thirds having only a share of 15 per cent of the total. The distribution can be even more skewed when one analyses samples of animal life particularly of small organisms. However, such a distributive pattern does not mean that the uncommon species are not important for determining or maintaining the characteristics of an ecosystem.

Another feature of biodiversity in a natural environment is that the diversity has a relationship with the size of the organism.

Diversity is greater in small organisms than in large. We will, for example, find a larger variety of mites than mammals in a forest. Besides, the extent of diversity also depends on the conditions of existence of the living organism. The diversity is reduced where the conditions of existence are severe or geographically isolated—as, for example, in the arctic or in an island.

Human activities, however, create selective pressure on the biodiversity of a natural environment and tend to reduce it. First of all, economic activities in the primary sector such as agriculture, fishery, forestry, etc. try to modify the concerned ecosystem. Economic objective would like to target a crop species to become the dominant species in an agricultural field. Even in such a situation the natural tendency of diversity tends to persist. If no herbicide or weed control measures are applied, even a grain field will show that one food crop is associated possibly with 10 other species of herbaceous plants with a share of about 7 per cent of aggregate standing biomass. In view of the natural tendencies for diversification, it is not surprising that whenever we try to control the growth of other non-target species in the field, a large amount of energy would be required as subsidy to the field to prevent such growth. Besides, the interdependence among species plays an important role and function of an individual species in an ecosystem. Elimination of some of these species may so alter the condition of the existence of even the protected species (as in the case of agricultural crops or floriculture, etc.) that the latter may require directly or indirectly energy subsidy from outside the ecosystem for survival or growth. The same reasons would explain high requirement of energy in the form of mechanical and chemical work.

The major point of conflict between the human economy and nature's ecosystem arises from the impact of human activity on bio-diversity. Since any production system gives rise to wastes some of which are inorganic and non-biodegradable containing toxic hazardous elements and flowing into the sink of nature, the economic system is introducing new limiting factors like pollution into the ecosystem. The sewage and industrial waste pouring into a stream or chronic overdose of insecticides in agriculture or forests would affect the species structure of the ecosystem. As the new limiting factors might be killing for the conditions of existence of many species, the diversity will go down which is often accompanied by boom in population of the surviving species in the system. If we have any biodiversity index, it can in fact be a good measure of level of pollution due to the pressure of economic activities on the ecosystem. It would, however, also indicate the effect of impact of human intervention to maximise the biomass yield of the target crop species in an agricultural field or of the timber species in social forestry.

For the construction of any index of biodiversity one has to consider the two aspects of biodiversity – (a) variety component of species and (b) evenness component or the distribution of relative abundance. The variety component is given by just the absolute number of species in the domain of life forms over which we are defining the index. The evenness component is determined, on the other hand, by the evenness of distribution of importance across the different species as given by their respective availabilities in terms of measures like the amount of standing biomass. The maximum biodiversity in a domain is given by the combination of the maximum number of variety of species with perfectly even distribution of the weightage of importance as given by, say, the standing biomass.

Both the mass and variety of distribution of different species give rise to different kinds of values. The mass is related with use value, while variety has given rise to both use value option and value. It is, however, the short or medium run objectives which have induced human beings to maximise the use value and therefore the yield of the desired species using their knowledge base and providing energy subsidy, if necessary. Such optimisation has often led to mono-culture or at least the removal of several other species from the surroundings. However, biodiversity is also itself to be considered as a resource as such with high option value. Some of the biotic species with no use value as of today, may be considered to be of immense value for medicinal or industrial or other purposes in future with the increasing scale of the human system and the expansion of knowledge base of humanity. With the tremendous potential of biotechnology to contribute in the 21st century to the eco-friendly development process, and the emergence of new innovated products of great welfare significance, biodiversity would have a high preservation value.

Economics of Choice of Biodiversity

The major problem of analysis of preservation of biodiversity arises from the absence of an analytical framework of workable cost-effectiveness within which, at least in principle, the basic issues of choice can be raised and discussed. Most of the current discussions of endangered species completely lacks theoretical underpinnings that could guide policies. The main underlying issue would be how to determine the basic priorities for maintaining or increasing biodiversity and rank the biodiversity preserving project options. The recent work of Metrick and Weitzman has developed an interesting approach to handle this problem (Metrick and Weitzman, 1998). The core problem in this respect is to specify the objective that we are trying to preserve. If we consider the unit of analysis of the preservation problem at species level, the overall value of a species would be the sum of the two components which contribute to the objectives or rationale of preservation: (1) the direct utility of the species and (2) the diversity added by the genes of the concerned species. The latter is the basis of option values while the former contributes not only to the use value but also sometimes to the existence value. A project or action for preserving a species or biodiversity, would improve the survivability of the species. The improvement in survivability would be measured by the difference in the probability of survival between if no such measure would have been taken and if such measures are taken. The expected gain of taking preservation measure would be the sum of the direct utility (U_i) and diversity value in term of distinctiveness (D_i) multiplied by the improvement in the probability of survival (Dp_i). This gain is to be weighed against the cost of preserving the ith species (C_i) which is measured in terms of the opportunity cost of enhancing its protection. Thus $R_i = (D_i + U_i)\frac{\Delta p_i}{C_i}$ would yield the benefit to cost ratio which may guide the ranking of alternative biodiversity projects (Sengupta, 2001).

One major problem of course arises in quantifying the four factors of the above formula ¾ utility of a species, distinctiveness of a species, change in survivability of a species and the cost of enhancing the survivability. Several proxies may be thought of for use to represent these factors.

As biodiversity is an important issue of economic choice it is important that the matrix of species giving variety and weightage of importance adopts itself to the strength and variety of energy and other material inputs available in a given geographic and climatic conditions. One has to note here the ecological phenomenon that nature always tries to maximise biodiversity given its constraints of resources, climate and geography but not at the cost of reducing energetic efficiency of the ecosystem. It is also a fact that biodiversity is correlated with the stability or resilience of an ecosystem which would have in turn a positive relationship with the wellbeing of the existing species structure including the humans. It would however be challenging to quantify this aspect of benefit of resilience in terms of avoidance of irreversible losses.

By stability the ecologists mostly mean reversion of the structure and function of nature to the original state after an experience of an exogenous shock. This is different from the physicists' way of defining the equilibrium after any perturbation. In an ecosystem with low biodiversity and concentrated specialised structure, there is efficient exploitation of the energy and the nutrients which would be relatively abundant in availability than in a situation of higher biodiversity and dispersed structure. However, a low diversity and high energy ecosystem will have a tendency to boom and bust as the ecosystem is not replenished with the nutrients which were fast depleted by the boom, through the bio-geo-chemical cycles within the relevant time frame. Growth and decay of algal booms in a lake or rise and fall of yield of an agricultural land producing only one crop illustrates such a situation. In a tight energy and resource situation, with a high biodiversity, on the other hand, most of the energy and nutrient resources will be stocked in the biomass of the diverse species. As a result the rate of drawl of such energy/resources from the ecosystem would be relatively moderate permitting the required balance between regeneration and drawl of the resources, and would lead to a more stable behaviour of the system.

Besides, the diversity is particularly valuable for the integrity and functioning of an ecosystem as the diversity of plant and animal species and micro-organisms help the ecosystems to organise themselves to cope with the external shocks and stresses. Diversity would also matter at its different levels taxonomic of classification. Genetic variability enables a given species to survive since as environmental condition changes due to shocks some individuals would stand a better chance for survival than others due to the variation of genetic specificities. A totally genetically homogeneous species would be facing a greater risk of extinction due to the risk of being unsuitable for adaptation to the new conditions. Existence of a large number of species in a taxonomic group similarly would contribute to a greater chance of survival at least at some species level of the group so that species diversity of a higher order may be sustained. There are however certain ecosystem processes or characteristics of the functioning of the ecosystems which are crucial for also creating conditions for adaptability of individual species or organisms to adjust itself for survival in the new regime after the shock or stress. However there is a vast amount of uncertainty regarding the reorganisation of the ecosystem's functioning and the behaviour of their determining fundamental factors or processes which can only ensure if an ecosystem stands the chance of survival or not (Pearce, 2001).

As an ecosystem may flip over to a new eco-regime in an unstable situation, involving an irreversible change due to external shocks, it may give rise to problems of serious uncertainty regarding the future state of primary productivity and possible survivability of certain species. As the sustainability of economic development would require stable behaviour of the ecosystem, biodiversity becomes a very important condition of sustainable development apart from its being such a valuable resource with high option value. The positive contribution of biodiversity to the resilience of the ecosystem should also be counted as an indirect utility or use value. A precautionary approach has often been adopted regarding the policy of conservation due to the factor of uncertainty. If diversity is critical for the functioning of the ecosystem, reduced diversity would amount to reduced probability that the ecosystem will survive. Hence the choice has been often to conserve biodiversity at least of such order which if fallen short of is likely to cause the collapse of the ecosystem due to non-linear behaviour of some of the ecosystem variables and the existence of threshold at such levels of values of the variables. Hence the argument has also been that the value of the diversity can be approximately represented by the value of the functions of the ecosystem or alternatively experienced in terms of values of ecosystem products of environmental goods and eco-services at the threshold.

Preservation or Development?

Any policy decision regarding the preservation of the ecosystem or its enhanced protection in the interest of conservation of biodiversity would however often lead to the difficult choice issue between the preservation and development. Such an issue of basic economic choice of preservation of biodiversity is again linked with the choice of land use where the option of land use change for development may lead to some change in an ecosystem causing habitat destruction which would enhance the probability of extinction of some of the species. The opportunity cost of not changing the land use for some development purpose is the benefit value of the development foregone. This would provide the benchmark for comparing the value of flow of ecoservices and other natural products from preservation for taking the decision. Alternatively in some other project the cost of improved protection of a spot of biodiversity, i.e. of reducing the probability of extinction of species, may have to be compared with the flow of additional direct and indirect use values that would be obtained from such conservation of species. The discounted present equivalent value of such future flow of ecosystem services may be the value of the ecosystem which would be inclusive of the value of resources as well as that of the diversity contained within itself and should not be interpreted just as an aggregate of the economic value of the individual environmental resource stocks. The totality of the value flow would be not only the values of the individual resources but also include the value of the positive externalities arising from their interaction but internalised into the ecosystem as a whole which cannot all be captured by the valuation of the individual components of a habitat or ecosystem by the marginalist principle and then by adding them up. It is in fact the total economic value of the concerned ecosystem of an identified habitat or the total stock of biological resources contained in it which can be assessed by appropriate methodological choice encompassing all the aspects of its value including the diversity factor of the biotic resources. In case a species is endemic to the concerned geographic area or ecosystem the local extinction would amount to global extinction. The method of valuation in the absence of a market would require the local or global distinction in respect of extinction to be clarified or specified in each context so that the total economic value may correctly reflect such an aspect of criticality.

The usual framework adopted in evaluating biological resources is that of the total economic value comprising both use and non-use values. The use values are related to the actual use made of the resource and the latter would be related to individuals' willingness to pay for such values. The use value can be direct like the one derived from the ecosystem products like timber, firewood, and non-timber forest products which are often private goods and marketable with prices signalling the values. There are also use values arising from the public characteristics of the ecosystem goods or services like those of tourism or water sports, biotic resources as a store of scientific information with enormous scope of applications in agriculture or pharmaceuticals, etc. These values are often reflected in the entry fee for amenity services of a national park or drug prices or seed prices or patent prices estimated using indirect revealed preference or household production or other approaches of valuation of the concerned environmental goods and services. There are indirect use values related to ecosystem services like micro-climate control, water flow regulation, soil conservation, etc and ecosystem resilience which would all have again public good character and may be estimated by using stated preference methods of contingent valuation by asking direct questions to respondents in respect of possible values of such services. Besides all these, individuals may value an ecosystem and its resources because of the option value for possible future use of the resources or the information stored in it or quasi-option value, i.e. the value that might accrue if diversity is maintained, otherwise lost. The methods of valuation of the different components of such an ecosystem or habitat resources would depend on the precise object or component of valuation, its private or public character, the stakeholder who derives the direct or indirect utility and on the vehicle of payment for value, etc. (Abramovitz, 1997).

Concluding Remarks

How can we finally assess the overall impact of human intervention on biodiversity? One can in the ultimate analysis look at the human appropriation of net primary production of the world as an indicator of such stress. Ecologists of the Stanford University estimated that of the global net primary production (NPP) of 225 billion metric tonnes, share of 60 per cent of it being on land which is available as a food resource for all animal organisms. Humanity is now directly appropriating a share of 3 per cent of the total global primary output and about 4 per cent of that on land (Vitousek et al., 1986 and Ehrlich, 1988). Such estimates consider all the energy that has flown upto the concerned tropic level which supports the incremental biomass ¾ directly consumed by human beings as food, fodder, energy or industrial raw materials. Human beings also indirectly use NPP as the biomass consumed in fire for forest clearance, crop wastes, NPP of pasture land wasted (or fodder not consumed by livestock), etc. With the inclusion of such indirect uses the share of human appropriation rises to 30 per cent of the total photosynthetic growth of output, a staggeringly high share. Again if we consider the NPP that is annually foregone due to conversion of land from more productive use in the natural system to less productive ones (for example, forest converted into agricultural farm land, or pasture, or grass land converted into desert owing to human interferences, marsh into urban settlements), the potential NPP on land in a year is reduced by about 13 per cent and the humans' share in the unreduced potential NPP of a year goes up to 40 per cent. This estimate does not take account of reduction of the potential NPP due to the pollution arising from human activities. If, however, human beings command over 40 per cent of net photosynthetic products on land for their direct and indirect uses, a doubling of human population and economic activity would mean appropriation 80 per cent of similar net primary production. How would other species on land survive in such a situation of doubling the scale of human kind size and operation? It is beyond doubt that in such an eventuality there will be serious loss of biodiversity and retention of only selected species. The world would look like Sahel or China where nature has low primary productivity and has been subjected to over use by the human kind.

The extinction of species and organisms would have its primary impact on human society through the impairment of ecosystem services. All plants, animals and micro-organisms exchange gases with the atmosphere and their biotic composition thus contributes to the maintenance of a mix of gases in the atmosphere. Destruction of biodiversity may result in such a change in the gas mix in the long run which may end up with rapid climate change and agricultural crop failures. As already noted, destruction of forests would deprive humanity not only of timber, but also of many medicinal options for the future. Destruction of insect species may cause decline of pollinations and affect the pest control services by ecosystem resulting in sudden devastating pest outbreaks. And finally, with the loss of species humanity loses irreversibly, part of the genetic library of the planet which has immense actual and potential benefits towards human well-being. Besides, the abundance of genetic variations across and within species enables the species to successfully evolve in response to long term environmental changes. Loss of biodiversity may therefore destabilise the ecosystem by robbing its power of resilience as already noted. As ecosystem services falter, human mortality from various respiratory and epidemic diseases, natural disaster and famine may lower life expectancy to a point which would possibly be as depressing as nuclear winter. As human civilisation is a construct of superstructure over the base of natural order, the loss of biodiversity in terms of its destructive potential seems to be the most serious threat to it in the long run, next only to a nuclear holocaust.

In view of the interdependence among the various species including human beings as explained above, the biophysical limit of human appropriation of NPP needs to be ascertained and taken seriously into account for the sustainability of our development process. The biodiversity conservation and economic development have their certain important complementarities which also need to be emphasized here. The problems of the humans in the tropics have mostly been biological in origin, overpopulation, habitat destruction, soil deterioration, malnutrition, disease and insecurity of food and shelter. To resolve these problems biodiversity can be used as a resource and not as an obstacle. For food supply, humanity has come to depend only on 7000 kinds of plants for food, while there are 75,000 edible plants in existence, although most of them are lying untested and fallow. What is important is to conserve different plant and animal species, convert most of their option values into actual use value in the human economic system, and harvest carefully at an optimum rate so that they are not threatened of extinction due to overuse. Economic motivation can in fact play a positive role in conserving and using a species rather than destroying it. This would require certain restraints on consumerism which are destructive from the ecological point of view and therefore changes in human preferences and values. Like environmental quality, the biodiversity needs itself to be recognised as a service rendering good which though not marketed, should enter the preference function of individuals as consumers. The economic policy modelling needs to recognise the relevance and significance of such structural change in preference to function based on deep ecological consideration. While such reorientation of analytical framework would yield useful and important results in respect of the optimal level of species diversity and the optimum share of humanity in the net photosynthetic output of the planet, new initiatives in appropriate reallocation in land use and in the introduction of technology, values and institutions need to be taken to realise the welfare potentials of the biodiversity resource.

References

Abramovitz, Janet N. (1997), Valuing Nature's Services, *State of the World*.

Ehrlich, R.R. (1988), The Loss of Biodiversity in E.O. Wilson (ed.) *Biodiversity*, Washington D.C., National Academic Press, USA.

Global Footprint Network, htt://www.footprintnetwork.org/en/index.php/GFN/

Metrick, A. and Weitzman, M.L. (1998), Conflicts and Choices in Biodiversity Preservation in *Journal of Economic Perspectives*, Vol. 12, No. 3, pp. 21-34.

Pearce, D. (2001), Valuing Biodiversity: Issues and Overview, in *Valuation of Biodiversity Benefits: Selected Studies*, Organisation for Economic Cooperation and Development.

Sengupta, R. (2001), *Ecology and Economics: An Approach to Sustainable Development*, New Delhi, Oxford University Press.

Sengupta, R. (2011), *Ecological Footprints*, Dissemination Paper, Madras School of Economics.

Vitousek, P.M., Ehrlich, P.M., Ehrlich, A.H. and Matson, P.M. (1996), Human Appreciation of the Products of Photosynthesis, *Bioscience*, Vol. 36, No. 6, pp. 368-73.

2

Status of Access Rights of Civil Society to Forest Resources in India

Ajit Banerjee

Abstract: The paper examines the status of forest fringe dwellers rights for the harvesting of forest products for household requirements and to sell a portion of their collected products at the local market. Although equally important, the paper will not include the access of corporate and industrial sectors for the sake of conciseness. About 67 million hectares of total forest covers in India, is owned by the government. These forests are classified as Reserved Forest, Protected Forest, Protection Forest, Village Forests and Unclassed State Forests, most of which, are managed by the state Forest Departments. Based on the forest categories, the access rights for the native dwellers differ considerably in terms of harvesting of forest products.

Introduction

This paper will discuss the status of only the civil society, especially the forest dwellers and those who live on the forest fringes, with respect to their rights of accessing the forest products. The corporate and industrial sectors, although equally important, will not be included in the discussion for the sake of brevity.

More than 90 per cent of the Indian forest covers (about 67 million hectares) is owned by the government. These forests are notified as Reserved Forest (RF), Protected Forest (PF),

Protection Forest (Pr.F), Village Forests (VF) and Unclassed State Forests (USF), most of which, are managed by the state Forest Departments (FD). Hence, strictly speaking, the rights on the forest land and the property on it belongs exclusively to the government.

Status of Access Rights of Civil Society

Forest covers in India, although mostly owned by the government; certain aspects of access rights over them are contested. For example, very large areas of forests found in north-east India are classified as Unclassed State Forest. The local inhabitants, however, claim community ownership of these forests as they are using them for centuries. There are again some areas in Madhya Pradesh where the state ownership is diluted to a certain extent by rights of the local people on the forests resources. These are called *Nistar* rights which are legally sanctioned by the government. These rights are officially recorded by the state with respect to the supply of specific quantities of forest products such as bamboos, firewood, etc made to individual families. About 0.47 million hectares of state owned forests in Orissa (Patnaik, 2005), are managed by local people as self-initiated community forests. Although legally these forests are owned by the government, 4481 groups composed of a small number of families have taken over for protection and management of specific forest blocks close to these communities. The groups do not allow the Forest Department to operate in the forests managed by them.

In addition to the above mentioned contested forests owned by the states, the Government of India (GOI) and the state governments have by executive orders in 1990 introduced what is called 'Joint Forest Management' (JFM) in state-owned forests. Such areas in the country amount to about 17.3 million hectares (Bahuguna, 2004) and are jointly managed by the state government and local groups numbering 84,632 (as of 2004). In this arrangement, the village groups, referred to as *Forest Protection Committee (FPC)* or *Vana Sangrakshan Samity (VSS)*, are entitled to use Non-timber Forest Produces (NTFP) from the forest blocks attached to the group and a part of the net income derived by the FD when they sell the forest timber. The groups are also empowered to protect the forests.

In the recent past, the Indian Parliament has enacted legislations with respect to people's forest rights. One is called PESA which is a constitutional amendment and the other is called Indian Forest Rights Act, 2006. PESA provides rights to the *panchayats* in declared tribal areas to manage the NTFP of the associated forests. By the Indian Forest Rights Act 2006, the GOI is authorised to transfer state-owned forest areas (under certain restrictive pre-conditions) to local tribal individual families or communities inhabiting in or around the forests and using the forest produces and those who have been forest users for at least 75 years.

In addition to the above, there are blocks of tree-lands in the country established by farms and social forestry. These forests belong to the private owners or village communities. Such tree-lands add up to about 8.1 million hectares. These are extensively spread in the country, each tree-land block being about 0.1 to 1.0 ha. There are others of sizes less than 0.1 hectares but the numbers and total areas of these are not known. We will call them private or collective forests.

Thus, we see that forest ownership though primarily resting with the government has actually some virtual ramifications in respect of access to the land and forest produces, as follows in Table 1 below-

The nature of virtual ownership in Table 1 designated by serials 1-8 for categories of forest owned mostly by the State is varied as will be evident from the table and discussion below.

Forest Access in Serial 1 (of Table 1) Forest Categories

The categories of forests listed in Serial 1 include RF, PF, PrF and USF. All these forests are owned by the government. Acts, rules and regulations prohibit use of the forest produces in these categories by outsiders unless permitted by the authorities concerned. This is especially true for the RF and PrF; in other forests there may be some concessions of using the forest resources, but they relate only to some of the NTFPs. For example, NTFPs such as firewood, medicinal plants, leaves,

Table 1: Indian Forests: Legal and Virtual Access

Serial	*Forest Categories*	*Legal Ownership*	*Virtual Ownership*	*Area in Million Hectares approx. (rounded)*
1	RF, PF, PrF, VF, etc.	State/GOI	Exclusively government but substantially used sometimes surreptitiously as a matter of right by local people	64.00 (This area includes some of those shown under 2,3,4,5,6,7)
2	RF, PF	State/GOI	Concession of Nistar rights	8.00
3	USF	State/GOI	Ownership claimed by local tribal people as customary right holders	13.63
4	RF, PF Government	State/GOI	Occupied and managed by local communities as in Orissa	0.47
5	RF, PF	State/GOI	JFM concessions to JFM groups by executive orders	17.00
6	RF, PF, USF	State/GOI	PESA allows rights over NTFP management and benefits to the Tribal area *Panchayats* (not fully operationalized yet)	Not Available
7	RF, PF, USF	State/GOI but ownership being transferred to individuals and communities under certain pre-historical conditions	Ownership of certain parts of the forests being transferred to individuals or rights to communities by Forest Rights Act 2006	Ongoing; may add up to 4-5 million ha.
8	Private Forests, village common land forest	Raised by individuals or small groups of people in private land near home as home gardens, near farms as farm forests and in the village common land as collective forests	Dominantly privately owned. Also small area under collective ownership	8.10

RF: Reserved Forests, PF: Protected Forest, Pr F: Protection Forests such as National Parks, USF: Unclassed State Forests, VF: Village Forests sponsored by the State gums and resins are permitted to be collected on token payments. The state administers the forests on the strength of the Indian Forest Act of 1927.

The de facto situation, however, is different. People inhabiting in or on the fringe areas adjacent to the forest are mostly poverty-stricken and are dependent partially on forest produces for their primary subsistence. They also sell some of the produces they collect to the local market for supplementing income. These collections are often surreptitious, exposed to, sometimes violent confrontation with the state Forest Department guards, litigation or bribe transactions.

These accesses cannot be considered to be legitimate and yet there are substantial back-up arguments in their favour. It is well known that the people living near the forests are among the poorest in India. One of the reasons cited for the apparently unlawful activity is that their legitimate customary rights on the forest have been usurped during the colonial period by forest acts and which are being followed in the post-independence period as well. In India it is estimated that approximately 250-350 million people (Poffenberger and McGean, 1998) are forest dependent for their subsistence. This situation with a large number of people deprived of adequate subsistence for various reasons and continuing to depend on the forest produces and the government insisting on legal ownership is a dilemma of forest access.

Forest Access in Serial 2 (of Table 1) Forest Categories

These forests are also state-owned with one difference referred to as *nishtar* rights. These rights are officially documented in favour of individual families. Concessions under these rights include annual supply of NTFPs, especially a specific quantity of firewood to certain individual families. However, with increase of population, families having *nishtar* rights and others without it created a conflicting situation. In addition, enlisted families also grew in size and the amount of produce provided to them was insufficient. *Nishtar* rights therefore have become virtually obsolete in the states where it prevailed. As such *nishtar* now has got a very uncertain status.

Forest Access in Serial 3 (of Table 1) Forest Categories

This category includes unclassed state forests (USF) dominantly in north-east India. In states such as Arunachal Pradesh, Nagaland, Tripura, Mizoram etc., people's status of accessing the forests is weak and is often contested by the state. Both the government and the people claim ownership over these forests. Local tribal people practise shifting cultivation in the hilly areas which the government does not approve of. The forests are often denuded due to a short cultivation cycle. The government is trying to introduce agro forestry in these areas where people have the choice of management.

Thus, serial 3 forest category areas can be considered to have currently limited choice of access which are likely to be further curtailed in future.

Forest Access in Serial 4 (of Table 1) Forest Categories

Substantial RF and PF areas (owned by the state) especially in Orissa and a few other states were being managed as coppice forest by the state Forest Department but degradation of the forests continued. The local people in small groups started protecting the degraded forest blocks near them as they saw degradation caused local water shortage, soil erosion, etc. They, however, stopped forest authorities from entering those forests or say anything about their management and protection. Forests have improved dramatically because of people's protection. These people have access to the forest blocks under their control but they cannot take away the timber or poles as state guards do not allow it. The access to these forests therefore is anomalous.

Forest Access in Serial 5 (of Table 1) Forest Categories

These forests also belong to the government but because of the executive order mentioned earlier, the local people (due to introduction of Joint Forest Management: JFM) are entitled to certain concessions in respect of access to forest resources. They are also entitled to protect the forest and to get a share from the sale of timber.

Although the JFM system does not provide any ownership to the users and is backed only by executive orders instead of any legislative support, JFM does for the first time provide some relief and concessions to the local people. Because of JFM, local people are, without any harassment, at liberty to collect NTFPs, etc. The total area covered by JFM is about 17.3 million hectares (Bahuguna, 2004) and consists of mainly degraded forests.

There are many pitfalls and failures in JFM as well (Banerjee, 2007) but overall it is a step towards improvement in access of the forest products by the forest fringe people and forest inhabitants. In brief we can say that JFM is a partial concession that allows the local people access to the forest products.

Forest Access in Serial 6 (of Table 1) Forest Categories

PESA refers to the concessions granted by the government to the people over the forest produced in the areas declared as 'tribal'. The major concession is that the local panchayat will be administering management of NTFPs in the state-owned forests under their jurisdiction and is benefited in return. This has not become operative in many states.

Forest Access in Serial 7 (of Table 1) Forest Categories

The Forest Rights Act of 2006 and its rules of 2008 are under implementation in all the states of India. According to this Rights, the transfer of ownership/use rights, under certain historical conditions, are being made to individuals/communities fulfilling the conditions. We estimate that transfer of ownership and allocation of forest use rights will add up to about 5-6 million hectares of forests now owned by the government.

Implementation of the Act and Rules are found to be substantially short of intention of the Act and is under scrutiny by different NGOs and other such organisations. In any case this Act is a definite improvement in respect of ownership, access and use of forest produces by some of the forest dependent people.

Forest Access in Serial 8 (of Table 1) Forest Categories

These tree lands are all privately owned. The people who are the owners of these tree lands have themselves raised the trees on them, sometimes with seedlings freely supplied by foreign donors, states or by the local banks. The owners are at liberty to access the produces and dispose of them.

There is, however, a great objection made by the state regarding the disposal of the trees outside the private area where these trees were planted. This objection is due to transit rules which every state has imposed on the removal of trees. The intention is that the tree lands should not be reduced to meet the economic gains of the owners as over cutting of tree lands will lead to ecological imbalance of the country.

In brief, we can say that in spite of the fact that the government owns most of the forest covers in India, the native forest dwellers are granted a certain amount of access to them. This has been achieved sometimes by repeated use by the local people often surreptitiously or by forceful occupation and sometimes due to the concessions granted by the government itself by executive orders and legislations. Besides, individual land owners also raise trees and access them as private property. There is, however, no doubt that overall the whole situation of access to forest and forest products is normally controlled by state authorities.

Some More Relevant Issues on Forest Access

There is a conservative view that unrestricted access to forests of people at large, especially the poorer forest dependent people will lead to forest deterioration and deforestation. This is the majority opinion of the civil society of the country. They believe that 'avoidance' of access has brought about a distinct, relatively favourable difference in the quantity and quality of the forests under the custodianship of the government. There is no doubt that as of today the state-governed forests are much better preserved than those of the village collective forests. In fact, some of the latter have completely disappeared. One therefore can easily conclude that access of the people to the forests without control is not the right thing to preach.

The other opinion is that unrestricted access is akin to 'tragedy of the commons' and is not the alternative to state ownership. The alternatives are: farm forestry which has attained a tremendous success in the country. Home garden is another example; Collective forestry as in Orissa and Siwaliks or Joint Forest Management in the states are examples of success stories. So collective forestry, the details of which are yet to be fully developed, need to be seriously considered. The group further points out that although state-owned forests, especially Reserved Forests are better preserved, there is statistical data to show that their quality is also deteriorating with reduction in biodiversity and some of them are even reverting to degraded forests. The Forest Department has increased forest guards that also did not do well in protection tasks. There were therefore frantic efforts to introduce participatory methods like JFM, PESA and lately FRA. The question of transferring ownership as I propose or at least liberally accessed with some conditionalities, is an issue that has to be addressed if we wish to keep the forests useful, friendly to people and materially, socially, and ecologically sustainable.

However, this can be easily said but in reality liberal access may have so many adverse ramifications. The two most important are corrupt leadership in all forms of decentralised institutions and lack of forestry training amongst the masses. In spite of these possible problems, it is necessary to counteract them as there are many forest dependent people and many of them are very poor and will continue to remain so for the next few decades. In a few words I would say that access of the poor people to the forests has to be ensured which would mean that management of forests, participation in planning, implementation and benefit distribution with equity should be a part of management. To ensure that people's institution can successfully perform these tasks, forestry training of the native people (and not value-addition to economic produces alone) is necessary. Another important aspect would be to enforce 'avoiding selfish leadership' that rears its head every time decentralisation is resorted to.

References

1. Bahuguna, V.K. (2004). An Overview in 'Root to Canopy'; Winrock International and Commonwealth Forestry Association-India Chapter, New Delhi.
2. Banerjee, A. (2007). Joint Forest Management in West Bengal In *'Forests, People and Power'* ed. by Springate-Baginski Oliver and Piers Blakie; Earthscan.
3. Patnaik, S. (2005). Community Forest Management in Orissa: Community Forestry. April; RCDC, Bhubaneshwar, Orissa.
4. Poffenberger, M. and McGean, B. (2005). *Village Voices and Forest Choices.* Oxford India Paperbacks, New Delhi.

3

Property Rights and Access to Forest Resources

Anurag Modi

Abstract: Thakur Bhabhootsingh, the tribal chieftain of the forested territory of Bori in Hoshangabad district falling in the then Central Province of India was the first the victim of the colonial strategy of usurping forest resources from the tribal community in the name of "Forest Management". Until 1864 there was considerable local population of aboriginal tribes who practised *dhaya* or "shifting" cultivation, but thereafter the tribal populations were induced to settle elsewhere and the forest was closed for grazing. Ironically, independent India went on to follow the British legacy and has perpetuated the injustice described in its own documents. Around 1997 the government under the direction of the Supreme Court initiated the processes of settlement of rights in Protected Areas of the country. Tribal people now occupying land and residing in 'Bori', designated as a wildlife sanctuary in independent India, submitted their claims to the District Collector. They received the reply that their rights had already been settled at the time of it being declared reserved (i.e. in 1865) and there were no more rights to be accounted for. This shows how the property rights and access to resources has been the story of state power, beginning with the British. The central idea of this paper is to show how forest-dwellers' access to forest resources has reduced with every major policy initiative in recent times. While there have been new policy frameworks none of them address the fundamental question of forest-dwellers having the first right over the use and management of forest resources. On the contrary, in a continuation of the colonial mindset, forests are treated as state property, and forest dwellers are regarded as a threat. Policy initiatives such as JFM use the fig leaf of democratic decentralisation to strengthen the state's hold on forests while people's access to forest produce for subsistence is further reduced. More recent policy shifts propelled by the World Bank, such as the Green India Mission, treat forests as a commodity that can be valued in the markets for their role as global carbon sinks. This line of thinking appropriates forests for the global commons, while duplicitously blaming the forest-dweller for destroying forest resources by their bona fide use that is now global property. In this paper I will try to relate with the grassroots level as witnessed by me in the last 17 years (1994 to 2011) as a founder member of a mass tribal right organisation named *Shramik Adivasi Sanghthan* working in Betul, Harda and Khandwa districts of Madhya Pradesh.

Introduction

Thakur Bhabhootsingh, the *Adivasi* (tribal) chieftain of the forested territory of Bori in Hoshangabad district; falling in the then Central Province of India was the first victim of the colonial strategy of usurping forest resources from *Adivasi* community in the name of "Forest Management". In 1859, around 10,000 acres of land under his control were confiscated as punishment for his rebellion against the British. Bhabhootsingh was traced and hanged at Jabalpur jail in 1861. Only then did it become possible for the British to seize his territory and place it under the control of the Forest Department. Until 1864 there was a considerable local population of aboriginal tribes, who practised *dhaya* or "shifting" cultivation, but thereafter the *Adivasi* populations were induced to settle elsewhere and the forest was closed for grazing. Ironically, independent India went on to follow the British legacy and has perpetuated the injustice described in its own documents. Around 1997 the government under the direction of the Supreme Court initiated the processes of settlement of rights in Protected Areas of the country. *Adivasi* people now occupying land and residing in "Bori", designated as a wildlife sanctuary in Independent India, submitted their claims to the District Collector of Hoshangabad. They received the reply that their rights had already been settled at the time of it being declared reserved (i.e. in 1865) and there were no more rights to be accounted for.[1]

This shows how the property rights and accesses to resources has been the story of state power usurping community resources in the name of scientific management, beginning with the British. Forests were a major source of revenue and resources to build infrastructure to enhance administrative and military power of the then British Empire. The British have created absolute property rights over *Adivasi* land by creating the Forest Department, thereby restricting *Adivasi* people's access over forest resources. Tribals' access to forest resources is directly related to their basic survival. With independence nothing much changed for the local community, successive governments continued with the policy of holding property rights inherited from the British. While in forest villages, *Adivasi* children often die of diarrhoea and malnutrition; women folk are anaemic, *Adivasi* people are denied basic rights over resources, the law enforcing authority shows the selective approach and they act as a law unto themselves. The *Adivasi* people are illegally detained; handcuffed and paraded in public; denied bail even in bailable and compoundable offence by the Forest Department; even their minor children of 8 to 13 years of age are not spared and they too are sent to jail on the charges of helping their parents making "*Jhopda*" on forest land.[2]

The central idea of this paper is to show how forest-dwellers' access to forest resources has reduced with every major policy initiative in recent times. While there have been many new policy frameworks in the last two decades, none of them address the fundamental question of forest-dwellers having first right over the use and management of forest resources. On the contrary, in a continuation of the colonial mindset, forests are treated as state property, and forest dwellers are regarded as a threat. Policy initiatives such as JFM use the fig leaf of democratic decentralisation to strengthen the state's hold on forests while people's access to forest produce for subsistence is further reduced. More recent policy shifts propelled by the World Bank, such as the Green India Mission, treat forests as a commodity that can be valued in the markets for their role as global carbon sinks. This line of thinking appropriates forests for the global commons, while duplicitously blaming the forest-dweller for destroying forest resources by their bona fide use that is now global property. In this paper I will try to relate with the grassroots level as witnessed by me in the last 17 years (1994 to 2011) as a founder member of mass *Adivasi* right organisation named *Shramik Adivasi Sanghthan* (SAS) working in Betul, Harda and Khandwa districts of Madhya Pradesh (MP), India.

Colonial Appropriation

According to Pathak (1994), "British administrators in the 19th century viewed vast tracts of Indian forests as impediments to the prosperity of the colonial exchequer, as these lands could otherwise be utilised as revenue-yielding property". Thus, forests were rapidly razed to the ground both for revenue earned from timber supplies and for maximising land revenue by putting the cleared tracts into cultivation (Guha, 1994). The growing ship-building industries in England in the 1800s and the expansion of the railway network in India in the 1850s further spurred the demand for timber, leading to rapid deforestation. The risks inherent in unregulated logging were noted by some imperial officials, and they created the Forest Department to protect and govern the use of forests. They pointed out that continued exploitation of forests would severely impair the potential of forest stock to yield timber, and they advocated insulating forests from the pressure of local use. Towards this end, legislation to curtail the previously free access enjoyed by village communities was proposed. A debate ensued within the colonial bureaucracy, finally resulting in the passing of the Indian Forest Act of 1865.[3]

The Forest Act of 1878 had the provision of Reserve Forest and extension of government control over it, leading to curbs on *Adivasi* access to forests on vast tracts. For example in 1876 forest reserves covered 2.39 per cent of land area of Mandla, and by 1891-92, in 15 years, half the land was annexed and converted into reserved forest. The usurpation campaign continued in other parts of the country and invited oblique criticism from elements within the British bureaucracy itself. Thus, the collector of Nasik, E.N.B. Erskine, felt that expropriation of forests would damage *Adivasi* interests. The procedure laid down for their guidance would seem to be absurd, he wrote, "Fancy a Bhil or a Koli being told to present the officer about to enquire with a written notice, stating the nature of his rights within the forest. I would venture to suggest that no Bhil or Koli would ever give in his written notice. Could we then say that all his rights have lapsed?"[4]

Contrary to the situation in the hill tracks, malguzars from the farming communities in the plains were given access to land. "The malguzars were thus given a stake in the extension of arable land as they could increase productivity and generate more revenue. In contrast forest-dwellers, who were largely tribals, lost out in a variety of ways. Under the Bengal Tenancy Act, a minimum period of occupancy of twelve years was required for tenants to secure full occupancy rights. As Rangarajan (1996) says, since *Adivasis* practised shifting cultivation they could never get tenancy rights.

Colonial Legacy

The same trend has continued even after independence. The forest-dweller remains in the clutches of the Forest Department bureaucracy that is wedded to the colonial Indian Forests Act 1927. Neither the legal framework created by the British, nor the attitude of landlordism inherited by our successive government has changed. Even today *Adivasi* hamlets are looted and burnt down to ashes, *Adivasies* are being victimized by way of false cases and imprisonment in jail, and beaten up for asserting their rights over resources. [5]The attitude of landlordism of successive states, flowing from the British, can be further understood from the following examples. The working plan of 2010-11 to 2019-20 of Betul North forest division and a range of west forest division says all the reserved forests of the plan area have been declared reserved in 1878, the protected forest covering 103 blocks was notified in the year 1965, 1966 & 1967. But the settlement proceeding in protected forest is yet to be completed and pending with sub divisional officer (revenue department).[6]

Mitra and Gupta (2009) rightly observe, "the forest policies of colonial India continued into the postcolonial period, as exemplified by the National Forest Policy of 1952, which further reinforced the right of the state to exclusive control over forest protection, production, and management. Just as the fulfilment of imperial needs was the priority of colonial forest policy, the demands of commercial industry became the cornerstone of postcolonial forest policy. While communities were excluded from using forests, many industries were granted raw materials at extremely low prices. Large tracts of forests were diverted for agriculture, hydroelectric projects, and other development projects in the years after independence. It is estimated that between 1950 and 1980, the rate of diversion of forests to sites of commercial industries was about 150,000 ha per year (Saigal et al., 2002)".

Experience as an Activist

During the initial years of the *Shramik Adivasi Sanghthan* (SAS) between 1995 to 2001 we found that in *Adivasi* areas the inhuman practice of *Begaar* (forced labour) and *Nistari* (coercive expropriation of menial labour, hospitality and material in lieu of permission for accessing the forest) had continued well into independent India and formed a live element of forest-dwellers' everyday lives.[7] Women folk of the village are forced to work in the local official residence of the village forest officer; doing all household chores always threatened by fear of sexual exploitation. Men folk are forced to work for free for forest officers. And under *Nistari* they are forced to bribe forest officers with their share of each crop they grow and every minor forest produce they collect; often with a bottle of liquor, chicken etc. Yet they have to pay heavy bribes for repairing their houses and if caught getting *Nistar* from forest without paying the bribe, they are often tied to a tree or locked in the forest office and beaten badly. The officers of the Forest Department continue to function as feudal lords and consider *Adivasis* as their subjects. The SAS organised local *Adivasis* and through the SAS they could assert their rights over forest resources.

When these *Adivasis*, with the encouragement of the SAS resorted to legal recourse it became a routine experience for us to find that the police would refuse to file an FIR based on our complaint. Even today, if at all an FIR is filed, it is not pursued and the investigations are invariably dropped. On the other hand, the Forest Department takes retaliatory action by filing multiple false and frivolous cases against the *Adivasis* as well as SAS activists. *Adivasis* are arrested and are often denied bail by the Forest Department even in the case of bailable offences. However, contractors engaged in illegal excavations in reserve forests are patronised and are allowed to let go by paying a meagre fine of Rs. 1000, if at all. Even the lower level judiciary is often unable to come to the rescue of the wrongfully detained tribals, and has not been acting judiciously. A number of instances can be quoted where judicial officers have displayed lack of application of mind and acted rather mechanically on the request of the Forest Department. When, villagers of Ghorpadmall and Kabra village in Betul district had filed the complaint against corrupt forest officials, who had not paid their due wages, at SC/ST Police Station, Betul, 20 false cases under the Indian Forest Act 1927 were slapped against them. Though, the sections imposed on the *Adivasis* were bailable and compoundable, those arrested were produced before Judicial Magistrate Bhaidehi who had granted three judicial remands of 15 days and they had to languish in jail for 45 days before they could secure bail.[8]

Policy Intervention by the World Bank

With the onset of the globalisation era in 1991, the World Bank has played a major role in policy changes in the forestry sector in India. A study of the World Bank's documents leaves one in little doubt that a process of further reducing the accesses of the local community on the forest resources is on the cards as commercialising every inch of the world's forest has been slowly but steadily being implemented for 25 years now.

Earth Summit

At the Earth Summit, held in Rio de Janeiro in 1992, a policy principle was laid down that in addition to each nation state's sovereign rights over its forests, the world's forests would be "global public goods". This has signalled the arrival of international players in the game, adding a new dimension to a conflict over access to forest resources that was thus far limited to the state and local populations. The World Bank was a major force behind this, having prepared the ground prior to the Rio Earth summit in its "Forest Strategy" of 1991. This brought the following changes in India:

(i) The Indian government legalised and universalised JFM institutions.

(ii) By mid-1995 the World Bank and many international funding agencies began funding various forestry projects across India.

Global Forest Strategy of May 2003

According to its Renewed Global forest strategy of the World Bank, a major challenge before it is the commodification of forests. Marketing of the eco-services and certification of logging activities in the coming years is going to be one of the biggest businesses in the world. The Bank anticipates a huge eco service market, estimated around 4.7 trillion dollars a year. This is more than ¼ of the world's GDP. The certification of forests will bring in another $5 billion worth logging market to the fold of big market forces and reduction in concession of another $ 10 billion. It also talks of reducing concessions to increase the government's revenue. The concessions are not specifically defined but, many of the community's rights over forests are considered concessions. The Bank has developed a strategy for the prevention of illegal felling, ending of subsidies on forest produce, and for efficient revenue collection. Eco service would mean increase in protected areas, discouraging the local community from extracting their bona fide needs directly from the forest, creating alternative means like solar cookers etc. The strategy includes increasing the forests designated as 'protected areas' from the current 50 million hectares to 100 million.

To achieve this, the World Bank envisages policy changes that are evident in its statement, "Because their values are complex and ownership often ill defined, forests are not entering the market at their full economic value." There is another statement which further strengthens the point: "Till the long pending issue of *Adivasi* rights are settled market biggies won't enter the forest."[9]

Unlocking Opportunities 2006

The World Bank document "India Unlocking Opportunities for Forest-Dependent People in India", released in February 2006 talks of how through regeneration and conservation the community can gain. All this led to major policy changes

The Bank's strategy and policy changes in India –

(i) The Bank knows quite well that with the hue and cry about *Adivasi* rights violation market forces will find it difficult to enter the forestry sector. Hence, prior to this the finalisation of the long pending issue of forest dwellers' rights over forests in India has begun by way of drafting the "Forest Rights Bill".

(ii) The Indian government offered commitment in WTO on eco-services. It has also agreed to remove the restriction of access to the scheduled area under V and VI schedule of the Indian Constitution. The offer was made on August 24, 2005 by the Indian delegation in the Council for Trade and Services.

Payments for Ecosystem Services (PES) a New Threat

Under Carbon Credit, Clean Development Mechanism Payment for Ecosystem Services is going to be a major agenda. An Interim Report of the Planning Commission Government of India released in May 2011 titled "Low Carbon Strategies for Inclusive Growth" under subhead 'Key Elements of Mission Strategy' says, "Drivers of degradation", e.g. firewood needs and livestock grazing will be addressed using inter sectoral convergence (e.g. livestock, forests, agriculture, rural development, energy, etc). Under the PES system the local community will be paid a certain amount in lieu of the carbon they either will not generate by restricting use of fuelwood or they will earn through regeneration of forest. That means restricting the local population's bona fide needs and access to the resources. It works on the theory that vigorous natural regeneration frequently occurs once grazing and cutting pressures cease, halting and reversing patterns of soil and biomass erosion thus the global climate change agreements and financing systems could further support and accelerate local initiatives that are recreating millions of hectares of carbon sinks. The future CDM, which will manage carbon-offset credits, will likely be a mix of international organisations, government bureaucratic agencies and private sector market mechanisms

Ministry of Environment and Forest (MOEF) Agenda

Under "Payments for Ecosystem Services (PES)" the MOEF has brought out a policy paper recently in 2011 "Green India Mission" which is going to be pivotal to all the future forestry projects and it is important to know the facts as placed by MOEF.

"The land use includes –

- Increased forest/tree cover on 5 m ha of forest/non-forest lands and improved quality of forest cover on another 5 m ha (a total of 10 m ha).
- Improved ecosystem services including biodiversity, hydrological services and carbon sequestration as a result of treatment of 10 m ha.

10 m ha of forest/non-forest lands and includes –

- Qualitative improvement of forest cover/ecosystem in moderately dense forests (1.5 m ha), open degraded forests (3 m ha), degraded grassland (0.4 m ha) and wetlands 0.1 m ha;
- Eco-restoration/afforestation of scrub, shifting cultivation areas, cold deserts, mangroves, ravines and abandoned mining areas (2 m ha); c) bringing urban/

semi-urban lands under forests and tree cover (0.20 m ha); and d) agro-forestry/social forestry (3 m ha)."[10]

Critical Analysis

The social forestry project was initiated in 1980 in India. From 1985 to 1993 the World Bank and USAID initiated the National Social Forestry Project in the States of Gujarat, Himachal Pradesh, Rajasthan, and Uttar Pradesh with the National Ministry of Environment. Likewise many social forestry projects have been initiated across the country. According to the Ministry of Environment and Forests' (MOEF) own data, till 1999, 31.21 million hectares of forest plantations had already been undertaken. Now, the land use shown in the National Mission for a Green India (Under the National Action Plan on Climate Change) will amount to community members further losing all their accesses to the common lands of all kind. It includes public lands under the revenue department and classified as revenue wastelands/land with forest growth under various names like *Chhote Bade Jhad Ke Jangal*, public lands with other government agencies, grazing lands under *panchayats*. It also includes private land and talks of regulatory changes in the legislation and regulations that govern this public private interaction and thereby increase the incentives for small-scale private participation in generating forest-based incomes, as well as free up. Not only that but in the name of institutional policy and legal measures, community accesses to conserved areas and sacred groves will also be further reduced. Now with all these, accesses over common forest resources will almost cease, as right will be valued in terms of money and will be further reduced to concessions through various methods

It says, "Lok Vaniki in MP: Recognising the constraints to private forestry, an attempt was made in Madhya Pradesh to deregulate for long rotation species as well, for farmers willing to get management plans in place for their forests prepared by a chartered forester. A key provision of the rules is that farmers who develop management plans to manage their forests under Lok Vaniki are provided a regulatory waiver from the web of pre-existing rules governing harvesting of trees on private lands."[11]

We however, know from our experiences in Betul District of MP, teakwood standing on the *Adivasi* lands were usurped by a proxy *Adivasi* person. A contractor manages all the due permission for felling the pre-existing naturally grown trees on the *Adivasi* land in lieu of pittance and it also provide them with the opportunity to illegally fell the trees from nearby government forest.

Critical Analysis of Joint Forest Management (JFM)

Critical analysis of JFM is important as this has become a universal and legalised institution, with the entire future programme and funding targeted to pump through it. As per MOEF Press Release of May 22, 2011, "Joint Forest Management (JFM) is aimed at regenerating and sustainably using forests through involvement of local communities. At present, there are more than one lakh JFM Committees involving 220 lakh people living in and around forests". With JFM, the state Forest Departments have got more men and resources at their disposal to keep these *Adivasis* at bay from the resources and are engaged in pitting the community against each other. With the Green Mission India, the JFM institutions are going to become stronger, and the local population's accesses to the forest resources is going to decrease to quite a large extent as most of the community land will fall under green cover, as Clean Development Mechanism and other "Eco Payment Services" are going to be one of the biggest businesses in the years to come.

Harda Model of JFM

This is an important example as it has been acclaimed as one of the most modern and effective models of JFM on which most of the future policy is based. The experiment of participatory forest management called joint forest management (JFM) started way back in 1989 in Rahatgaon and Temagaon forest range of Harda forest division. The JFM was formalized by the Madhya Pradesh Government in 1990-91 and the driving thought behind the JFM was to reduce *Adivasi* communities' (forest dwellers, indigenous) pressure on forest. The various programmes and rules made under the JFM were also aimed at this. FPCs were formed in each forest village. Through these FPCs *Adivasis* were given solar cooker, biogas plants were installed in the villages and restrictions were imposed on use of forests by the *Adivasi* community for their daily needs. To lure the *Adivasi* communities towards JFM, in a few villages various developmental schemes under various governmental plans were taken up. The JFM programme in itself was supported by various international agencies like the world food programme. By the year 1994-95, the area was also brought under the World Bank Funded MPFP.

Community's Grievances

In 10 years, from 1990 to 2000, the *Adivasis* of Harda forest division were so annoyed with the JFM programme that the first demand they put forward before us, during our (Shramik *Adivasi* Sanghthan, SAS) first entry in the area in 2000, was to abolish JFM programme at once. Initially a few protest rallies by SAS at Harda Collectorate were focused on this. *Adivasies* told us that due to restriction put on their daily forest need (Nistar) they are even unable to repair their houses.

Experts View –

(*i*) The *Jan Sunwai* (Public Hearing) on Forest Rights at Village Indpura, Harda District, May 26, 2001 with the panel for the public hearing consisted of Ms Madhu Sarin, Dr. Nandini Sundar and Rakesh Diwan is enough to prove the case. The report said, "The villagers' feelings about JFM can be gauged from the fact that all the villagers present said by voice vote and a raise of hands that they do not want JFM. They want the JFM committees to be disbanded as these have become a means of increasing the exploitation of *Adivasis*, rather than benefiting them. JFM has also created conflict between villages."

(*ii*) **Village Forest Protection Committees in Madhya Pradesh** – An update and critical evaluation by Emily Caruso, Forest Peoples Programme and Anurag Modi, *Shramik Adivasi Sangathan* says, according to *Adivasi* communities throughout MP, JFM was effectively imposed on them without appropriate consultation during project identification, planning and implementation, and has resulted in the marginalisation, displacement and violation of the customary and traditional rights of the *Adivasis* in the state. The central state policy of eviction of forest encroachers has been a feature of the implementation of JFM, through which many *Adivasis* have lost land and access to essential forest resources. According to local activists, there were 56 JFM project-related shootings in Madhya Pradesh during the five-year JFM period, some of which resulted in the death of *Adivasi* community members. There was the case in 1997, in Mandlia and Dahinala, when two *Adivasi* people were killed by armed forces as they tried to defend their crops.

(*iii*) **PUDR Report** - The latest report suggests that there has been no let up in the atrocities. The People's Union for Democratic Rights (PUDR), Delhi in the Harda *Report of a Fact Finding*, The Struggle for Forest and Land Rights December 2009 says, "Deep rifts within and between different *Adivasi* villages and groups on the question of land rights was observed as a result of this. Those employed as watchers and receiving a monthly salary of Rs. 3000 were looked upon as government agents spying on members of their own community. It was observed that many of the watchers employed came from different *Adivasi* groups residing in the same village, leading to conflicts within communities as a result of financial disparities between ordinary villagers and forest watchers, to contested bans on grazing in the forest and collecting timber for individual use and curtailment of *nistar* rights". "The strategy clearly has many long time costs associated with it, such as increased social and economic hierarchies, breakdown of local networks within communities, and so on which directly contradict the letter and spirit of what the 2006 Act aims to achieve."

(*iv*) **MP Forestry Project** – The Bank revised its policy on the basis of reactions to its earlier 'Forestry Projects', undertaken in various states in India between1990-2000. These projects were met with bitter opposition, especially in undivided Madhya Pradesh, where Mass Tribal Organisations' (MTOs) were able to bring all the ill effects of World Bank's Forestry Project (WBFP) to the light, especially on the ground of decreasing *Adivasi* people's accesses over forest. Through a joint mission with the World Bank (under which representatives of the World Bank, Madhya Pradesh Forest Department and *Adivasi* rights organisation toured the project area to review the project). As during the report writing MPFD and later World Bank backed out, the MTOs brought out unilateral report in May 1999, on the basis of most of the already agreed points. The mission concluded that the MPFP has had a severe negative impact on the *Adivasi* communities of Madhya Pradesh. The report has shown how the World Bank failed to comply with its own safeguard policy on indigenous people. Major failings and problems with the project that have been highlighted are –

- Lives of millions of *Adivasi* people and other forest dwellers have been adversely affected by the MPFP.
- The traditional and customary rights of indigenous people and forest dwellers are being denied and their right to livelihood is threatened.
- The entire project is based on an erroneous assumption that the use of forests by local communities is responsible for the destruction of forest resources.
- The project led to increasing tension and conflict between the Forest Department and local communities.

Climate Change Programme a Criticism

Under Carbon Credit, Clean Development Mechanism is going to be the major agenda under the Green Mission of MOEF. The

Handia range of Harda Forest division has been chosen as one of the districts in India where the climate programme has been planned in 2001. Though the agreement was signed in April 2011 between the German Development Corporation and the State Development Authority of Madhya Pradesh, the planning was afoot since 2001.

"Levels of carbon leakage through fire and illicit felling have declined dramatically in Rahatgaon Range, while this has not been the case in Handia. In Rahatgaon, before the formation of FPCs, commercial head loading of firewood was uncontrolled. By the end of 2000, the FPCs studied in Rahatgaon Range allowed only two head loads of firewood (18 to 22 kg. each) per week for each household. The area impacted by ground fire has also been reduced from an estimated 50 per cent of the range to only 5 per cent. Illegal logging that averaged 10-15 trees (20-30 GBH) per hectare annually before protection is now insignificant. Such a scenario is possible for Handia CCA under the proposed project."[12]

Forest Rights Act: False Promises

The much talked about Forest Rights Act (FRA), 2006 has failed to undo historical injustice and recover the community's right over forests. For example, right claims have hardly been processed and it is only right over Tendu Patta (Kendu leaves) collection and two places for worshipping have been recognised in Harda Forest division. Whereas the community of the village gets its benefit of *Nistar* uses, not only from the forest spread over various forest ranges within the division but also from other districts. For example, *Adivasis* from Revenue village Jodimau, manage their needs of forest produce, such as, bamboo from Bod Forest (5 kms), babar grass from Bori Sanctuary (20 kms) and so on and so forth. The *Adivasi* community's accesses to various places of their annual worship has not been considered as their rights.

The MoEF/MoTA Committee report says, "There has been no substantial progress on Community Forest Rights. The claims being reported under CFR category are either pertaining to Sec.3(2) (diversion to non-forest purposes) or claims to minor public spaces such as burial sites, cattle grazing, threshing grounds, ponds, or sacred sites. There is a lot of confusion in the minds of the implementing agencies between development rights and CFRs. There is also lack of awareness about the CFR provision among local communities." The Ministry of *Adivasi* Affairs July 20, 2010 says that "A scrutiny of reports received from the States so far reveals that till June 30, 2010, only 1.76 per cent of the forest rights claims filed relate to community rights."[13]

Forest Act, 1927: A Big Hurdle

The Forest Act, 1927 is based on the colonial legacy and its provisions have been the prime reason of restricting communities' rights over forests. The act forbids community members from even entering the reserve forest unless otherwise permitted. The Section 64 of the act also empowers forest officers to arrest without warrant. The basic idea of the act was restricting the community's accesses to forest.

Discussion and Conclusion

Under Clean Development Mechanism (CDM), the international corporations got interested in India's forests and all the new policies are tailor-made and preconceived to accommodate their agenda that a developed country can continue to generate carbon emission in excesses to their legal limit provided somewhere someone else is made to sacrifice his rights. Under Payment for Eco-Service System, by paying some cash compensation through JFM, developed countries sought to reduce local communities' accesses over forests. Now JFM will go to any length to implement the agenda proposed and to the extent of replacing the role of the Forest Department in controlling the community's accesses over forests. The Community's bona fide needs proposed are to be met through alternative means.

- With introduction of JFM policy a new dimension was added in the pre existing conflict. The JFM institution with legal teeth and manpower leads to authorities using this very little paid army at their disposal to increase their control over the local community.

- By introduction of JFM the government can save both money and manpower as they use these committee members as their field level staff. Otherwise, covering millions of hectares under various forestry projects would have required the government to spend a great deal of money on establishment and this would also have placed the government in direct conflict with the community.
- JFM is a bigger threat than *Salwa Judum*. The *Salwa Judum* is limited to a certain area, whereas there are a hundred thousand JFM committees across the country. Secondly, in *Salwa Judum*, community members are used as a Special Police Officers, but they have no legal status and their existence is under scrutiny of the Supreme Court of India. Whereas, in JFM, executive members of the committee are deemed to be public servants while removing encroachments or doing any other committee work. Thereby the JFM has created legal hierarchy among otherwise cohesive and egalitarian *Adivasi* community.
- Moreover, as we have seen creating an alternative resource base through plantation and substituting grazing by stall feeding has been a great failure and it leads to the community's gradual loss of right to accesses. Secondly, cash compensation to the *Adivasi* community does not work. Thirdly, while we are talking of land for land in the rehabilitation policy, how can we have a policy which so drastically reduces communities' accesses over forests?
- There are bound to be power games in any institution. The individual's right to accesses over forests should not be subjected to any institutional monitoring and control, especially when it is a designed control and funded by the Forest Department or any authority. The JFM is not a traditional institution and its framework has been designed by the Forest Department. Institutions create hierarchy, as otherwise everyone was an encroacher in the eyes of the Forest Department but

> not for the community. Now an executive member or often, a person employed under JFM as a watchman, perceives his own community's bona fide use as an illegal activity.

We must also remember that welfare schemes run by government cannot suffice as a substitute to forest resources as all these schemes are controlled by an institution where a common *Adivasi* does not have any say. A Tribal's accesses to resources are directly related to the tribal's survival. This can be understood from the following example: on November 19, 2010, in Bakhari village under Bathri Panchyat of Jamai Block from Chindwara District, Madhya Pradesh, 6 members of Jugarlal Korku's family; his wife Rasiya (40), sons Jaysing (27), Kalu (18), Chaklu (15), Palesigh (12) and daughter Sukhwanti (10) died, after consuming stale chapattis of the previous night made out of mango kernel. Jugarlal's ration card and job card given under the NREGA scheme did not have an entry. However, when *Shramik Adivasi Sangathan* checked his job card on the NREGA website, in 2008-09 for 78 days of work payment of Rs. 7,549 was shown and in the year 2009-10 for 71 days of work Rs. 6,596 payment was shown against his name.

Accesses to forest have been their way of life for *Adivasis*, not merely a means of deriving livelihood. For example, catching small fish in the river is a very tedious job in terms of labour involved, and if valued in monetary terms it will be just 20 per cent of a day's labour. For *Adivasi*s, however, fishing is a part of their lifestyle, fun and sense of being. We all do certain things unique to our culture. *Adivasi*s' life and rituals revolve around forests and it is very important to know all that to decide the issue of their accesses to forests –

- Their pilgrimage places lie along the rivers and hills in the forest.
- Each clan has its own deity and it has its own place somewhere deep in the forest called *'Dev Khala'* (deity's place) and every year all the members of the clan have to perform collective offerings/sacrifices.
- During the *Hari Jiroti* (most important of tribals' festival

which marks the beginning of festivals), *Adivasis* consume honey which is found inside the tree trunk.

- In Gonds, *Sat Phera* (taking seven rounds) of Salai's (*Shorea robesta*) pole is a mark of the marriage.

This concept of sole proprietorship has to be broken. After independence the government has abolished the '*Zamindari* System' in revenue's area and the concept of 'tiller as the owner' was enacted way back in 1954; whereas, no such application of principle was applied in the forest areas. We are yet to come to the terms that the so-called forest resources has been the *Adivasi* home for generations and the British had usurped it and coined the concept of forest as a separate entity. The successive governments of independent India have proved no better.

The main issue is not where to end but where to begin. All the present day thinking is based on the basic premise which flows from the British legacy that is forests are our main concern and *Adivasi* people are a hindrance to it. All our efforts are directed towards reducing their 'interference' into 'our' forest. Therefore, our primary concern is forest and not human beings in flesh and blood. Whereas, the forest cannot be saved without the *Adivasis*' active involvement. To have an effective solution to this historical conflict of interest between the state and the real owner of these resources, one has to have the courage to accept the moral burden of denying people the right to live which nature has offered them. The *Adivasi* people are required to be given territorial rights as has been the case in many countries. Now would the community be able to manage it? The strategy should be worked with the community rather than imposing a ready-made JFM committee on them.

References

1. *Working Plan Report for Bori Forest, in Hoshangabad Forest Division,* Year 1909-1919.
2. World Bank Forest Strategy of 2003.
3. *Working Paper Series Julian L. Simon Centre for Policy Research April 2002,* History of Conflict over Forests in India: A Market Based Resolution by Arnab Kumar Hazra.

4. Rangarajan, M. (1996). *Fencing the Forest; Conservation and Ecological Changes in India's Central Providences 1860-1914.* Oxford University Press: The University of Michigan.
5. *Land and Cultural Survival: The Communal Land Rights of Indigenous People of South Asia, edited by Jayantha Perera 2009, Chapter 7 Indigenous People's Forest Tenure in India, Kinsuk Mitra and Radhika Gupta.*
6. *National Mission for a Green India (Under the National Action Plan on Climate Change) 52 A Draft Submitted to Prime Minister's Council on Climate Change Ministry of Environment and Forests, Government of India.*
7. *Working Plan of 2010-11 to 2019-20 of Betul North Forest Division and a Range of West Forest Division, MP.*
8. MoEF/MoTA Committee on Forest Rights Act Implementation of Forest Rights Act in Madhya Pradesh: Report of field visit, May 20-24, 2010 by Devendra Pandey and Sharachchandra Lele
9. World Bank "Forest Strategy" of 1991.
10. Village Forest Protection Committees in Madhya Pradesh: An Update and Critical Evaluation, Emily Caruso, Forest People's Programme and Anurag Modi, *Shramik Adivasi Sangathan,* October 4, 2004.
11. Jan Sunwai (Public Hearing) on Forest Rights at Village Indpura, Harda District, May 26, 2001 with the panel for the public hearing consisted of Ms. Madhu Sarin, Dr. Nandini Sundar and Rakesh Diwan.
12. Mass *Adivasi* Organisation's Report on Joint Mission on World Bank Funded MP Forestry Project, May 1999.
13. The Struggle for Forest and Land Rights in Harda Report of a Fact Finding People's Union for Democratic Rights, Delhi December 2009.
14. *A Case Study of Handia Range of Harda District in MP, published in 2001 from Harda Forest Division, Madhya Pradesh, India on Communities and Climate Change: The Clean Development Mechanism and Village-based Forest Restoration, A Collaboration of Community Forestry International, Inc. and The Indian Institute of Forests)*
15. The World Bank document "India Unlocking Opportunities for Forest-Dependent People in India" released in February 2000.

Notes

1. The colonial encounter with Thakur Bhabootsingh is recorded in "Working Plan Report for Bori Forest, in Hoshangabad Forest Division, Year 1909-1919")

2. Preliminary Offence Report, POR no. 370/04 dated June 19, 2007 of Bhoura Range, North Betul Forest Division, MP.
3. Mitra, K. and Gupta, R. (2009) Land and Cultural Survival: The Communal Land Rigths of Indigenous People of South Asia, in Perera, J., *Indigenous People's Forest Tenure in India,* City: Publisher.
4. Rangarajan, M. (1996) *Fencing the Forest: Conservation and Ecological Changes in India's Central Provinces 1860-1914.* New Delhi: Oxford University Press.
5. Special Leave Petition no. 12393/2011, Shramik Adivasi Sangahthan vs State of MP.
6. Working Plan of 2010-11 to 2019-20 of Betul North Forest Division and a Range of West Forest Division, MP.
7. Jan Sunwai (Public Hearing) on Forest Rights at Village Indpura, Harda District, MAY 26, 2001 with the panel for the public hearing consisted of Ms Madhu Sarin, Dr. Nandini Sundar and Rakesh Diwan.
8. PIL 1064/2010 of MP High Court Shramik Adivasi Sangathan vs. State of MP and others.
9. World Bank Global Forest Strategy 2003.
10. (*National Mission for a Green India (Under the National Action Plan on Climate Change) 52, A Draft submitted to Prime Minister's Council on Climate Change, Ministry of Environment and Forests Government of India).
11. (*National Mission for a Green India (Under the National Action Plan on Climate Change) 52, A Draft submitted to Prime Minister's Council on Climate Change, Ministry of Environment and Forests Government of India).
12. A Case Study of Handia Range of Harda district in MP, published in 2001 from Harda Forest Division, Madhya Pradesh, India on Communities and Climate Change: The Clean Development Mechanism and Village-based Forest Restoration a Collaboration of Community Forestry International, Inc. And The Indian Institute of Forests).
13. MoEF/MoTA Committee on Forest Rights Act Implementation of Forest Rights Act in Madhya Pradesh: Report of field visit, May 20-24, 2010 by Devendra Pandey and Sharachchandra Lele.

4

Property Rights and Decentralised Forest Governance: How Far the Objectives Have Been Achieved

S.R. Balabantaray

Abstract: The degradation of forest resources creates dual complexity of reducing the changes of the present generation to earn their livelihood and also compromise on the ability of the future generation to meet their needs. This goes in contrary with the dual objectives of the concept of sustainable development. In order to attain the goal of sustainability of resources, at the theoretical level it is witnessed that there is decentralisation pertaining to the rights, use and management of forests but the ground reality has something else to offer. The present paper seeks to analyse the property rights pertaining to forests prevalent in the Indian context. It also highlights the decentralised forest governance. Decentralised forest governance has been an issue for more than two decades and the paper seeks to examine how far the process of decentralised forest governance has been successful in addressing the intermittent problems of forest exploitation. Failure of the state with respect to centralisation policies in maintaining the forests demanded for a fresh approach and thus emerged the decentralisation mechanisms in the Indian forestry sector. Decentralisation mechanisms were thus adopted to ensure that a better management of the forests can be done by the communities and once the rights over the forests can be transferred to the local people they can manage the forests in an efficient manner much better than the state. The objectives thus set were basically the sustainable management of the natural resources. And now that it has been a long time since the decentralisation mechanisms have been adopted in the Indian context the paper documents how far the desired objectives of the decentralisation policies have been met. All the data presented in this paper has been derived from secondary sources done by an overview of the literature available on the forestry resources. The primary objective of the paper is to analyse how far the decentralisation policies have been successful in India.

Introduction

Forests, all over the world, are considered to be important aspects of the individual's life and livelihood. They have numerous uses out of which keeping the environment healthy, supporting the domestic needs of individuals, checking soil erosion and facilitating rainfall are the primary ones. Over decades the degradation of forest and deforestation has been an issue of serious concern not only in parts of India but in the entire world. Throughout the world, forests are increasingly endangered by heavy deforestation caused due to ever increasing human population and the emanating needs from the population for agricultural and housing services. There has been an increasing concern regarding the depletion of forest resources (Guha, 1983). In India this phenomenon is not of recent origin but has been persisting for a long time. Degradation of forests results in the reduction of productivity thereby giving rise to a chain of complex problems. The problem of degradation creates the dual complexity of reducing the chances of the present generation to earn their livelihood and also compromises on the ability of the future generation to meet their needs. This is contrary to the dual objectives of the concept of sustainable development.[1] Sustainable development of the forests resources is a challenging task provided the complexity of the nature of the problem. The natural resource regime always faces a tough job of extreme exploitation on the one hand and on the other there is a constant pressure to keep a check on the over exploitation of the natural resources so that they will remain for the future generation.

The present paper seeks to analyse the property rights pertaining to forests prevalent in the Indian context. It also highlights the decentralised forest governance. Decentralised forest governance has been an issue of more than two decades and the paper seeks to examine as to how far the process of decentralised forest governance has been successful in addressing the intermittent problems of forest exploitation. Failure of the state with respect to centralisation policies in maintaining the forests demanded a fresh approach and thus emerged the decentralisation mechanisms in the Indian forestry sector. Decentralisation mechanisms were thus adopted to ensure that a better management of the forests can be done by the communities and once the rights over the forests can be transferred to the local people, they can manage the forests in a manner much better and more efficient than the state. The objectives thus set were basically the sustainable management of the natural resources. And now that it has been a long time since the decentralisation mechanisms have been adopted in the Indian context, the paper documents how far the desired objectives of the decentralisation policies have been met. All the data presented in this paper has been derived from secondary sources collected from an overview of the literature available on the forestry resources. The primary objective of the paper is to analyse how far the decentralisation policies have been successful in the Indian context.

In India the problem (deforestation and degradation of forests) has a rather long history which has plagued the Indian social set up right from the colonial period. There was a radical alternation in the property rights pertaining to the forests after the arrival of the British. People failed to claim their rights over the forests and consequently lost their control over the natural resources. The British thereby limiting private property rights changed the forestry usage in India (Saxena, 1997). These steps were initiated by the British to ensure that they became the sole users and owners of the forests. No trees were felled without the prior permission of the British. The British used to fell heavy logs of trees for fulfilling their various needs. The needs included building of railway networks for the purpose of transport and communication. Forests were heavily chopped off to accommodate the needs of the construction of railway tracks. Ship building activities also required huge quantities of timber which required massive felling of trees. The British were also in favour of cultivation as it ensured them greater and better revenue and also it enhanced their hold on India (Guha, 1987). This resulted in a scenario where the tribal or the indigenous people were completely devoid of the natural resources of which they have been an integral part since time immemorial. Even though there was a sharp reaction against the policies which prohibited the tribal communities to access the forests but the British suppressed these agitations. Speaking in a nutshell the British exploited the forests in India to the maximum possible limit to derive large benefits from the natural resources.

Since prior to independence the British exploited the natural resources wilfully, it was expected that the situation would improve after independence. It is, however, not true that the problem came to a halt after the departure of the British, instead it tended to grow in magnitude. In independent India, the state was the sole authority of forest management. It took the entire responsibility on itself to safeguard the forests against the threat of degradation. However, the degradation did not stop, only the people who were responsible for degradation changed. The post colonial era witnessed a new set of people who exploited the forests namely, contractors, businessmen, timber mafia, common people and government to some extent. Contractors are engaged in commercial exploitation of the forests for satisfying their selfish needs. They are also backed by some of the forest officials to whom they pay certain bribes. Such an activity tends to weaken the small forest owners and causes degradation of forests on a massive scale. For quite a long period of time forests were viewed as sources of timber (Nathan and Kelkar, 2001) and a means of revenue generation. People, generally, were engaged in gaining self benefits thereby overlooking the larger interests or the interest of the community.

Instant profits were much focussed upon at the cost of the degradation of forests.

Guha (1997) has pointed out that after the attainment of independence, the need for industrialisation increased to be at par with the developed nations. There was a growing and widespread assumption that industrialisation could be of great help to take India along the lines of development. Thus the building up of industries was given extreme support. This tendency resulted in the negligence of the ecological concerns and the environmental issues were completely sidelined. The then policy makers failed to realise the need of the hour and the intensity of the situation which could be grave in the later phases. The lack of visionary approach and a complete failure on the part of the policymakers to focus on a distant future resulted in immediate gains but in the long run it was to yield greater trouble. The negative repercussions are felt today when there is the high incidence of excessive degradation of forests. Now since the forests face the problem of excessive denudation, there is widespread concern to search for alternatives to save the natural resources from degradation. The desperate search is on to look into the issues that have been primarily responsible for the cause of loss of forestry cover. Moreover, the search is also to look for the alternative options available that can facilitate the protection of the natural resources.

Immediately after independence the need was largely felt for "development" which cannot occur (as realised by the then government) in the absence of industrialisation. As a result of which there was a liberal approach towards the process of industrialisation. The government did not have a strict mechanism to check the high growth of the industries. This gave rise to wood-based industries on a large scale which in turn required a heavy amount of raw materials to meet the requirements ultimately resulting in large scale deforestation. The growth of wood-based industries was also supported on the grounds of greater revenue generation for the country and creation of employment. The wood-based industries in India are constantly being encouraged as it provides incentives for the state exchequer. These industries generally enjoy subsidies in raw materials and a variety of other concessions. There are instances from Karnataka where the paper industries were supplied with bamboo at the rate of Rupee one per tonne which was far cheaper than the persistent market price. This was done to enhance the industrialisation process in the country and in the meantime the lager perspective of saving the forests was entirely lost. This clearly envisages as to how the various state governments have a liberal attitude towards the wood-based industries in the name of development.

Apart from the growth of industries the exploding rate of population growth put persistent pressure on the forests. Currently, India has a population of above 200 million approximately. This huge amount of population tends to put an enormous degree of pressure on the forests for infrastructure and livelihood. The ever increasing population demands more agricultural land to feed them. Since the amount of available land is fixed and that population is ever increasing; therefore, the available land must be used for agricultural purposes and that land has to come only from the vicinity of the forests. Hence the need arises for clearing the forests. Even use of large tracts of land become inevitable for the purpose of irrigation projects taking into account the fact that India is predominantly an agricultural country with a substantial amount of its population dependent on agriculture and the lack of periodic rainfall makes things worse. Therefore a situation arises where the need for the irrigation projects are heightened and since these irrigation projects tend to safeguard the productivity of the crops the forest lands are diverted for the purpose of building of irrigation projects. Moreover, housing, creation of dams and urban developments also require land to satisfy the demands of the bulging population. This land can be made available only by clearing the forests which has been the contested debate in the present day era.

Forest degradation has not been halted in most of the developing countries in spite of the fact that there have been several policies to combat the rate of forest degradation and ensure a sustainable management of the forests. Instead the rampant degradation of the forests is constantly on the rise.

There have been a number of empirical studies pertaining to the causes and effects of forest degradation and deforestation. Of late it has been realised that the practices by people which are highly unsustainable in nature and the property rights which seem to be conflicting are the primary underlying causes of forest degradation. The loss of forestry cover has very serious implications for the conservation of soil and water (Gadgil, Prasad and Ali, 1983). Taking into account the role played by the forests in the economy of any developing country there is a serious need for saving the forests for the ecological balance. In India for a period of more than two decades (from the late 1960s to the early 1980s) the extent of forest land diverted for non-forestry purposes is reported to be over 2 million hectares (Agarwal and Garg, 1987). And this by no means is a small figure which clearly envisages the scenario of the forestry sector in India prior to the advent of community managed schemes which are largely prevalent in the forestry sector in present day India.

Centralisation in India

Owing to the excessive denudation and degradation of forests, independent India launched the national forest policy in 1952 for proper maintenance of the natural resources. The need of the hour was to conserve the forests through an efficient management of the natural resources. But there seemed to be another hidden objective of the government which was to gain the maximum benefits from the forests. The central emphasis of the policy was to maintain 60 per cent of geographical land in hilly regions and 20 per cent in the plains under forest cover. The forest policy of 1952 which served to be the perfect base for the centralisation of the forest emphasised that village communities should refrain from the use of the forests and the forests should only be used for "national interest" (Saxena, 1997). The national interest included defence which is an essential requirement for any country for ensuring security against other enemy countries, communication and vital industries which serve the purpose of development. High valued plantations like eucalyptus having a higher commercial value, were given much emphasis which could generate greater revenue. The government was keen on generation of revenue rather than looking at the interests of the people. The policy of 1952 also ensured that non-timber forest products are supplied on a regular basis for the process of modernisation sponsored by the state.

The period after independence witnessed larger control of the government over the forests thereby limiting the role of people and the tribal/indigenous communities over the forests. Government took the initiative of having supreme control over the forests to ensure that it can use the natural resource for its gains thereby overlooking the gains of the people heavily dependent on the forests. This was the era where the indigenous communities were deprived of their basic rights into the forests and as a result of which they failed to collect the forest usufructs. The people living in abject poverty and the ones completely dependent on the forests for their livelihood had to face extreme hardships to meet their daily requirements. The centralisation of the forests was also supported in many quarters owing to the fact that the open access regime resulted in a situation where people exploited the natural resources. Hence it was expected that if once the state gains control over the natural resources, the process of degradation of forests can come to a halt.

The centralisation policies, however, adopted by the government completely sidelined the needs and demand of the people heavily dependent on the forests. Instead it was keen on diverting the forest uses for the purpose of industries. In the name of development the rights of people over the forests were heavily curtailed. People refrained from the forestry uses taking into account the fact that the centralisation policies adopted by the government and the forests were used for the purpose of revenue generation and expansion of the industries which could facilitate the development process in India. Persistent failure on the part of the public sector has resulted in the adoption of the decentralisation mechanisms.

Decentralisation

Before going into detailed discussions of decentralisation it is important to highlight why decentralisation is required.

Decentralisation is not a new concept in the forestry sector. Decentralisation aims at increasing the forestry cover which has been at stake owing to the excessive exploitation of the natural resources. At the theoretical level decentralisation refers to the improvement in the resource allocation, enhancing the efficiency, enlarging the level and accountability as well as ensuring equity at the level of the stakeholders. Decentralisation is often supported on the grounds that needs and requirements of the local people are best known by the local governments and not by the national government at the centre. Moreover it is easier to increase the accountability of the local leaders than leaders at the centre. It also aims at bringing the state closer to the people thereby increasing local participation and building social capital. Through decentralisation employment opportunities are being created and it tends to reduce poverty alongside improving the means of livelihood of the people heavily dependent on the forests for earning their livelihood.

Literally the term "Decentralisation" refers to the moving away from the centre. The shedding of powers, rights and responsibilities from the governmental agencies and transferring the same to the non-governmental entities is called as Decentralisation. It can be defined as redistribution of power and authority which initially rested with the central governments but now is growingly being devolved to the local levels. It is described as an act where the power is transferred to institutions or the actors involved. The transfer of power occurs at different levels in different places, it may be from central government to local government, individuals to the private sector and government to community managed organisations. Basically decentralisation in the forestry sector implies private ownership of the forests. Here private ownership refers to a set of people or we can say a community who are believed to manage the forests in the best possible manner.

Decentralisation is very often assumed as the devolution of responsibility for resource management to the local people at the lower levels (Agarwal and Ribot, 1999). Decentralisation is viewed as the allocation of the decision-making rights to the subunits of any organisation. In case of the property rights regime decentralisation refers to the transfer of the authority at all levels to the people at the grass root level. The rights thus ushered are to be enjoyed by the community as a whole and not by any individual independently. This also includes the transfer of the entire decision-making authority regarding the resources. In the process the people enjoy a relatively greater degree of autonomy pertaining to the roles they play in the natural resource management. Decentralisation also allows the farmer to make certain changes feasible for the forests suiting the conservation of the forests. It also gives the scope to the people to plant the trees of their choice rather than the revenue generating species.

By channelling greater benefits to local authorities and local people, decentralisation is believed to provide incentives for local populations to maintain and protect local resources. Giving away the entire control of the natural resource (forests) to the community ensures that the accountability of the public sector is enhanced. Once the community is bestowed with the use and ownership of the forests the onus is on the community to manage the natural resources. The decentralisation in forest resources was a response to the demand made by the people to transfer the rights as the state was unable to manage the forests in a full-fledged manner. This transfer of the use and ownership rights can also ensure the effectiveness in the management of the forests.

The trend of increasing decentralisation of natural resource management from the central government to that of the local bodies is visible among several developing countries (Nygren, 2005; Bartley, Andersson, Jagger and Laerhoven, 2008; Tacconi, 2007). Several countries are shifting natural resource management responsibilities to the community organisations. Decentralisation has been viewed from many quarters as the provision of the efficient services. But decentralisation cannot be narrowed down to such a specific definition. It does not only imply providing the services efficiently but also the devolution of powers in a real sense (Agarwal and Ribot, 1999) where the communities would have a voice in the decision-making process pertaining to the natural resources. The majority of national governments in Asia, Africa and Latin America have claimed to have enacted the decentralised provisions in the arena of environmental management (Agarawal, Ribot and Larson, 2006).

Emergence of Decentralisation

Resounding failure on the part of the government bureaucracy called for decentralisation. Large scale illegal logging and uncontrolled deforestation have been attributed to weak governance structures. Prior to the advent of decentralisation, the natural resources were managed by the state which failed to perform and meet the expectations of the people. The natural resources continued to degrade on a regular basis. The search for alternatives were made to find better and effective ways of the management of forests and also owners of the forests who can be bestowed with the forest rights to ensure that the natural resources are best managed and conserved. The next best possible alternative was to shift the power base from that of the bureaucracy to the local people or the community who were believed to have a better understanding of the natural resources since the fact that they are close to the natural resources and they live in the natural setting. The community ought to have a better and brighter knowledge about the scheme of things pertaining to the forests. The problems in the forestry sector are driving many countries to reconsider the role of the state in the administration of the forests. The increasing trends in forest deforestation are forcing many governments to shift the approach from centralised systems of forest governance and direct forest implementation of government programmes to schemes of decentralisation.

The decentralisation policies of natural resource governance became quite popular in the mid 1980s. Taking into account the failure of the state to conserve and manage the forests common people were viewed as a solution rather than a problem. Decentralisation was assumed to increase democratisation of the natural resources management by allowing the local populations to make decisions on the control and use of the local services (Nygren, 2005). When the decentralisation is in real practice, local people feel a greater sense of ownership and this ensures that these people work with a greater degree of commitment towards the conservation of the natural resources. Decentralisation guarantees that people will be the sole owners of the forests. Hence, a sense of belongingness encourages the people to work more and efficiently.

Decentralisation as a process became a quite admired means for the national governments to settle the competing claims over the natural resources. There have been a large number of empirical studies which have highlighted the conditions in which decentralisation has succeeded in the successful management of the natural resources. Even though the empirical studies were being made in different geographical conditions and varying natural settings, most of the literature suggests similar findings which prove that decentralisation is a probable solution to the conflict over the natural resources.

Paradigm Shift

Even though there was an elongated debate over decentralisation but there was a paradigm shift only in the late 1980s. Community participation for the management of forests came into the limelight in the late 1980s when the urgency of the situation was realised. The growing degradation of the forests finally opened the eyes of the Indian government and it chanced to formulate some policies to ensure a check on the depletion of the natural resources failing which disastrous outcomes were on the cards. There was a constant pressure on the government from several quarters to transfer the management and user rights to the community due to the fact that it (government) failed to maintain the momentum of maintaining the forests. Therefore, the search for alternatives was on which facilitated the management of the forests by the community. The role of institutions can be highlighted here whose presence mattered the most due to the fact that it kept a constant vigil on the unlawful activities (forest exploitation) of the common people. Thus it facilitated the formulation of a new forest policy which could accommodate the desired objectives of maintaining the forests and meeting the needs of the forest dependent communities.

The beginning of 1980 saw a paradigm shift in the forestry sector which almost changed the fate and face of the forestry sector in India. A new forest policy (National Forest Policy, 1988) was enacted in the year 1988 which had a different approach on the offering altogether. This policy emphasised environmental stability, soil conservation, maintenance of ecological balance and above all meeting the basic requirements of the people. The policy set the national goal of having one third of the geographical area under forest cover. The basic objectives of the national forest policy 1988 are as follows (MoEF, 1988):

- To maintain environmental stability through preservation and restoration of ecological balance.
- To conserve the natural heritage of the country preserving the remaining natural forest with a vast variety of flora and fauna.
- To check soil erosion and denudation in the catchment areas of rivers, lakes, reservoirs in the interests of soil and water conservation, for mitigating floods and droughts and for the retardation of siltation of reservoirs.
- To meet the requirements of the fuelwood, fodder, minor forest produce and small timber of the rural and tribal population.
- Checking the extension of sand dunes in the desert areas of Rajasthan and along the coastal tracts
- Increasing substantially the forest/tree cover in the country through massive afforestation and social forestry programmes, especially on all denuded, degraded and unproductive lands.
- Encouraging efficient utilisation of forest produce and maximising substitution of wood.
- To increase the productivity of the forests to meet the essential national needs.
- To create a massive people's movement with the involvement of women, for achieving these objectives and to minimise pressure on the existing forests.

The focus suddenly shifted from "conservation of forests" to "sustainable management" of forests. In the earlier forest policy the government only focused on the conservation of the forests. But it was realised that it did not yield significant and positive results and degradation of the forests continued like before. The earlier policies barred people from access to the forests but this policy ensured that there is scope for involvement of local people, local knowledge and local wisdom in a wide range of activities such as protection, preservation, proper utilisation, sustainable management of the forest resources. Decentralisation was thus viewed to be the best possible alternative for the management of the forests so as to serve the dual objectives of halting the forest degradation and meeting the needs of the indigenous communities.

Problems in Decentralisation

Decentralisation has been the key word for almost over two decades in the environmental sector where the need of it is largely felt. Most of the decentralisation policies are flawed in their design (Agarwal, Ribot and Larson, 2006). The policies thus formulated are at the apex level. There is less knowledge regarding the grass root reality among the policy makers and the problems of the field. So the policies thus formulated either do not work or might work for a specific period of time and then fail to respond to the issues. The local/indigenous people are never consulted while formulating the policies and thus they are formulated by a certain section of people who have limited knowledge of the natural resources. Moreover some of the policies thus formed are good in design but the same fails to be implemented in the best possible manner. Even though government has pronounced decentralisation in the forestry sector but still the government bureaucracy (government officials in the forestry sector) hesitates to transfer all the power.

Joint Forest Management

National Forest Policy is said to have brought about significant changes in the forest management in Indian history. It proposed the creation of a massive people's involvement (also women) to protect the forest resources. It also aimed at providing a framework of norms for participatory forest management. It is basically viewed as a partnership between the forest department and the village community for the proper management of the forests and ensuring sustainability. It could help in solving the problems related both to the causes of the sustainability of the forests and alleviation of poverty among the village community.

On June 1, 1990, the Government of India adopted a National Joint Forest Management Resolution, which set guidelines for partnership between local communities and the state forest department for the protection and management of the state-owned forests through formation of Forest Protection Committees (FPCs). The earlier approach of the state was the protection of the forests, that is, to guard the forests against encroachment from the village community. However, the new approach was the responsibility of managing and maintaining the natural resources that will be jointly shared by the Forest Department and the village people. Such will also be the case with the profit thus generated from the forest. The circular supporting JFM initiatives, as well as earlier and subsequent state level government orders, provided specific guidelines for the recognition of community forest protection activities.

Property Rights

The state for long has been the sole owner of the forests and has been deciding matters pertaining to the forests. Management issues and governance of the forests was done by the state. But this increasing and overwhelming control of the state over the forests is discarded by many people. The state as the sole controller of the forests failed to produce the desired results. Pertaining to the fact that the state was the sole owner of the forests for a longer period of time did not ensure that the forests were well managed. Owing to the bleak picture of the forestry sector, the state has been severely criticised for failing to maintain consistency in conserving the natural resources. The state as the sole owner of the forests is not accepted everywhere. Often people question the authority of the state over the forests as on what grounds the state enjoys the power to manage and govern the forests. The indigenous people around the forests and the ones dependent on the forests consider the forests to be their own property. Therefore, there is a constant tussle between the indigenous people and the state over the user rights of the forests.

The basic problems in the natural resource management is due to the absence of clearly defined property rights and at times the lack of enforcement of the property rights (even if there is the presence of any property rights) leads to an open access situation. The open access situation is a very problematic phase where every individual tends to derive the maximum from the natural resources thereby reducing the amount for the other members. The open access situation thus develops a free ride mentality among the individuals who tend to derive as much as they can from the natural resources. The people generate a feeling that if they do not exploit the resources then somebody else will and thus they will be deprived. It is not that if they stop extracting their maximum possible benefits, others will stop as well. So why should they sacrifice their share and thus engage in exploiting the natural resources? Thus arises a scenario of competitive mindset among people who tend to constantly struggle with the members to derive from the natural resources to the utmost. In the meantime, however, they tend to forget that there is a limit of extraction from a natural resource and once the resource is extracted beyond the level of regeneration then it tends to deplete.

Resources may be classified under three broad categories:

Public Property: The ownership is bestowed with the government and the decisions pertaining to the resource is solely taken by the government. In ancient times forests fell under the category of public property where the government was the sole decision-maker of the forests and it decided the scheme of things pertaining to the forests.

Private Property: Both the ownership and user rights are with a single individual as he is the owner of the particular resource. Since the forests are a state subject they cannot be treated as an individual property. Either it has to be a public property or a common property.

Common Property: This resource is jointly owned by a group of people or, to be specific, is owned by a community.

The user rights are enjoyed by the community and the decisions pertaining to the resources are collectively taken by the community. All the stakeholders have a user right and they tend to derive their particular scheduled share from the natural resource.

These days the forests are known as common property whose use and ownership rights are bestowed with the community. This change has been introduced due to the decentralisation mechanisms adopted in the forestry sector since the community was the next best alternative available for the management of the forests after the failure of the state to manage it. However, there is still a long way to go in terms of complete decentralisation. Property rights are devolved but the extent to which these rights have been devolved needs a careful analysis. In many cases people are not aware of their rights. Still there is the hegemony of the forest department over the forest resources.

Conclusion

Although on pen and paper or at the theoretical level it is witnessed that there is decentralisation pertaining to the rights, use and management of forests but the ground reality has something else to offer. Analysis of the real practices at the community level gives an entirely bleak picture of the visions of decentralisation of the government. The theory and practice vary widely and on a large scale. By decentralisation, the government proposed for a complete transfer of authority from the Forest Department to the local communities which included all aspects pertaining to the forests (use, management and ownership). The real practice, however, has an altogether different story to narrate of places where there is high existence of government bureaucracy to make things worse. The forest department (officials of the forest department) still have a strong hold over the forests. The officials are not prepared to shed their age-old powers. However, it is not only the officials who are to be blamed alone; the inefficiency of the village communities to grab their rights should also be highlighted. They make decisions on vital matters thereby giving no room for decentralisation which still remains only a myth. The concept of decentralisation is yet to be achieved in its complete form.

Local decision-making must ensure that there is the existence of popular participation. Unless and until there is popular participation (which has been the core objective of decentralisation), proper management and better conservation of the forests will fail to materialise. Therefore, keeping this in mind the local users must be given a special place while taking some of the important decisions pertaining to the natural resources. The question arises here of who will take the initiative for ensuring people's participation. Some argue that the stakeholders must take the initiative for increasing participation. However, some others argue that since the people living adjacent to forests are tribal communities and they are at a lower rung of development, they must be facilitated to participate.

A vivid discussion on the common property resources suggests that the role of institutions is highly significant to check the excessive exploitation of the forests by native people. Absence of strict rules and regulations facilitates people to derive their maximum possible benefits from the natural resources thereby leading to an open access situation which in the long run results in the degradation of the forests. So the organisations or the communities working for the conservation and the management of the forests must ensure that they have strict institutions (set of defined rules that are working) which can facilitate the cause of decentralisation. Decentralisation as a concept emerged due to the failure of the state to manage the forests. So if the communities fail to have institutions then decentralisation cannot be a success. Therefore, a constant effort must be initiated to ensure that the rules thus formulated are implemented and strict vigil must be kept so that the certain degree of punishment, like imposition of fines, is given those who dare to violate the rules in order to deter them from unlawful activities.

In many Asian countries the participation of women is significantly low (Capistrano, 2008). Women who seem to be potentially half of the workforce are deliberately kept away from the decision-making process. Social barriers prevent women from true participation in the decision-making process of the communities thus formed for the protection, conservation and management of the forests. Speaking of participation, only mere attendance in the meetings does not ensure taking part. People have to play an active and vigilant role while taking important decisions pertaining to the natural resources and for doing this they have to be empowered enough. Empowerment can come only when people are aware of their rights, duties and responsibilities. Once people are made aware of the scheme of things going on around them and they have access to education, they will be able to handle the situation in a better manner. If people are not self-sufficient or empowered enough then they will be dependent on other people (officials of the Forest Department, intermediaries, village headmen and local elites) to take decisions on their behalf which has been the scenario in most of the participatory models of development. Self-sufficiency can be attained through a standard level of income. But in a developing country like India where a significant proportion of the people live below the poverty line, this objective is difficult to be achieved but not impossible. The level of awareness can be increased once the people are educated.

Funding seems to be a major point of concern among the communities who are given the chance to manage the forests. The communities managing the forests are the ones living in or around the forests. And most of the people belonging to these forest management communities are not economically well off. Hence they cannot bear the burden of excessive finance incurred in the activities of managing the forests. Here the role of the state is extremely crucial, where the state should not neglect the rural communities and must cater to their needs and demands wherever and whenever it is required. There should be substantial funding available to these communities or the groups who are engaged in the activity of community management of forests. Unavailability of appropriate funding is never going to help the cause. Decentralisation cannot be achieved if there is lack of appropriate funding to the communities manging the forests, since the unavailability of finance would restrict the community people from governing the resources in the best possible manner. Proper funding by the state would ensure that the communities will take up their job in an active manner. Moreover the central government must make provisions to make the administrative services available for the communities managing the forest resources.

Technology must be made available at the grass root level to make the process of decentralisation a success. Communities living in and around the forests have little access and even less knowledge regarding the variety of technology available in the schemes of forest management. The state, or the technical experts to be precise, can come in handy in helping the communities managing the forests to work wonders. Once the community is given the opportunity to combine their indigenous knowledge and the technology if at all it is being made available to them, then the forest management will be able to reach new heights. The availability of technology on a timely basis to the communities also serves as a vital issue because untimely offering of the technology is not going to help the communities in any way.

Undoubtedly there have been significant changes in the forestry sector which have taken place after the policies, programmes and devolution have taken place. Several instances speak of the success stories of the community managed systems. The efforts of the communities managing the forests have been noteworthy. At least one can say that the years following the formulation of the 1988 forest policy has brought about some positive changes in the Indian forestry sector. However, the fact must also be kept in mind that it has been almost more than two decades of decentralised forest governance and two decades are by no means a small time. The success that was expected from the community managed systems has not been met. Still there are several inherent issues like (participation of women, proper management of the forests) which need to be answered on an urgent basis. The policies thus formulated have certain loopholes which are being misused by a certain section of the society. The role played by the communities can be said to be work in progress where the desired targets are not being met. Real participation should be the primary focus and steps/ initiatives must be taken to achieve the desired objective. And real participation includes the decision-making of all the stakeholders in all the important issues. The devolution of powers should ideally reach the grassroot level and the women members must also actively take part in the decision-making process pertaining to the forestry activities in the forestry committees of which they are the members. It is easier said than done. Still there is a long way to go where one can witness decentralisation in full form.

Decentralisation can only be a guaranteed success if people from all quarters can come together and join hands, shedding their age-old rivalries and setting aside their selfish interests. Working together will largely enhance the probability of success. The forest officials, the government authorities and the common people are all required to work and serve with a common purpose and noble cause which can facilitate decentralisation in its real form and true sense both in theory and in practice. If some more time is given to the communities to work towards the management of the forests and if they are supplied with the demanded help by the state on time, then things can get much better.

References

Agarwal, A. and Ribot, J.C. (1999), "Accountability in Decentralisation: A Framework with South Asian and West Asian Cases", *The Journal of Developing Areas*, Vol. 33, No. 4, pp. 473-502.

Agarwal, A., Ribot, J.C. and Larson, A.M. (2006), "Recentralising While Decentralising: How National Governments Reappropriate Forest Resources?" *World Development*, Vol. 34, No. 11, pp. 1864-86.

Agarwal, S.K. and Garg, R.K. (1987), *Environmental Issues and Researches in India*, New Delhi: P.L Printers.

Bartley, T., Andersson, K., Jagger, P. and Laerhoven, F.V. (2008), "The contribution of Institutional Theories to Explaining Decentralisation of Natural Resource Governance" *Society and Natural Resources*, Vol. 21, No. 2, pp. 160-74.

Capistrano, D. (2008), "Decentralisation and Forest Governance in Asia and the Pacific: Trends, Lessons and Continuing Challenges", in C.J.P. Colfer, R.D. Dahal and D. Capistrano (eds) *Lessons from Forest Decentralisation: Money, Justice and the Quest for Good Governance in Asia-Pacific.* London: Earthscan

Gadgil, M., Prasad, S.N. and Ali, R. (1983), "Forest Management and Forest Policy in India: A Critical Review" *Social Action*, Vol. 33, No. 2.

Guha, R. (1983), "Forestry in British and Post-British India: A Historical Analysis, *Economic and Political Weekly,* Vol. 18, No. 44, pp. 1882-96.

Guha, R. (1997), "Socio-Ecological Research in India: A Status Report", *Economic and Political Weekly,* Vol. 32, No. 7, pp. 345-52.

MoEF (1988), Government of India, Resolution, National Forest Policy, 1988.

Nathan, D. and Kelkar, G. (2001), "Case for Local Forest Management: Environmental Services, Internalisation of Costs and Markets" *Economic and Political Weekly,* Vol. 36, No. 30, pp. 2835-45.

Nygren, A. (2005), Community-Based Forest Management within the Context of Institutionalised decentralisation in Honduras, *World Development,* Vol. 33, No. 4, pp. 639-55.

Saxena, N.C. (1997), *The Saga of Participatory Forest Management in India,* Indonesia: CIFOR Publications.

Tacconi, L. (2007), "Decentralisation, Forests and Livelihoods: Theory and Narrative", *Global Environmental Change,* Vol. 17, No. 3-4, pp. 338-48.

Notes

1. Sustainable development is defined as "the ability of the present generation to meet their needs without compromising on the ability of the future generations to meet their needs." The dual objectives of sustainable development can be said to be meeting the needs of the present generation on one hand and on the other keeping some of the resources for the future generation as well.

5

Joint Forest Management in Bengal: A Human Nature Cooperation

N.C. Bahuguna

Abstract: Destruction, disturbance and diversion of forest areas together with sharp increase in human population resulted in the reduction of forest cover in West Bengal. The change over from the colonial system of forest management to the Joint Forest Management (JFM) programme in south-west Bengal through a process of evolution began to resuscitate the forests in the state. This programme created a bond between the forest staff and the fringe area people. The creation of Forest Protection Committees institutionalised the system. The success of the programme got the global focus and the programme spread throughout the country. In spite of hurdles, the programme bridged the political, caste and religious lines. Women's empowerment was the biggest success of the programme. In other areas the Joint Forest Management programme was either created or imposed. The creation had a mixed reaction and the imposition of the programme was a complete failure.

Introduction

Darjeeling was once covered with thick forests. In 1844, Mr. Fortune brought *Cryptomeria japonica* seeds. Slowly this plant replaced the natural forests. Hunter (1876) mentioned that in around 1856-57 the tea industry was established. Introduction of tea, cinchona, potatoes and orange cultivation wiped out the remaining forests.

An old inhabitant of Oodlabari in north Bengal recollected that the place was a thick forest when he arrived there in 1934. The only habitation was a timber depot, established in the year 1912. Now, however, the town has a population of more than a hundred thousand.

In Birbhum, a great famine occurred in 1770. Almost 1500 out of 6000 villages were wiped out (Mazumdar, 1875). Official reports of 1772 show that much of the cultivated land relapsed into jungles through which a small body of sepoys forced their way with difficulty. They marched for 120 miles through extensive woods, all in a state of a perfect wilderness throughout the way. Tigers and bears visited the camps every night. The report of 1863 mentions that the area became a barren waste. Presently, hardly any forest is exists there.

In the beginning of the nineteenth century, Sundarban extended upto Dampier Hodges line. Now the Sundarbans is restricted to approximately 10,000 square kilometres which is less than half of the forest area that existed in the 18th century (Danda, 2007).

Destruction, disturbance and diversion of forest area had been the main reason of reduction of forest cover in the state and elsewhere. Sharp increase in the human population with a high density in the country has directly contributed to this destruction. However, in the last couple of decades, in spite of all these adversities, the forest cover has risen from 14.32 per cent in the year 1988 to 16.67 per cent in the year 2007 (Anon., 2010). This increase in the forest cover can be attributed to the Joint Forest Management (JFM) programme.

Chronological Achievement of Joint Forest Management (JFM) in Bengal

The success of JFM can be ascribed to the failure of the century-old colonial system of forest management. The increase in human population, with the growing need for more land and more natural resources together with degenerating human values and decreasing fear of law, began to erode the forests at a rapid pace. The impact was more visible in south-western Bengal, where a new trend of forest destruction started. Initially only the habitual forest offenders entered the forest area for timber theft. The weak legal framework encouraged more and more people to tilt towards this illegal business. Sometimes, the inaction or involvement of the forest staff also encouraged them. The access to easy money motivates the youth to take a short route to illegal activities. The adjoining villagers initially ignored such offences. However, seeing the forest resources getting out of their reach, they could not resist being involved in the affair. One fine morning, every villager from a village entered the forest area. The news spread of the neighbouring villages like wildfire. By the time the forest staff prepared for action, a sea of people flooded the forest. By the evening, the entire forest patch disappeared. Only the bushes obstructed the visibility from one village to another. In south western Bengal, the forest patches are interspersed by the human habitations in a mosaic pattern. The epidemic of mass looting soon spread from one patch to another, crossing the geographical boundaries of the districts. Except for a few big chunks of forests, the wilderness had vanished from Purulia, Bankura and Medinipur in the early 1980s.

With the disappearance of forests, the forest offenders also disappeared. With the foresters' guns rusting in the vaults, the forest staff began to roam freely in the villages without fear of assault. At the same time with the frightening power of the staff gone, the common man image of the foresters started encouraging the people to develop a friendly relationship with them. With more and more interactions, they began to know and feel the pain of each other. The staff realised that every villager was not a thief. The villagers also felt that foresters were not corrupt. Slowly this closeness penetrated into their personal relationship.

JFM: Not Just a Give-and-take Relationship

The concept of JFM was not just a give and take relationship between the forest department and the people. Its roots lay in the mutual respect for each other. The forest staff became a part of their social network. Their presence at any function and religious ceremony raised the social status of the organiser. Their physical and financial inputs together with their independent and impartial view helped in reducing the distress and miseries of the poor. In return, the people began to extend their support to the official duties of the staff. Their call for forest protection became a concern for the entire village. The villagers extended voluntary service when the staff required manpower to overcome the forest offenders. Intially this system was limited to a few pockets where honest and competent staff were posted. In other areas, the staff did not take much interest. Thus, this trend did not extend horizontally. However, with the vertical rise of this trend, it reached the senior officers and was picked up at a certain level of hierarchy. From that level it began to spread roots downwards.

During this period, a few officers were transferred from north Bengal, where fire power had failed to deliver the desired result. The love from the people in pockets of south Bengal changed their hearts. In spite of friendly relations at the root level, the public anger against the department had not subsided. The meetings invariably started with verbal accusations about the staff and often ended with appreciation of each other. In the initial years, it was a traumatic experience for the officers to face the people. But with more and more interaction, the trend changed. The blame game converted into flower shower. With like minded officers joining the region, a healthy competition started and JFM spread its roots to the south-western Bengal.

To institutionalise the system, Forest Protection Committees (FPCs) were created from among the fringe area people. All the adult villagers were made its members. Forest jurisdiction was identified for each FPC. Initially, they did not have rights in these forests except for the collection of Non-Timber Forest Produce (NTFP). Slowly, they were involved in the management of the forest as well. This involvement inculcated a feeling of belongingness among them. They decided to optimise the use of forest resources and minimise their requirements. Instead of axing the trees and branches for their daily fuel requirement, the poor villagers began to use twigs, leaves and pods as firewood. Encouraged by the response of the people, a concept of micro-plan was floated. This concept created an impression that the FPCs would be flooded with money.

JFM: Bridging the Forest Department and Villagers

Initially it was an arduous task to handle the errant villagers, who attended the micro-plan meetings. While the poor villagers expected more work and more wages, the leaders among them intended to pocket the major booty. At one of the first meetings, their expectation turned into shock when the same old schemes were announced. They asked what the difference was. The setback was so big that the leaders decided to boycott the meeting. But the villagers' bond with the staff was so strong that in spite of the disappointment the gathering paid no heed to their leaders. The front seaters left the meeting only to return when they saw the public was still attending the meeting.

The meeting was organised to identify sites for some community development works like ringwells, hand pumps, road maintenance, etc. The other works targeted economic upliftment of poor individuals. Everyone at the gathering wanted to benefit from all the schemes. The Divisional Forest Officer (DFO) declared ringwell as the first item. Almost everyone raised their hands to get the ownership of the well. It was difficult to manage the crowd as the leaders lost interest. The DFO then asked who all covered more than a kilometre to fetch water. There were many raised hands. With distance limit raised to two kilometres, the demand was restricted to a few families in a village. The DFO had almost finalised the village, when a voice appeared from the crowd. A person, who had not raised his hand, had to traverse much more distance, but being a member of the lower caste he did not dare to raise his hand. A few people, however, in the crowd broke the caste barrier and spoke for him. No one raised objections. He was the first beneficiary in the allotment of the ringwell. The shortlisted village also got the same benefits, in spite of the second priority. Suitable sites were chosen for other wells as well. Similarly, other works were also distributed among the villages and villagers.

It had taken almost an hour to convince the people to attend the meeting. It was a chaotic scene when the first item was announced. But thereafter, it was smooth sailing. The greedy people began to disappear. The needy people took over. They continued staying, irrespective of party lines, cast line or religious line.

After the distribution of schemes, the villagers were asked whether the distribution was fruitful or old procedures should be followed. They unanimously aproved the meeting and showed their satisfaction. They said that in the past the villagers often did not reap the benefits as the works were taken up without evaluating their requirements. The micro-planning had seen its first success.

The subsequent success was not so smooth. The senior officers could not conduct meetings everywhere. There were hundreds of FPCs in every division. The DFOs had to depend on the lower staff. The lower staff, who were instrumental in the formation of FPCs, found themselves in an adverse situation when false promises began to flow in the adjoining areas. A few smart fellows handled the pressure. For others, the friends began to turn into foes. It was a Herculean task for the senior officers to bridge this communication gap. They had to spend a lot of energy in spreading the clear message through repeated meetings with ground level officers. Much of the success of the JFM programme depended on the funds made available to conduct such meetings. Frequent interactions gave them an opportunity of bringing innovative ideas to the table. To create a positive image at such meetings, the officers and field level staff invariably projected their new initiatives.

The interaction among the staff began to spread beyond the departmental boundaries. Various departments, which had to achieve physical and financial targets but did not have target groups, were involved. The Forest Departments had target groups readily available for the targets of other departments. The FPC meetings proved to be the confluence of the targets and the target groups. The Animal Husbandry Department had some targets under the cattle immunisation programme. It was a tedious job for their field staff to persuade every villager to take up such work. At the same time, the villagers had cattle but no department to take care in case of need. Thus the FPCs provided a readily available platform for the Animal Husbandry Department as well as the villagers. The same was true for all the other departments dealing with the rural schemes. With the Forest Department becoming a power centre, a few power hungry elements began to raise their eyebrows. Undeterred by their envious feelings, the forest staff continued their efforts to make the JFM programme more successful.

Gender Equality and the JFM

Initially, the FPC meetings were attended mainly by the male members. The women members of the poor families still continued stealing firewood for their daily needs. Although illegal, the forest staff did not object to this pilferage. They requested the ladies to avoid cutting the trees in a polite tone. Such interactions and atmosphere gave an opportunity to the staff to convince them to attend the meetings. Slowly, women's participation in the meetings began to increase. However, the FPCs were still male-dominated. The women did not have the final say. To encourage them, female membership in all families was made compulsory. Thus all the adult members of the family were automatic members in the FPC. This had far-reaching consequences. During the Fourth Regional Steering Committee meeting of Mangrove for Future, an international body consisting of UNDP, IUCN, FAO, UNEP and many other international organisations, a woman in her address said,

> When I was a child, I had to abide by the decision of my father. When I got married, I was governed by my husband. We were poor. So I used to go to the forest for firewood collection. The Forest Guard would shoo me away. Even in the forest, I was dominated by a male. At the meetings, I was silenced simply because I was a woman. The men would say, what did we women know? I used to ponder whether my life had a meaning? Then there was a change. An FPC was formed. I was made an independent member. For the first time, I was allowed to speak without interruption. Thereafter, with the help of the Forest Department, we formed a self-help group. With this, I began to earn money on my own. Suddenly, my status changed. I became a bread-earner in the house. The same ideas which were discarded a few years ago became examples for others. Today, I got the opportunity to speak in the presence of this august gathering and everyone is listening.

Present Scenario of JFM Success Story

The success of the JFM programme was appreciated throughout the world. International channels broadcasted its success. The programme began to spread its roots in the state of West Bengal as well. With the programme gaining momentum, the concept of usufruct sharing cropped up. It was decided that 25 per cent of the revenue earned from timber would be given to the FPC members in south-west Bengal. This order encouraged the villagers towards better involvement. This concept also attracted the people with vested interests. Some NGOs began to demand 50 per cent share for the villagers. Middle men cropped up with this instigation. Before the formation of FPCs, all the villages in the vicinity of the forests used to earn benefits in some form or other. As they did not have any rights, the people of distant villages also shared the advantage of legal or illegal activities. At least the poor villagers did not mind covering long distances to meet their firewood need. But the formation of FPCs became restricted to fringe area people only. With all the rights given only to the fringe area people, the Non-FPC villages began to distance themselves. It was in spite of the fact that the initial formation and planning involved all forest dependent villagers. With the expectation of earning handsome money, a few elements began to disrupt the friendly environment. Inter-FPC rivalry began. In the wildlife areas, where usufruct-sharing was not possible, Eco-Development Committees (EDC) were set up. Compared to FPC areas, more funds were pumped for community development works in EDC areas. With this instant benefit, the FPCs demanded conversion to EDCs.

Conclusion

With time, players in the JFM programme changed. Different officers in different areas began to implement JFM programmes differently. The concept spread throughout the country. The concept which was implemented by the people for the people became the programme of a few officers sitting in closed chambers and a few NGOs who appeared from nowhere. In south-west Bengal where it evolved, the JFM programme still prevails in spite of all adversities. In other areas, where JFM was created, there are mixed results. In areas where JFM was imposed, it has completely failed.

The JFM programme might not have brought substantial economic changes but the programme crossed political, caste, or religious barriers. In addition, it helped women's empowerment. In areas where this programme failed, JFM never existed for the villagers. For those, who are unaware of the evolution of the JFM programme, it is an outdated concept.

References

1. Anonymous, (2008-09), Mangrove for Future (MFF), E-Newsletter. Issue No. 7.
   The Site MFF-Wetlands International in:
   http://www.google.co.in/search?q=bahuguna+MFF&ie=utf-8&oe=utf-8&aq=t&rls=org.mozilla:en-US:official&client=firefox-a. Accessed on 20.08.2012.
2. Anonymous, (2010), State Forest Report. Directorate of Forests, Government of West Bengal. Aranya Bhawan, LA-10A, Salt Lake, Kolkata.
3. Danda, A. (2007), *Surviving in the Sundarbans: Threats and Responses*. An Analytical Description of Life in an Indian Riparian Commons to Obtain the Doctor's Degree at the University of Twente, The Netherlands. Printed by YES in Kolkata, India.
4. Hunter, W.W. (1876), *A Statistical Account of Bengal Volume X, Districts of Darjeeling and Jalpaiguri, and State of Kuch Behar*. Trubner & Co., London.
5. Mazumdar, D. (1975), *West Bengal District Gazetteers: Birbhum*. Government of West Bengal, Calcutta.

6

Contribution of Human Interventions Towards the Sustainability of the Joint Forest Management Programme in South West Bengal

R. Mukhopadhyay and S.B. Roy

Abstract: While people around the globe are struggling with the challenges of depletion of forest ecosystems and associated biodiversity loss, there have also been examples of positive human interventions to reverse the process. Human interventions, in this context, are considered as all the planned activities of the members of a social group with a definite purpose in the form of social action. Such human intervention could be from the society or those made by the public sector with the involvement with society. Joint Forest Management (JFM) has emerged from South West Bengal as one of the viable management options to check the process of degradation of the forest resources with a set of planned interventions made both by the community and the Forest Department. The satellite imageries show that the forest has started regenerating and there has been an increase in the area under forest cover especially in the JFM areas of West Bengal. The present study has been carried out over an area covering 155 Joint Forest Management Committees (JFMCs) of Bankura and West Midnapur districts of West Bengal to understand the role of human interventions in sustaining the JFM programme in South West Bengal. The study shows that human interventions by the community members organised in the form of the JFMCs are the most important determinant for the success of JFM. Human interventions in terms of institutional arrangements to protect the forest, as developed and implemented by the Joint Forest Management Committees (JFMCs), have turned out to be the most important factor influencing the JFM programme in this region. The result points out that the strong institutional arrangement and control mechanism developed by the JFMCs are contributing towards the achieving of the desired goal of protection and conservation of forest resources even without any marked village development incentives.

Introduction

Forests are essential for human beings to survive and provide various associated ecosystem services in the form of provisioning services through various timber and non-timber species; regulatory services like providing shelter belts, checking soil erosion; supporting services like soil nutrient recycling and checking hydrological cycles as well as cultural services. All such ecosystem services help people in meeting their survival needs. Degradation of forest resources thus has a strong negative impact on the survival of the mankind at large.

West Bengal, like many other states of India witnessed massive degradation of forest resources especially in the south western part of the state coupled with tense relations between the Forest Department and the community members during the 1970s and 80s. Joint Forest Management (JFM) has evolved as one of the management options to reverse the process by involving the forest fringe dwellers as partners in protection and management of the forest resources in West Bengal during the 1980s.

Background

The first government order of JFM in the country was issued in the state on July 12, 1989 with the "objective to re-establish moribund *Sal* and other hardwood forests in the districts of Midnapur, Bankura, Purulia, Bardhaman and Birbhum". JFM is an initiative to bring together the Forest Department and the people for the cause of forest conservation with clearly defined and mutually agreed roles and responsibilities and benefit sharing mechanisms. It is for the first time that any state Forest Department in the country has agreed to share 25 per cent of the net sale proceeds of timber with the forest fringe dwellers organised in the form of Forest Protection Committees (FPCs) after fulfilling the functions and duties stipulated in the government order.

It has always been a challenge to the development practitioners as to how to sustain the initiatives and actions of such community institutions that are created and recognised by the government to meet a cause of managing common and public resources. People struggle to find the factors that would contribute towards the sustainability of the programme and the institutions.

In JFM, a group or collection of individuals organises itself explicitly for the purpose of pursuing forest conservation on a sustainable basis jointly with the Forest Department and share rights, responsibilities and certain interests together in a cooperative way as an association that ultimately leads towards taking the shape of a social system (Roy, 1996). The sustainability of the JFM programme can only be achieved, ultimately, at the level of maintaining the human interventions and actions by the JFMC as an institution.

After the initiation of JFM it has spread in all parts of South West Bengal and presently 3735 Joint Forest Management Committees (JFMCs) are managing 326010.1 ha of forest in this region. The reports of the Forest Survey of India and State Forest Reports have stated that the degraded forests have started improving after the adoption of JFM in West Bengal since 1989 and thus there has been a reversal in the process of degradation.

Objectives of the Study

The present study has been carried out to examine how the human interventions by the JFMC members and the Forest Department have contributed in sustaining the JFM programme in this region and among all the interventions which one has turned out to be the most important factor for sustainability of the programme.

Gradation of JFM to Assess the Sustainability of the Programme

Joint Forest Management involves management of a complex system where cultural, ecological and economic elements form a web of human and environment interaction. This web provides checks and balances of cultural values with ecological and economic implications governed by state bureaucratic and people institutions. Each system has components, which are interdependent and interrelated. Each component, say, social/ bureaucratic, ecological and economic, is interwoven with the other in such a fashion that isolation of any hampers others (Roy, 2003). Therefore, we cannot measure the success of JFM by taking into account any one of the elements such as social, economic or ecological.

Purpose of JFM as Stated in the Government Order

JFM as a programme has been adopted in West Bengal with the purpose for the development of the degraded forests and the forest prone to forces of degradation through involvement of people vide the order no (4461-For/D/IS/16/88 dated 12.07.89, modified as 5971 dated 3.10.08 for South West Bengal). JFM requires the members of JFMCs and the Forest Department to act as partners with clearly defined duties and functions as well as benefit sharing arrangements. As stated in the purpose of formation of JFMCs, the success of JFM will be measured against the development of degraded forests in terms of its regeneration status, density and diversity of species. Involvement and the degree of participation of the JFMCs are the means to achieve the stated goal.

Human Interventions Under JFM

Human interventions are undertaken both by the Forest Department (FD) and JFMC. The FD interventions are categorised into five constituent parameters:

I. Institutional arrangements by the Forest Department to

ensure protection from illicit felling, grazing, pest control and communication with JFMC (FDIA).

II. Interventions for development of forests through plantation, soil moisture conservation and silviculture management (FDFM).

III. Interventions for village development, social development, providing productive assets and micro-planning involving the JFMC members (FDVD).

IV. Interventions for distribution of benefits to the JFMCs in terms of timber sharing, wage generation, corpus fund to the JFMC/SHG (FDBD).

V. Interventions for capacity building of the villagers through training (FDCB).

Similarly interventions by the JFMCs are categorised into four constituent parameters:

I. Institutional arrangements to ensure protection of forests against illicit felling, fire, grazing, encroachment, pest control, information exchange within JFMC, social action against offenders and monitoring the rules and norms (JIA)

II. Roles in forest development related activities like plantation, SMC measures and silviculture operations (JFD)

III. Developing communication and network with Panchayati Raj Institutions (PRI) and neighbouring JFMCs (JCN)

IV. Developing and managing community funds and assets (JFD)

The success of JFM depends on how coherently the JFMC members and the Forest Department work together to set out the rules and norms and act together for their implementation.

Methodology

The study is descriptive-cum-exploratory in design. Primary data is collected from the JFMC members through structured interviews, focus group discussion and participatory rural appraisal as well as interviews with the officials and staff of the Forest Department. Statistical methods like correlation and regression analysis was used for analysis of the data. Scores for each constituent aspect of each set of human interventions is calculated from a predetermined set of responses. A numerical four point scale of 0, 1, 2 and 3 has been used to assign scores to the responses. Scores of each of the parameters have been calculated through summation of the scores assigned to the various constituent aspects of each parameter.

Data is collected from 155 JFMCs of Bankura and West Midnapur district following the random sampling method.

Results and Discussion

All the sample JFMCs in South West Bengal under the study can be considered as first generation JFMC as all of them were formed during the late 1980s and early 1990s.The JFMCs are mostly initiated by the FD but with very active support from PRI. West Bengal Forestry Project (1992-1999), meant for supporting JFM in South West Bengal, initiated in the year 1992 and the support from the Ford Foundation for capacity building of staff and JFMCS also helped in spreading the programme in the region during the early 1990s.

The status of JFM has been classified by the researchers into four categories A, B, C and D considering the regeneration status of the forest, crowd density, occurrence of forest offences, encroachment, timber share received by the JFMC and coordination between the Forest Department and JFMC. JFM gradation is considered as dependent variable.

It is seen that the maximum percentage of JFM, i.e. 39 % are in Grade B. While, 34% are in Grade A, 20% are in Grade C and 7% are in Grade D.

Table 1: Correlation of Constituent Parameters of JFMC with Gradation of JFM in SW Bengal

	JFM Gradation	*JIA*	*JFD*	*JCN*	*JFA*
JFM Gradation	1				
JIA	0.76	1			
JFD	0.62	0.57	1		
JCN	0.34	0.32	0.20	1	
JFA	0.66	0.50	0.54	0.13	1

It is observed in Table 1 that all the four constituent parameters of JFMCs have a positive correlation with gradation of JFM in South West Bengal. Among these, JIA has the highest correlation (0.76) followed by JFA (0.66) and JFD (0.62). However, from the above table it becomes clear that JIA alone may contribute significantly in the functioning of JFMCs. It also stands true in the agro climatic context of the *Sal* dominated forest of South West Bengal. The agro climatic condition of the area favours the *Sal* species to regenerate from the coppices on their own if protected from the uncontrolled grazing, fire, uprooting of stumps, etc without many inputs. Thus, protection of young saplings after coppice felling stands out to be the most important factor to regain the vigour of the forest. JFMCs in the area are making an effort to maximise the protection initiatives under the JFM programme in the area.

Table 2: Simple Regression Model of JFMC and FD Interventions in SW Bengal

Model	*Inter-vention*	R^2	*Adjusted* R^2	*Coefficient of X Variable*	*E*	*F*	*T*	*Z Test*
1	JFMC	0.69	0.68	1.84	0.10	336.98	18.35**	0.5
2	FD	0.48	0.48	1.37	0.11	144.35	12.01**	0.5

** = significant at .05 level

Among the single factor models, it is seen that JFMC intervention is the predominant one among the two sets of interventions with a value of 0.69. The result indicates that JFMC interventions alone can explain 69 per cent of the variance in the gradation of JFM. Therefore, JFMC interventions are certainly the most significant one for gradation of JFM.

As JFMC turned out to be the most significant contributor towards the gradation of JFM, in the next step simple regression analysis is done with the constituent parameters of JFMC interventions, i.e. JIA, JFD, JCN and JFA with JFM gradation to understand the most significant parameters of JFMC interventions in terms of gradation of JFM.

Table 3: Summary of Step-wise Regression Analysis with JIA, JFD, JCN and JFA in SW Bengal

Factor		R^2	*Adjusted* R^2	*Coefficient of X Variable*	*E*	R^2 *Change*	*F*	*T*
	Model 1							
JIA		0.58	0.57	1.41	.09		208.55	14.44**
	Model 2							
JIA	0.63	0.62	1.10	.11	.05	129.33	9.89**	
JFD				.39	.08			4.66**
	Model 3							
JIA	0.64	0.63	1.04	.11	.06	89.73	9.16**	
JFD				.39	.08			4.65**
JCN				.16	.07			2.12**
	Model 4							
JIA	0.70	0.70	.86	.10	.13	91.61	8.05**	
JFD				.22	.08			2.72**
JCN				.18	.07			2.61**
JFA				.52	.08			5.96**

Among the above sets of step-wise regression models containing the various constituent parameters of JFMC interventions, it is seen that JIA is the most important factor that has explained 57 per cent of the variance of gradations in its single factor model with a high regression coefficient (1.41). Inclusion of independent variables, JFA in the model changes 13 per cent of the variance in gradation of JFM. For the model at all levels the statistics for the estimated coefficient is significant at .05 level. These are therefore fairly accurate. For the model including all parameters, the estimated coefficient of JIA is significant at 0.05 level. However, with the addition of independent variables with JIA in the model the regression coefficient of JIA decreases.

Thus, from the above model it becomes evident that including the parameters of JFA and JFD with those of JIA improves the model though with a reduced slope.

The above results are consistent with the observations made from correlation analysis in Table 1.

The JIA interventions that has the strongest relation with the gradation of JFM as is found through Regression Analysis clearly shows its impact on gradation of JFM in the two districts. The average JFM gradation score of Bankura is 78 per cent compared to 44 per cent in West Medinipur. The regression coefficient of JIA (1.41) has a high value that proves that even a smaller degree of changes in the intervention as an independent variable brings a higher degree of changes in gradation of JFM.

Institutional Arrangements Developed and Implemented by the JFMCs

It is found that JFMCs have developed and are following certain rules for protection of forest against illicit felling of timber, uncontrolled grazing, fire, encroachment, etc from outsiders and from those in the same village who infringe on a widely accepted and desirable set of rules developed on a consensus basis. Wide and inclusive participation of JFMC members in designing, implementing and monitoring such norms have been a key to the success of JFM in the state.

In the initial years, emphasis was on exclusionary protection to ensure regeneration of degraded forest. Thus, the initial years of JFM saw stringent restrictions on the use of forests. However, with improvement in the forest condition and institutionalisation of the norms, the need to have regular vigil in terms of patrolling becomes less. The nature of offence that occurs now is insignificant in terms of cutting small poles. It is due to the strict vigil that JFMCs consider the minor offence also as illicit felling.

Uncontrolled fire is one of the major threats for forests. It not only damages the young plantation but also causes loss of biodiversity both in terms of flora and fauna. It is found that the forest fire in most cases is caused intentionally by people. People set fire to clear the undergrowth for creating a passage, for collecting NTFPs like *Sal* seed and *Mahua* seed, to create space for cattle grazing, etc. After putting the undergrowth to fire, the grasses and small plants come out in a vigorous way that can be used as fodder. It may often occur through unintentional acts of the people also as they throw the lighted parts of cigarettes in the forest. Such kind of fire problem is more severe in case of South West Bengal during the dry season.

JFMC members are taking part in controlling such fires by creating and maintaining the fire line as a part of preventive measures and creating awareness among the people. In many JFMCs they do not maintain the fire line but try to control fire when it breaks out. It is very important as in the dry forest the fire spreads very fast. So they have to take prompt action to control it before much damage has been caused.

Though people in South West Bengal graze their animals in forest areas but they follow the rule of not grazing them in new plantation area. The plantation monitoring Report of the state also supports the fact that the average survival rate of plantation in South Bengal is more than 80 per cent.

Encroachments in the forest pose a serious threat for its management and development. Controlling encroachment is one of the most important functions of the JFMC. They have to put a lot of effort in evicting as in most of the cases it is done by the villagers of the same village. The group dynamics, village politics are to be dealt with very sensitively.

In most of the JFMCs in South West Bengal JFMCs charge a fine, depending upon the magnitude of offence, ranging from Rs. 100-500 that is deposited in the JFMC account.

JFM has started formally in 1989 and have completed two decades of its journey. JFMCs have been formed as an institution under the programme. According to Tuckman and Jenson (1977), the formation of any group passes through five stages:

(a) Forming – This is the initial stage when the group comes together and members begin to develop their relationship with one another and learn what is expected of them. This is the stage when team building begins and trust starts to develop. Group members will start establishing limits on acceptable behaviour through experimentation. During the initial stage the facilitators had to make concerted efforts to build the trust and confidence of the people.

(b) Storming – During this stage of group development, interpersonal conflicts arise and differences of opinion about the group and its goals surfaces. If the group is unable to clearly state its purposes and goals or if it cannot agree on shared goals, the group may collapse at this point. It is important to work through the conflict at this time and to establish clear goals. During this phase likeminded committed people are identified who can form the group by developing a consensus.

(c) Norming – Once the group resolves its conflicts, it can now establish patterns of how to get its work done. Expectations of one another are clearly articulated and accepted by members of the group. Formal and informal procedures are established in delegating tasks. In this stage the group members develop their own norms, rules, regulations, control mechanisms to run the group and starts functioning accordingly.

(d) Performing – In this stage the group members start performing their jobs to achieve the purpose and goal of the group. The members develop a strong feeling of group identity, and interdependence with each other. They would also like to take up challenging activities to show their abilities. The role of the outside facilitator starts becoming more passive from this stage.

(e) Transforming – In this stage the group members set new agenda, revisit their priorities and the group takes a new shape.

The JFMCs in West Bengal, especially in South West Bengal, have gone through the stages of Forming, Storming, Norming and are now at the Performing stage. FD as the initiator and facilitator had to make a great effort during the first three stages. It is but natural that the FD who has taken the lead to promote and support JFM in the early days does not intervene much now especially in South West Bengal. Though the Beat Officer is the Member Secretary of the JFMCs, it has now taken shape to manage the functioning on their own and is emerging as a self-regulating autonomous institution in South West Bengal.

Sustainability of JFM

JFM has completed two decades of its journey in the state. At this stage it is very important to understand how the major stakeholders, i.e. the JFMC members and the FD considers the future about it to ensure sustainability of the programme.

Though the perception varies among the individuals at different times but in general it reflects whether they have the clarity of purpose and goal of the programme and their ownership with it. In general, it was found that JFMC members consider the improved relationship with the Forest Department coupled with improved forest as the most important benefit of the JFM programme. Improved relationship has brought self-confidence, self-respect and autonomy within them. Improved forests give them returns in terms of NTFPs as well as timber share. People consider them as the byproduct of improved relationship and trust. The people in South West Bengal thus consider the role of JFMC as prime for the success of JFM or it can turn out otherwise if the JFMCs do not perform their duties. The JFMC effort was considered so vital for the success of JFM that when people were questioned on its non-existence, 86 per cent replied that the forests would be destroyed.

On the other hand, forest officials opined that JFM is a viable option for managing the forests with less conflict and improved output in terms of forest productivity and quality. They have also shared the view that now with improved relationship they have increased the authority. It is not in terms of "Gun Power" rather by improving the "Personal Power" of trust and confidence that they can take action against the offenders with collective support from JFMC.

All of them have observed that there has been a reduction in the rate of offences after formation of JFMCs. It is the JFMC members who catch the offenders and report to the department.

Conclusion

The JFM movement in West Bengal is attaining maturity. The JFMC members themselves are playing the most important role for the JFM as they have significant correlation (0.83).

It is found that human interventions, especially the institutional arrangements become the major determinants of sustainability of JFM. Wherever, the human interventions are designed to win the trust of people by giving them due recognition, the options have emerged to solve the problems related to resource management and resource endowment. On the other hand even though the policy and the resources remain the same, yet variations in human interventions in terms of functioning of JFMCs has resulted in micro level variations of sustainability of JFM even within the same agro-climatic regions. Overall, the result shows that the interventions designed and implemented by the JFMCs are the most important determinant for sustainability of JFM. The JFMCs in the region are by now time tested as they have completed two decades of existence and their efforts have shown positive results in terms of regeneration of the degraded forest. Therefore, in the context of South West Bengal care should be given to maintain the spirit of the JFMCs for sustaining their institutional arrangements.

Bibliography

Agarwal, C. and Saigal, S. (1996), *Joint Forest Management in India : A Brief Review.* SPWD Working Paper, New Delhi.

Blaike, P. and Baginski, O. Springate (2007), in Oliver Springate Baginski and Piers Blaike (eds) *Forests, People and Power: The Political Ecology of Reform in South Asia,* The Earthscan Forestry Library, London, pp. 1-21

Banerjee, A. K. (1996), Some Observations on Community Forestry, in M. Victor (ed.), *Income Generation Through Community Forestry.* Bangkok : RECOFTC, WLN. Vol. XI No. 31.

Banerjee, A.K. (2004), *Participatory Forest Management in West Bengal: A Review of Policies and Implementation,* Working Paper 3, ODG Dev University of East Anglia and Ramakrishna Mission, Kolkata, pp. 27-36.

Banerjee, A.K. (2007), Joint Forest Management in West Bengal in Oliver Springate Baginski and Piers Blaike (eds) *Forests, People and Power: The Political Ecology of Reform in South Asia,* The Earthscan Forestry Library, London, pp. 221-58.

Bebbington, A.J. (1999), *Capitals and Capabilities: A Framework for Analysing Peasant Viability, Rural Livelihoods and Poverty,* Int. J. World Development, 27(12), 2021-2044.

Champion, H.G. and Seth, S.K. (1968), *A Revised Survey of the Forest Types of India.* Manager of Publications, Government of India, Delhi.

Dutta, M., Roy, S., Saha, S. and Maity, D.S. (2004), Forest Protection Policies and Local Benefits from NTFP: Lessons from West Bengal, *Economic and Political Weekly,* February 7, pp. 587-91.

Guhathakurta, P. and Roy, S. (2000), *Joint Forest Management in West Bengal: A Critique,* WWF for Nature, India, pp. 28-32 and 112-25.

IBRAD (2007), *Study on Effectiveness and Functioning of Joint Forest Management Committees in India*, Project of NAEB, MOEF, Government of India, Inter India Publications, New Delhi, pp. 1-20, 125-34

IIFM, Bhopal (2007), *C&I India Update*, Vol. 5, No. 2, IIFM ITTO Research Project, Bhopal, India, pp. 1-16.

IIFM, Bhopal (2009), *C&I India Update*, Vol. 7, No. 3 & 4, IIFM ITTO Research Project, Bhopal, India pp. 13-22.

Mishra, T.K, Maiti, S.K. and Mondal, D.K. (2004), Joint Forest Management in West Bengal: It's Spread, Performance and Impact in N.H. Ravindranath and P. Sudha (ed) *Joint Forest Management in India: Spread, Performance and Impact*, Universities Press, pp. 160-78.

Roy, S.B. (2003), Conceptual Framework for Criteria and Indicator for Assessment of Sustainable Development: An Illustration from Joint Forest Management; *Indian Journal of Landscape System and Ecological Studies*, Kolkata, Vol. 26, No. 2.

Roy, S.B. (1995), Social Indication Towards Institutionalisation of Development Programme: A Case Study from Joint Forest Management, in S.B. Roy (Ed), *Enabling Environment for Joint Forest Management*, Inter India Publication, New Delhi.

Roy, S.B. (1996), Social Institutionalisation towards institutionalisation of Development Programme; A Case Study from Joint Forest Management, *South Asian Anthropologist*, Vol. 17 (2); 81-87.

Roy, S.B., (1993), Forest Protection Committees in West Bengal, *Economic and Political Weekly*, 27 (29), pp. 1528-30

State of Forest Report (2009), Forest Survey of India, MOEF, Dehradun, pp. 163-6.

Tuckman, Bruce W. and Jensen, Mary Ann C. (1977), Stages of Small Group Development Revisited, *Group and Organizational Studies*, 2, 419-427.

7

Sustainable Management of Minor Forest Produce Through Joint Forest Management in Orissa: A Case Study of Lamtaput

R.K. Khosla

Abstract: JFM emerged as a participatory forest management strategy to protect the rights of the forest dweller by endowing them equal rights over forest resources. The JFM programme in Orissa was initiated much before the enforcement of this policy at the national level. The increasing resource pressure due to deforestation urged various communities and groups to begin protection of forests in the 1970s. By the late 1980s, the community forest protection group did spread throughout the state. The people's organisations under JFM namely, VPCs, VSSs and VFPCs have members both from tribal people and non-tribal people, but the bulk of them are those who depend on forests for their livelihood. The collection and sale of the minor forest products (MFPs) are crucial to their subsistence economy. The question of customary rights of tribal people to collect MFPs is the central issue of all forest policies, formulated from time to time. Nevertheless, ground reality based on the study of Lamtaput block proves that the traditional community forest management system is more participatory for the larger interest of tribal society. Although the JFM programme has spread quickly throughout the state but it was noticed that due to institutional problems, associated with the committee and lack of trust between community groups and the forest department, the programme has not succeeded in achieving its objectives. According to the NTFPs policy of the year 2000, the *panchayats* in Orissa were vested with the power of collecting and marketing of MFPs, which contradicts the JFM policy. Though the forestry sector in Orissa contributed a meagre revenue of 0.27 per cent in 2000-01 to the NSDP, the livelihood support in terms of MFPs is immense in sustaining a large number of forest-dependent people and tribals in particular.

Introduction

The concept of Joint Forest Management (JFM) has gained rapid acceptance in India in the 1990s. The central idea behind this new system of forest management was to transform the centralized, top down, bureaucratic forest management system introduced during the colonial rule to decentralised, participatory, local need-based management of forest resources *(Sarin, 1996: 1-3)*. The JFM programme seeks to share both the responsibilities and accountabilities between the Forest Department (FD) and local communities in managing the forests' resources. The JFM programme is the outcome of the realisation that without the active participation of local communities the fast depletion of forests cannot possibly be controlled and regeneration of already degraded forests will never succeed. The broad objective of JFM is to empower the local communities and make them come to terms with their rights over forests accompanied by their duties to protect and manage them. The programme is a strategy of sharing forest products and the responsibilities and decision-making power over forest lands between the Forest Department and local communities.

The initiation of a new forest management strategy was to protect the large scale destruction of forests by illegal commercialisation of forest resources and ensure substantial amount of Minor Forest Products (MFPs) for forest-dependent people as MFPs is an important source of livelihood for these people due to limited non-agricultural earning opportunities in rural areas. The need to reduce the large scale depletion of MFPs and to protect the interest of forest-dependent people, particularly the tribals, had urged the government to change the forest policy to adopt a participatory forest management system in the country. In this context the study critically analysed the role of the JFM model in managing the MFPs for the interest of the tribal communities. The study is broadly divided into two parts, the first part discusses the profile of MFPs of the country based on its annual production and the share that goes to the tribal communities. It also discusses the contribution of MFP in the economic growth of the country as a whole, at the micro and macro level and its importance in the household economy. The second part is based on a case study of Orissa. In this part the study concentrated on the impact of the JFM model in protecting and preserving the MFPs without disturbing the needs and interests of tribal communities.

Minor Forest Products in India

Forests constitute a major source of natural capital of the country. In India, the major source of both self-employment and indirect employment in forests is the collection, processing and sale of a wide range of MFPs. These include bamboo, cane, grasses, oilseeds, fibres, gums and resins, dyes, medicinal plants, spices, honey, leaves and seeds (Mitchell, 2003). The Minor Forest Products have had significant value in the life of the people living in and around the forest. It is estimated that 70 per cent of MFPs are collected in 5 states, i.e. Maharashtra, Madhya Pradesh, Bihar, Orissa and Andhra Pradesh, where 65 per cent of tribal population lives. MFPs are important raw materials for cottage, small and village industries and contribute to the national income through export and import substitution *(Report of the Expert Group, Government of India, 2004:114)*. A report of an Expert Committee set up by the Ministry of Environment and Forests (1999) has observed that some 50 million tribal people depend on MFPs for meeting their subsistence and income needs. The profile of MFPs and its annual production in India is being furnished in the following Table.

Profile of MFPs in the Country

Sl. No.	*Products*	*Annual Production (MT)*
1	Wild Edible Products	101200
2	Myrobalan	132250
3	Sal Seeds	709700
4	Mahua Seeds	697600
5	Neem Seeds	115000
6	Other Seeds	57500
7	Essential Oils	3160
8	Gum Karaya	15000
9	Katha	5750
10	Tans and dyes including cutch	222900
11	Bamboo	4716600
12	Fibres and Flosses	15000
13	Bendu Leaves	360000
14	Lac	30000
	Total	1,17,71,850

Source: Report of Expert Committee set up by the Ministry of Forests and Environment (1999). Quoted from Tenth Report, Standing Committee on Social Justice and Empowerment – 2005-06, (Fourteenth Lok Sabha), Ministry of Tribal Affairs, Grants-in-Aid to State Tribal Development Cooperative Corporations for Minor Forest Produce Operations, Lok Sabha Secretariat, New Delhi, December, 2005,

MFPs and Tribal People's Share

Minor forest produce provides substantial sustenance to the tribal communities particularly in the backward regions of our country. In some cases MFPs are the main source of cash income through which they meet the expenses of non-subsistence needs like health and education. In the report of the Expert Committee set up by the Ministry of Forests and Environment (1999) accounted tribals' share of MFP, details are as follows.

In the above table, the report states that tribal families mostly collect MFPs for self-consumption as well as for the sale of the non-consumable products to meet their domestic economy. Over the years it has been found that availability of MFPs is being drastically reduced which adversely affects the life style of the tribal families. Earlier they used to collect more amount

Tribal Share of MFP Market

Sl. No.	*Commodity*	*Tribal Share (In percent)*	*Procurement Value (Rs. in Crore)*
1	Hill Grass	100	150
2	Tamarind	65	60
3	Sal+Mahua+Other tree-borne oil seeds	100	100
4	Mahua Flower	100	15
5	Tej Patta	100	35
6	Siyali Leaves	100	35
7	Shikakai	100	10
8	Honey	25	15
9	Myrobalan	100	10
10	Sericulture (Muga/Tassar)	100	30
11	Shellac (Lac)	100	75
12	Gum (Karaya) & Others	100	15
13	Other Commodities	100	100
14	Estimated Supply	95	650

Source: Insight Management Consultants (2002). Quoted from Tenth Report, Standing Committee on Social Justice and Empowerment – 2005-06, (Fourteenth Lok Sabha), Ministry of Tribal Affairs, Grants-in-Aid to State Tribal Development Cooperative Corporations for Minor Forest Produce Operations, Lok Sabha Secretariat, New Delhi, December, 2005.

of forest products for self-consumption and a minimal amount to sell at the local market. The scarcity of MFPs by illegal commercialisation resulted in stiff competition among the tribal MFPs collecting families which leads to the collection of immature plant parts, leaves, flowers, fruit, barks, roots and tubers thereby causing damage to the mother plant and less returns to the forest-dependent community (Tenth Report, December, 2005: 7-9).

Contribution of MFP to National Account

The Gross Domestic Product (GDP) growth has for long been the key indicator for the country's macro-economic policy-making. Over the years the national income accounts suffered from the major limitation that they focused mainly on goods and services that are bought and sold in markets and ignore the non-marketed services such as natural assets. As a result, there exists an inconsistent treatment of man-made capital and natural capital. In assessing the cost and capital, the national income accounting neglects the new scarcities of natural resources, which threaten the sustained productivity of the economy and also overlook the degradation of environmental quality. The report of the Central Statistical Organisation (CSO) accounted the domestic products from forestry and logging from 1999-2000 to 2006-07, appended in the following Table:

Domestic Products from Forestry and Logging (Rs. in Crore)

Item	*1999-2000*	*2000-01*	*2001-02*	*2002-03*	*2003-04*	*2004-05*	*2005-06*	*2006-07*
Value of Output	19907	20443	21071	21211	20969	21417	21818	22212
Industrial wood	1818	1804	2478	2196	1676	1919	1905	1962
Firewood	16038	16710	16736	17192	17654	17770	18165	18548
Minor Forest Products	2051	1929	1857	1823	1738	1728	1748	1702
Less: repair maintenance and other operational costs	1991	2044	2107	2121	2097	2142	2182	2221
Gross domestic Product	17916	18399	18964	19090	18872	19276	19636	19991
Less: consumption of fixed capital	630	649	673	689	724	741	761	780
Net Domestic Product	**17286**	**17750**	**18291**	**18401**	**18148**	**18535**	**18875**	**19211**

Source: National Accounts Statistics, Central Statistical Organisation, Ministry of Statistics & Programme Implementation, Government of India, 2008, p. 153.

The above Table indicates that the value of output from the forestry and logging accounted was Rs. 19,907 crores in

1999-2000 and Rs. 22,212 crore in 2006-07. In the case of Minor Forest Products, the report accounted Rs. 2,051 crore in 1999-2000, whereas Rs. 1702 crore in 2006-07. The contribution of the forestry sector in Gross Domestic Product of the country is accounted Rs. 17,916 crore in 1999-2000, whereas Rs. 19991 crore is accounted in 2006-07. Finally, the Net Domestic Product of the forestry and logging indicates that Rs. 17,286 crore in 1999-2000, whereas Rs. 19,211 crore in 2006-07. The report clearly indicates that the contribution of MFPs in domestic products has been declining gradually due to the large scale illegal destruction of the forest cover in different parts of the country. A comparative analysis of state-wise value of output from MFPs from 1999-2000 to 2005-06, has been accounted by the Central Statistical Organisation (CSO) and is appended in the following Table.

State-wise Value of Output from Minor Forest Products (At Current Price)

(Rs. in Lakhs)

States/U.Ts	*1999-2000*	*2000-01*	*2001-02*	*2002-03*	*2003-04*	*2004-05*	*2005-06*
Andhra Pradesh	18378	17431	9109	10632	7698	9217	9217
Arunachal Pradesh	1300	4670	2780	2370	1160	127	127
Assam	606	624	646	668	704	750	750
Bihar	467	395	696	335	236	235	158
Goa	2	3	52	20	32	44	50
Gujarat	1827	636	646	543	936	550	1096
Haryana	475	290	393	473	54	626	573
Himachal Pradesh	7856	7961	8395	11122	11143	6091	6092
Jammu & Kashmir	1909	2945	2384	1943	2152	1061	1061
Karnataka	2837	2093	1858	1704	2783	5941	5941
Kerala	173	208	214	192	379	314	314
Madhya Pradesh	30599	32423	24673	25778	27971	38575	38575
Maharashtra	73419	62336	74196	62154	53928	42354	42661

Manipur	445	616	380	355	660	375	375
Meghalaya	569	716	909	1166	2310	2818	2818
Mizoram	433	454	384	453	461	525	525
Nagaland	11	18	23	9	10	22	22
Orissa	18065	19009	18476	19567	16860	12516	12516
Punjab	439	464	381	466	475	417	417
Rajasthan	1510	1693	1490	1121	1046	791	489
Sikkim	123	134	199	216	229	220	236
Tamil Nadu	3146	1977	2312	2421	3457	4555	640
Tripura	145	96	119	132	251	121	121
Uttar Pradesh	6387	5631	4347	4172	3750	335	342
West Bengal	1051	1140	784	695	453	410	410
A & N Island	12	16	9	4	4	20	16
D & N Haveli	0	0	0	0	0	0	0
Daman & Diu	5	0	0	1	1	0	0
Delhi	0	0	0	0	0	0	0
Lakshadweep	0	0	0	0	0	0	0
Puducherry	0	0	0	0	0	0	0
Chandigarh	0	0	0	0	0	1	1
Jharkhand	5062	5125	5675	5975	6444	9047	9047
Chhattisgarh	16194	19650	22220	24503	22904	18481	18388
Uttarakhand	11639	9567	8664	9121	12274	22435	22435
Total	**205084**	**198321**	**192414**	**188310**	**181259**	**178974**	**175413**

Source: State-wise Estimates of Value of Output from Agriculture and Allied Activities with New Base-Year 1999-2000 (1999-2000 to 2005-06), Central Statistical Organisation, Ministry of Statistics and Programme Implementation, Government of India, 2008, p. 165.

The above Table shows that the value of output from MFPs of the country was Rs. 205,084 in 1999-2000, whereas in 2005-2006 it was Rs. 175,413.00. At the state level, the report indicates that the major states, i.e. Andhra Pradesh, Bihar, Gujarat, Himachal Pradesh, Jammu & Kashmir, Karnataka, Orissa, Punjab, Tamil Nadu, Uttar Pradesh and West Bengal, the output value of MFPs has declined over the years. In the North Eastern region, some states, namely Assam, Meghalaya, Mizoram, and Nagaland the value of output of MFPs has increased, whereas in states like Arunachal Pradesh, Manipur and Tripura the trend has declined during the same years.

Contribution of MFPs at Macro and Micro Level

India's forests are endowed with vast natural resources, including minor forest products, i.e. medicinal plants, leaves, fruits, seeds, bamboo, canes, etc. MFPs provide diverse employment and economic opportunities to support rural livelihoods. Small-scale forest-based enterprises, many of which rely on MFPs, provide up to half the income of about 25 per cent of India's rural labour force. Nearly half the country's forest revenue and 70 per cent of export forest revenue comes from MFPs. The export potential of MFPs has been growing as the scope of globalisation increases and recognition of the health benefits of herbs becomes more widespread.

The role of MFPs in alleviating poverty, particularly for forest-dependent people, is now well recognised. The MFPs provide subsistence and cash income to millions of tribal and forest dwellers in India, as a major source for fuel, fodder, food, medicines, construction materials and livelihoods. In states like Orissa, Madhya Pradesh, Himachal Pradesh and Bihar more than 80 per cent of forest dwellers depend entirely on MFPs; 17 per cent of landless depend on daily wage labour, mainly consisting of the collection of MFPs and 39 per cent are engaged in MFPs collection as a subsidiary occupation. The proportion of household income from MFPs varies from state to state and from one area to another, at a rough estimate, it ranges from 5.4 per cent to 55 per cent.

As the market for natural products is growing, particularly for medicinal and aromatic plants and organic mountain products, the sustainable harvesting and management of these products offers an immense opportunity to improve livelihoods of local communities as well as conserving resources in India. Besides supporting livelihoods, the MFPs sector provides employment for the unskilled and semi-skilled rural poor. It is estimated that 1.6 million person-years of employment in India are derived from MFPs, while the forestry sector in total provides 2.3 million person-years of employment. In certain seasons, when there are no regular work opportunities, the MFP sector provides alternative sources of livelihoods. This sector also contributes heavily to the rural healthcare system (Rasul, 2008; Khare, 2000).

Dependence of Households on MFPs

The MFPs not only contribute to the economic growth of the country but also supports all the households of the country. The National Sample Survey Organisation (NSSO), in its 54th round report accounted the dependence of households on MFPs in the country as a whole and in four major states, i.e. Bihar, Karnataka, Madhya Pradesh and Maharashtra. The following Table shows the distribution of households in collecting MFPs—

Distribution of Households Collecting MFPs

States	*Firewood*	*Fodder*	*MFPs*	*State Total*
India	24744 (36)	6450 (9)	9365 (14)	67674 (100)
Bihar	2977 (40)	1117 (15)	582 (7)	7482 (100)
Karnataka	1666 (53)	539 (17)	304 (10)	3161 (100)
Madhya Pradesh	3184 (55)	516 (9)	1408 (24)	5812 (100)
Maharashtra	3222 (60)	679 (13)	514 (9)	5374 (100)

Note: Figures in parentheses denote percentage of households in each category.

Source: NSSO 54 Rounds (1999). Quoted from Mohanty, Pratap C., Role of Community Participation through JFM for Rural Development in India, Strength Based Strategy – 2006, p. 90. http://www.strengthbasedstrategies.com/PAPERS/MohantyP.

The above Table shows that the nature of dependence of households in four states (Bihar, Karnataka, Madhya Pradesh and Maharashtra) on Common Property Resources as measured by number of households collecting each of the three commodities, i.e. firewood, fodder and MFPs. The report states that firewood is one of the largest forest resources in all four states that the percentage varies from 40 per cent to 60 per cent, whereas the average rate of collection at India level shows 36 per cent.

The percentage of household collecting fodder is lowest, ranging from 9 per cent in the state of Madhya Pradesh to 17 per cent for Karnataka. The MFPs collection also involves low percentages of households, with the range varying from 7 per cent in Bihar to 24 per cent in Madhya Pradesh. The report further accounted the percentage of distribution of collected items in the four states. Details are given in the following Table.

MFPs Collected and Percentage Distribution of Collected Items

Minor Forest Products	*India*	*Bihar*	*Karnataka*	*Madhya Pradesh*	*Maharashtra*
Fruits	17,86	15.48	31.03	28.21	25.29
Roots, Tubers, Spinach etc	9.10	14.22	1.59	7.93	0.33
Gums & resins	0.61	—	—	1.65	0.16
Honey	2.96	1.83	9.28	2.21	2.30
Medicinal/herbs	2.72	0.69	—	2.38	0.49
Fish	16.93	19.72	11.41	4.96	16.91
Leaves	26.51	28.78	10.34	43.28	29.72
Weeds, Grass, Cane, Bamboo	23.31	19.27	36.34	9.38	24.79

Note: Column totals equal 100.
Source: NSSO 54th Round (1999). Quoted from *Mohanty, Pratap C., Role of Community Participation through JFM for Rural Development in India, Strength Based Strategy – 2006,* p. 90. http://www.strengthbasedstrategies.com/ PAPERS/MohantyP.

In the above Table the report shows that products such as leaves, weeds, cane grass and bamboo constitute the largest collections in our country. Madhya Pradesh stands first in collection of fruits and leaves (Tendu leaves for making village cigarettes) i.e. 28.21 and 43.28 per cent respectively. In Karnataka and Maharashtra, the collection of weeds, grass, cane grass and bamboo takes place as largest compared to Bihar and Madhya Pradesh (Mohanty, 2006).

The MFPs is one of the important sources for survival of tribal communities in rural society. Several studies demonstrate the importance of MFPs for survival and household economy of certain communities of society, i.e. tribal people. A study by Ghosal, S. (March, 2011) in West Bengal demonstrates the importance of MFPs for livelihood in the southern-western part of the state. The study states that forest communities, especially tribal people are highly dependent on the collection of forest products for their domestic as well as commercial needs. The importance of MFPs within the household economy is greater when other income sources from agriculture and wage labouring are limited. The poor transportation system, distance between remote tribal villages and the local market, limited availability of manufacturing products are other reasons for the high levels of dependence on MFPs (Ghosal, 2011).

JFM Programme in Orissa

In Orissa, the JFM programme was initiated much before the enforcement of this policy at the national level. With the increase in resource pressure due to deforestation, various communities and groups began to protect forests in the 1970s and by the late 1980s, the community forest protection spread throughout the state. On August 1, 1988, the Government of Orissa passed the nation's first forest policy resolution endorsing community management practices (Poffenberger et al., 1996). According to the 1988 resolution, villagers were granted certain concessions in the matter of meeting bona fide requirements of firewood and small timber. The Forest Protection Committees (FPCs) were constituted in each assigned village under the resolution. The Government of Orissa further modified the earlier circular to provide representation to women and minorities in the FPCs on the basis of the JFM guidelines issued by the Government of India on June 1, 1990. In order to make the forest protection drive more effective and transparent through involvement of local villagers, the Government of Orissa issued another resolution of JFM in 1993 (Orissa Development Report, 2002: 172-173), under which *Vana Samrakhyan Samitis* (VSSs) were constituted under the JFM programme. The forest protection committee, i.e., VSSs were constituted by members of both tribal and non-tribal communities. The well organised VSSs groups have been effectively involved in protection of forests and collects MFPs without harming the valuable trees in order to get better returns from the forests.

Contribution of MFPs in the State's Economy

Forests are an important source of non-tax revenue for the Government of Orissa. During the post-independence period several forest policies were adopted by the government to protect the forests and earn revenue from its resources. The report of the Economic Survey – 2003-04 of the Government of Orissa shows the year-wise collection of revenue value from 1998-99 to 2002-03 in the Table given below.

Revenue Receipt from Forest Products (Rs. in Crore)

Item	*1998-99*	*1999-00*	*2000-01*	*2001-02*	*2002-03*
Timber & Firewood	6.47	5.21	14.23	9.36	9.15
Bamboo	8.52	5.50	5.11	2.03	0.07
Tendu Leaf	63.50	74.50	55.00	69.00	75.00
Minor Forest Produce	—	—	—	1.33	0.62
Others	8.32	10.18	9.91	6.09	12.08
Total	**86.81**	**95.39**	**84.25**	**87.81**	**96.92**

Source: *Economic Survey – 2003-04, Government of Orissa.*

The above Table shows that during 1998-99 to 2002-03 the total value of revenue earned by the state government from the forest resources has increased over the years, whereas the account of each item in the Table shows that the value has been declining during the period except the revenue earned from *Tendu (Kendu)* leaf. The major challenge before the government is sustainable management of forest resources as despite several forest policies, illegal commercialisation of forest products could not be arrested systematically (Economic Survey 2003-04: 6/7-6/8).

The subject of customary rights of tribal people to collect minor forest produce is the central issue of all forest policies, formulated from time to time by the Government of Orissa. Historically, the ownership of government over forests and forest products has alienated the bona fide forest users of Minor Forest Produce (MFP) from securing benefits of subsistence from forests. Though the forestry sector in Orissa contributes a meagre revenue of 0.27 (Q) per cent (2000-01) to the Net State

Domestic Product (NSDP) (*Orissa Development Report, 2002:145*), the livelihood support in terms of Minor Forest Produce is immense in sustaining a large number of forest-dependent people and tribal people in particular. Indeed, despite numbers of forest laws and regulations in Orissa, tribal people find challenges to access the forest resources as per their need and requirement. Some of these pertain to issues related to ownership rights over forestlands and produce accessibility. It has also been found that due to active involvement of private organisations or forest traders, the forest department machineries are failing to protect the interest of tribal people in the form of ensuring right value to primary collectors of forest products and marketing arrangements at the local level. The absence of adequate attention to marketing infrastructure has also resulted in the under utilisation of existing forest potential of the state.

Despite the significant role of MFPs in supporting rural livelihoods and economy, the potential of the forest resources are still grossly underutilised and their contribution to poverty alleviation has remained minimal in the state. The people who collect and process MFPs receive minimal income even sometimes less than they would earn from wage labour. The authoritative forest policies and faulty management system at institutional level have contributed to large scale destruction of forest resources, particularly the MFPs. The following case study demonstrates the argument.

Study Area

The study was carried out in the Lamtaput block in the Koraput district of Orissa. Lamtaput block is situated in the southern part of Koraput district. Lamtaput block was selected because of two considerations; first, its high concentration of tribal population and second, its socio-cultural and economic proximity to the forest. The block is predominantly hilly and has a thin forest cover and the majority population in the block are tribal people. The tribal population of the block is 46.27 per cent (*District Statistical Handbook*, 2005: p. 9).

Methodology

For this study three villages were selected in the Lamtaput block and in each village thirty sample households were selected to collect data/information. During the fieldwork, a survey was carried out at sample households with the help of a structured questionnaire. During the field study a group discussion was also arranged with the community forest protection groups, non-government organisations and forest department officials to obtain information. A random sampling technique was adopted for the study considering the concentration of tribal population in the sampling villages. Prior to the fieldwork government documents, Census data was referred to identify the forest cover area of the study area and also the dependence of tribal people on forest resources. The secondary literature, i.e. journals, books and previous study report were also referred to obtain a comprehensive understanding of this study.

Source of Livelihood

In Lamataput block, most of the tribal people are forest dwellers. Traditionally, forest resources, i.e. Minor Forest Produces contribute to the livelihoods of the forest dwelling communities. Although the majority of tribal people are engaged in agriculture but the forest still forms the mainstay of livelihood and domestic economy. Mostly, MFP contributes to household self-sufficiency, food security, income generation, etc. Earnings from agriculture are generally not sufficient to maintain a tribal family in Lamtaput block for the whole year. It is because of low quality of agricultural land due to an undulating landscape and its low productivity, inadequate availability of suitable cultivable land in the hands of tribal people, use of traditional agricultural technology and scarcity of water resources for the lack of irrigation that has resulted in the low income or poverty of the tribal communities. Hence, the tribals generally supplement their food requirements as well as income through collection of MFP. The following Table shows the level of dependence of tribals on MFPs for their livelihood in the sample villages.

Source of Livelihood of the Sample Respondents

Name of the Village	*Agriculture*	*Forest Product*
Devgondna	13	17
Bhimariput	12	18
Hingeiput	09	21
Total	34	56

The above Table clearly indicates that the majority of tribal population depends on forests for their livelihoods. Out of the total 90 sample households of the three villages, 56 households have expressed their view that the major source of livelihood for them is forest products. The study learned that due to the long process of turning the forest cover areas into a source of revenue, illegal exploitation and commercialisation of forest resources have resulted in significant loss in the amount of MFPs production. Though the forest is the age-old source of subsistence for the tribal people but owing to large scale depletion over the years, they have been alienated from their common property resources.

Minor Forest Produce and Tribal Life

The tribal people have adopted the forest as their habitat. Their subsistence pattern, economy and social institutions, beliefs and practices are closely linked with the forest. The relation between them and forest has often been called symbiotic. The tribal depend on the forest and forest in its turn depends on them for the preservation and continuity. The social, religious and economic systems of the tribals revolve around the forest and they still like to live in their original natural abode consisting of hills and forests and practise their traditional way of living, i.e. rituals, customs, dance, music and belief system. A set of religious myths and social customs were built around the forests to ensure that the economically important trees were protected, human needs were met and the species that were more commonly available were equitably distributed. Above all, apart from socio-cultural and religious life, forests are the primary source of survival for the tribal people. The following Table shows the pattern of use of MFPs by the sample villages.

Pattern of Use of MFPs

Name of the Village	*Survival*	*Commercial Purpose*
Devgondna	21	09
Bhimariput	18	12
Hingeiput	19	11
Total	58	32

The pattern of use of MFPs by the tribal people shown in the above Table proves that out of the 90 household respondents, 58 households expressed that MFPs are the important source of their survival, whereas 32 households have said that they use the MFPs for commercial purpose. It is not possible to quantify the level of use of MFPs by tribal for different purpose and record the level of dependence of tribal people on MFPs because the collection of forest products takes place throughout the year, hence they have been depending on forests throughout the year. For commercial purposes, the seasonal forest products (*tamarind, tendu leaves, brooms,* etc) and to some extent firewood help them to earn some money by selling the MFPs at the weekly market.

Most of the tribal people collect fruits, roots, leaves, mushrooms, etc., for their family consumption. The seasonal vegetables which include different types of mushrooms, the jungle roots, are the most nutritious food item of the tribal families. For the social ceremony, the tribal community drinks wine, prepared using *Mahua* (*Madhuca indica*) flower. The healthcare pattern of the tribal people is also closely linked with the forests. The task of the women, on the other hand, is very crucial not only with respect to the collection of forest products but also to the processing and marketing at the local level. They are the primary collectors of MFP, i.e. various fruits, seasonal vegetables, fuelwood, jungle roots, *Siadi* leaves, brooms, etc.

Collection of the MFPs of the tribal families takes place with twofold objectives i.e. direct consumption and to meet the domestic economy by selling non-consumable products. Even in the socio-cultural ritual life of the tribal family, the women folk play an important role to gather various forest products to meet their requirements. At the same time, women in tribal society are more concerned with managing the forest resources and thus they never cause any destruction to the forest and the valuable trees/plants as it provides them with food, employment, household requirements, etc.

Community Forest Protection System

The Community Forest Protection (CFP) system is one of the oldest and traditional forest management practices that have informally existed in Orissa. The study of S. S. Negi (1996) demonstrates the CFP practice of Budhikhamari village in Mayurbhanj district of Orissa. The sal forests around this village had been devastated due to excessive biotic pressure. The situation had become so bad that regeneration of sal was almost impossible, which had an adverse impact on the life of the villagers. It was under these difficult conditions that the villagers formed a Village Forest Protection Committee at Budhikhamari for the first time and later in seven other villages. They achieved instant success through minimum use of forest products without degradation of forests and involvement in plantation activities. This initiative benefited the local communities immensely (Negi, 1996).

The CFP system existed in Orissa much before the JFM programme was introduced. The CFP system was controlled by the *Gaon Kutum* (apex body of tribal village). Forest protection committees are in operation in a formal way in all three villages, i.e. in Devgondna (*Maa Nakti Bhairabi Bana Surkhya Samiti*), Bhimariput (*Jangal Surakya Committee*) and Hingeiput (*Maa Thakurani Jangala Surakhya Committee*). The *Maa Nakti Bhairabi Bana Surakhya Samiti* in Devgondna village is the registered committee under the Rayagada Bana Khanda, Rayagada in 1998. The CFMs bodies are quite participatory primarily because they are constituted by homogeneous communities or a single village. Although these committees are independent formal bodies but they are controlled by the traditional norms and rules of the respective village.

The operation system of the CFP committee differs from village to village and a harmonious decision-making atmosphere prevails in the process of protecting forest resources. The forest protection pattern is quite interesting and systematic. In the first stage, the villagers select a *Dongor* (Big Hill) or *Kupli* (Small Hill), adjoining to their village. The committee of each village selects two to three persons to protect the forest area and in return villagers give them food grain as the labour cost of the day. The villagers equally use the forest products without causing any destruction. In this process the women folk of the village are also benefited through easy collection of MFPs. The *Gaon Kutum* (village committee) has drawn certain provisions according to which if any person goes against the norm of the village, the village body takes action following the provision of the village committee.

The worries of some part for these forest protection committees are the forest mafias and timber traders who smuggle timber and various MFPs at night. Though villagers often lodge complaints against the forest mafia at the forest officials, but the concerned authorities are not much interested in taking action against the defaulters because of high-handed corruption at the local official level. The authoritative control by the forest officials also goes against the interest of the rights of the tribal people and interest of the CFP committee of the village.

Status of Community Forest Protection Committee

Name of the village (*)	*Authoritative ownership of the Forest Officials over forest cover areas*	*Restrictions to use the Minor Forest Products*	*Illegal Commercialisation of Forest Products by the forest mafias/ timber traders*
Devgondna	25	21	28
Bhimariput	19	17	26
Hingeiput	23	27	19
Total	67	65	73

Note: * : As some respondents have given multiple answers to a single question so the addition of the total number of responses is not the same with the number of households interviewed, i.e. 30 households, but it is more than that.

The above Table shows that out of 30 sample households in each village, the respondents of each household had given multiple answers to the questions asked them relating to the functional status of the CFPs. The first challenge before the CFPs committee is the ownership of forest that out of the 90 household respondents of three villages, 67 households have said that though the forest protection committees are very active in protecting forest cover areas adjoining their village but over the years it has been found out that the forest officials have claimed the ownership of the forest cover areas which defeats the interest of the committees. The committee also states that the protection of forest cover areas is quite a challenging task. Almost 65 sample households mentioned keeping vigil on forest cover areas is quite challenging due to the increasing number of forest traders. The changing pattern of participatory forest policy does not create a conducive atmosphere for villagers to protect them from the restrictions in accessing the MFPs levied by the forest officials. The forest mafias and timber traders are other challenges for the CFPs to protect the MFPs from illegal commercialisation. In the three sample villages, 73 households agreed that illegal commercialisation of MFPs is prevalent. They have pointed out two crucial issues; first, whenever the CFP committee tries to resist the forest mafias, CFP members frequently receive life threats. As a result the CFP committees had to take further steps in this matter. Secondly, a number of times the CFP committees have also brought the issue of the illegal commercialisation to the notice of the forest officials but no action has been taken against the forest mafia. Also, the forest officials have failed to preserve and protect the resources. Thus, it clearly shows that CFP committees are losing its operational scope over the years.

Status of JFM Programme

Much before the JFM programme, the Government of Orissa allowed the local communities to protect Reserved Forests surrounding their villages and in return they were granted certain rights of usufruct in those forests. Then in 1990, similar provisions were extended to Protected Forests. Further, following the Government of India's resolution on JFM, the Government of Orissa adopted the policy in July 1993 to formalise the arrangement. This policy granted the communities usufruct rights to Non-Timber Forest Produce (NTFP) (Human and Pattanaik, 2000:34). The provision of the JFM programme endows power to the local level forest officials to constitute a committee at the village level and select the forest area to preserve and protect it. These provisions are equally applied in the area of study.

The study learned that the operational process of the participatory management of forest resources under the JFM programme has been found unsatisfactory. Despite implementation of the JFM programme, the colonial pattern of control over the forests and the MFPs is still very much in existence, where the issue of tribal right has been undermined by the state machinery. The authoritative control of the forest officials over the forest resources and non-recognition of the community forest protection committee are major shortcomings of the JFM programme in the study area.

Status of JFM Programme

Name of the Village(*)	*Lack of awareness among villagers of legal provisions of JFM programme*	*Forest officials: less responsible and more authoritative*	*Capacity building strategy missing in JFM system*	*Reluctance to grant rights to forest protection groups*
Devgondna	27	21	28	23
Bhimariput	21	29	19	21
Hingeiput	22	26	21	26
Total	70	76	68	70

Note: * : As some respondents have given multiple answers to a single question so the addition of the total number of responses is not the same with the number of respondents interviewed, i.e. 30 households, but it is more than that.

The JFM programme was initiated to build a participatory forest management system where the forest department and the forest dwellers enjoyed equal rights and responsibility to protect and preserve the fast depletion of forest resources. In the study area, this programme has not been accepted positively by wide sections of the rural society. There are a number of factors that are responsible for the weakness of the programme. The above Table shows that out of the 90 sample households of the three villages, 70 households have expressed their ignorance of the legal provisions of the JFM programme. Even the forest officials are not cooperative. They take no initiative in making the villagers aware of these provisions and this has proved to be a major setback for the success of the JFM programme. The study also learned that 76 households have stated that the forest officials are less responsible and more authoritative in managing forest resources under the JFM programme. In the study area the role of the forest officials has been that of dictating to the villagers instead of taking equal responsibility under the JFM programme. Further, 68 households mentioned that the capacity building strategy is missing under the programme, whereas 70 households have clearly pointed out the reluctance of forest officials in granting rights to the forest protection groups, especially where forest cover is healthy and valuable.

The new strategy of the forest management system is a great threat to the livelihood and domestic economy of the tribal communities. In Hingeiput village, the tribal people have stated that the forest officials are exercising their authority over the CFP committee in the name of the JFM programme, as a result of which the CFP is losing its autonomy over MFPs. The great deal of nexus between the local forest officials, traders and political leaders is also prevalent in the study area where illegal commercialisation of forest products are taking place on a large scale. Bhimariput and Hingeiput villagers have mentioned that after the implementation of the JFM programme, the forest officials have restricted the access of the tribal people over the forest products harvesting, whereas the forest traders and contractor were given a free hand to access the forest areas causing large scale destruction of forest resources. The poverty-stricken tribal people cannot understand the legal provision of the JFM programme, neither do they want to lose the source of their livelihood.

Conflict Areas of JFM Programme

The JFM programme came into force with enabling resolutions by the state government, permitting partnership with local people for ensuring an effective forest management. But the study explored that sustainable management of minor forest products is threatened owing to the absence of proper mechanisms required to implement the programme. In the present system of the JFM programme several shortcomings have emerged, particularly related to tribal interest. These include:

(i) The legal framework for joint management remains weak and controversial. First, the existing old rights and privileges of the dependent people in most degraded forests do not match the corresponding responsibility and often more than one village have their rights on the same forest. Second, the new settlers in a village who are deprived of such traditional rights resort to illegal practices.

(ii) Intra-village conflicts are some of the regular features. As forest track boundaries were not formally demarcated initially at the degraded stage, the conflicts begin to emerge as soon as valuable products are regenerated and green forest cover comes up. The boundary disputes between neighbouring Village Forest Management Committees are another threat to the success of JFM which begins once harvesting starts.

(iii) The recent Act for Extension of Panchayati Raj to the Scheduled Areas gives ownership rights over minor forest produce to the *Gram Sabhas* in the Scheduled Areas. The Lamtaput block falls in the Schedule Areas, where the status of village Forest Management Committees versus village panchayats has created a great deal of controversies, since the links between panchayats and JFM groups are fairly weak. Moreover, such committees do not have legal and statutory rights to manage forest resources on a sustainable basis.

Conclusion

The Joint Forest Management strategy was brought into operation in order to preserve and protect the forest resources realising the growing needs of local communities and large scale depletion of forest resources. The critical analysis of the study reveals that the JFM model of management of forest resources is unclear in the study area and it is far from meeting the expectation in the management of minor forest products. There are a series of contradictions, deficiencies and conflicts among the state machineries and tribal people. The JFM programme clearly stated that it is a strategy of partnership between communities and the state to regulate the use and management of forests. However, ground reality proved that the traditional community forest protection system is a more participatory model for the tribal communities. Although the JFM programme spread quickly throughout the state, it has been noticed that in Lamtaput block that due to lack of trust between community groups and the forest department, the programme could not achieve its objectives.

On the part of sustainable management of MFPs products, it has been revealed from the study area that CFP strategy is quite participatory and suitable for the tribal communities in order to protect the forest product. The JFM model is one of the best models in managing the forest products, but tribal people of the study villages say this model does not serve the interest of forest dwellers in free access of the MFPs. Therefore, after analysing the policy of the JFM programme and its present form of practice, in the perspective of sustainable MFPs, the study found that the programme needs a proper policy direction for its better future. In this perspective the following issues are being identified:

(a) The JFM programme should adopt a holistic approach of participatory, local need-based practice so that the responsibility and accountability of management of forest resources will be equally shared between the Forest Department and local communities. (b) The present form of JFM framework does not recognise the widespread Community Forest Protection (CFP) committee at the state level. This study learned that these committees contribute immensely towards the sustainable management of MFPs. Hence, a separate legal framework should be placed to recognise the CFP committee in rural areas. (c) Demarcation of boundaries of the forest areas protected by various CFP committees should be prioritised at first track level. For this, state governments should undertake a comprehensive survey of the CFP Committee engaged in protection of forest areas, with the help of the Forest Department and Civil Society Organisations so that the actual function of these committees will be revealed. (d) Nationalisation of marketing the MFPs should be promoted in order to prevent a market monopoly and subsequent exploitation of the primary collectors. Promotion of cooperative societies under the guidance of the government should be emphasised for better benefit of forest-dependent people. (e) The government should provide support to forest dwellers in the process of skill development training and capacity building on market so that the primary collector of MFPs would be capable enough at the marketplace in price fixation of their products. Finally, promotion of traditional knowledge on medicinal species should also be given emphasis in order to meet the growing demand of herbal medicine.

References

District Statistical Handbook, Koraput, Directorate of Economics and Statistics, Orissa, Bhubaneswar, 2005.

Economic Survey 2003-04, Directorate of Economics and Statistics, Planning and Coordination Department, Government of Orissa.

Ghosal, S., Importance of Non-Timber Forest Products in Native Household Economy, *Journal of Geography and Regional Planning*, Vol. 4 (3), March, 2011, pp. 159-68.

Human, Joe and Pattanaik, Manoj, *Community Forest Management: A Casebook from India*, Oxfam, 2000.

Khare, Arvind, Sarin, Madhu, Saxena, N.C., Palit, Subhabrata, Bathla, Seema, Vania, Farhad and Sathyanarayana, M., *Joint Forest Management: Policy, Practice and Prospects*, London: International Institute for Environment and Development, 2000.

Mitchell, C.P. et al, Non-Timber Forest Products: Availability, Production, Consumption, Management and Marketing in Eastern India, April 2003.

Mohanty, Pratap C., Role of Community Participation through JFM for Rural Development in India, Strength Based Strategy – 2006. Website: http://www.strengthbasedstrategies.com/PAPERS/MohantyP.

National Accounts Statistics, Central Statistical Organisation, Ministry of Statistics & Programme Implementation, Government of India, 2008.

Negi, S.S., *Forests for Socio-Economic and Rural Development in India*, New Delhi: M.D. Publications Pvt. Ltd., 1996.

Orissa Development Report, Planning Commission, Government of India, 2002.

Poffenberger, Mark et al., "Communities Sustaining India's Forests in the Twenty-first Century", in Mark Poffenberger and Betsy McGean (eds.), *Village Voices, Forest Choices: Joint Forest Management in India*, Delhi: Oxford University Press, 1996.

Rasul, Golam, Karki, Madhav and Sah, Ram P., "The Role of Non-Timber Forest Products in Poverty Reduction in India: Prospects and Problems", *Development in Practice*, Vol. 18, No. 6, 2008, pp. 779-88.

Report of the Expert Group on Prevention of Alienation of Tribal Land and its Restoration, Ministry of Rural Development, Government of India, 2004.

Sarin, Madhu, *Joint Forest Management: The Haryana Experience*, Ahmedabad: Centre for Environment Education, 1996.

Statewise Estimates of Value of Output from Agriculture and Allied Activities with New Base-Year 1999-2000 (1999-2000 to 2005-06), Central Statistical Organisation, Ministry of Statistics and Programme Implementation, Government of India, 2008.

Tenth Report, Standing Committee on Social Justice and Empowerment 2005-06, (Fourteenth Lok Sabha), Ministry of Tribal Affairs, Grants-in-Aid to State Tribal Development Cooperative Corporations for Minor Forest Produce Operations, Lok Sabha Secretariat, New Delhi, December, 2005.Website: http://www.dfid.gov.uk /r4d/PDF/outputs /Forestry

8

Economics of Forest Dependence: Evidences from Nagarhole National Park, Western Ghats of Karnataka

K. Raj

Abstract: Forest resources continue to support livelihood needs of an estimated 275 million people in rural India since the forest sector continues to occupy the second largest land cover after agriculture. National Parks and Sanctuaries cover about 5 per cent of the country's geographical area and these forests are not only inhabited by wilderness but also by indigenous forest dwellers for centuries. These communities besides, getting fuel wood, medicinal plants, food, fodder, wood for house construction, also earn about one-third of their income from the sale of non-timber forest products. Forest resources therefore, continue to act as an insurance or safety net for these communities particularly during drought periods apart from generating regular employment opportunities. On the one hand, depletion of forest resources in recent decades owing to various factors has affected local communities' essential livelihood needs. Consequently they have to spend 40-50 per cent of working hours in collecting forest produce. On the other, appropriation of forestlands by the government for in situ conservation has further deprived local communities' dependence on forests.

Against this backdrop, the study has been carried out in Nagarhole National Park in the Western Ghats of Karnataka state with the objectives of estimating the extent of dependence of forest dwellers on the national park for eking out their livelihood needs including collection of timber and non-timber forest products, employment and income generation. The study examines the degree of dependence on forests by communities living inside and on the fringe of the national park with contrast property rights regimes and ecological settings. Empirical data derived from the two distinct study sites show that high dependence on the national park by communities living inside the national park for subsistence needs, whereas, their counterparts depend on forests for commercial gains. This data includes occupations of household heads, collection of NTFPs and their types, quantities consumed and marketed, time spent in gathering each commodity, duration of consumption, prices of NTFPs in local markets. The methodology followed in assessing the extent of reliance on forest produce includes direct pricing method, cost of collection method, and direct substitutes method.

Introduction

India's forests are not only inhabited by wilderness but also by millions of indigenous forest dwellers for centuries. Forests, besides providing bona fide livelihood needs, have played a vital role in the socio-economic and cultural fabric of forest-dependent communities since time immemorial (Gadgil and Guha, 1992). "Today, in India there are about 100 million forest dwellers in the country living in and around forest areas and another 275 million for whom forests have continued to be an important source of their livelihood and means of survival" (Lynch, 1992 and Saxena, 2000). This implies that local communities in India besides, getting fuelwood, fodder, and timber for house construction also earn about one-third of their income from the sale of MFP (Raymond, 1997). These evidences have validated the importance of forests for meeting livelihood needs of local communities all over India. It is also a well established fact that the environmental, economic, historical, and socio-cultural ethos of forest-dependent communities have been nurtured by the forest ecosystem for ages. Simultaneously, these communities take a legitimate interest in protecting and managing the forest resources for their continued existence. They also inculcated the practice of living harmoniously with forests by eking out a sustainable livelihood. But appropriation of community managed forest resources by the authoritarian state as a state property resulted in the end of traditional management of forests. The emergence of state management of forests is mainly attributed to widespread appropriation of forests by the larger economy rather than the local economy. Consequently accelerated deforestation and the consequent environmental degradation led to the formulation of forest conservation and wildlife protection policies. However, the inherent weakness of these policies is that they offer little or scant attention to forest dwellers' livelihood needs and their stake over forest resources. Therefore, it is argued that the most important reason for fast depletion of forest resources is that historically forests have been conserved and managed by local communities in a sustainable manner. But presently, it is believed that the irresponsibilities and disempowerment of local communities in the process of community management of forests by the centralised decisions lead to loss of control over forests. As a result, the core objective of these policies designed for conserving forest resources is counterproductive following non-participation of local communities and the growing conflict between foresters and forest dwellers. In reality, sustained deforestation continues to cripple the government's effort of environmental conservation and also seriously constrain livelihood needs of forest dwellers that lead to unsustainable development. Achieving environmentally sustainable development by addressing concomitantly environmental conservation apart from unlocking sustainable livelihood opportunities to forest dwellers is absent in wildlife protection policies. Finally, the Government of India, viewing the urgency of this problem, passed the Scheduled Tribes and Other Traditional Forest Dwellers (Recognition of Forest Rights) Act (TFRA) 2006 in the parliament, towards realising inclusive and participatory forest conservation and management. However, many researchers have expressed reservations about the operation of this policy in practice mainly owing to overlapping of forest and wildlife policies.

In India, an unprecedented pace of deforestation in recent years has caused serious economic, environmental hazards and worsening of livelihood conditions. Therefore, India's forest ecosystem is viewed as one of the most 'critical ecosystems' or 'hotspots' of biodiversity. The country has lost annually 235 sq km forest cover in the last two decades. Unabated depletion of forest cover is a major source of concern for environmental sustainability and survival of local communities in the future, not to speak of meeting their livelihood needs. It is observed that continued denudation of forest resources would pose serious challenges to ensure environmental stability as well as sustaining economic well-being of the local communities. The sustainability of forest resources appears to be conditional on the harmonisation of forest policy with end users and managers. Therefore, the end users' perceptions on forest resources and their conservation and management priorities need to be taken into account in order to realise twin objectives simultaneously, viz. forest conservation and meeting livelihood needs in a sustainable way (Kothari et al., 1996). Therefore, it is justified at least in academic circles that participatory approach to forest management and conservation is the best alternative method to market mechanism and government (Chopra et al., 1990). Poffenberger et al. (1996) aptly observe that the successful management of natural resources does not happen unless the people associated with the resources actively participate in designing and executing the various ventures intended to improve their welfare. Further, people's participation in management of forests can minimise conflict, utilise natural ecosystems on a sustainable basis to maximise the flow of important products to communities, and generate income and employment opportunities. It is well acknowledged in recent times that people's participation in decentralised policy decisions plays an effective role in inclusive and broader economic development process rather than command and control policies followed by the government in the past. In this backdrop, the present study was undertaken in one of the rich biodiversity hotspots of the Western Ghats, viz. Nagarhole National Park to assess conservation and livelihood needs.

Biodiversity of Nagarhole National Park

The study area—Nagarhole National Park (NNP)—was rechristened as Rajiv Gandhi National Park (RGNP) in 1992. The park comprises an area of 643.39 sq kms spread over Kodagu and Mysore districts of Southern Karnataka was created in 1983 with the consequence of Wildlife (Protection) Act 1972 for the purpose of wildlife protection. The park is a part of the Bandipura Tiger Reserve (BTR) and it falls in Nilgiri Biosphere Reserve (NBR) comprising adjoining forests of Kerala and Tamil Nadu. The park represents one of the finest biodiversity hot spots among the protected areas of India. Conservation of this biodiversity 'hotspot' has received a worldwide attention including the World Bank's Global Environmental Facility (GEF) to launch India Eco-Development Project (IEDP) in 1996, by recognising its rich and unique biodiversity such as (fauna) large carnivores. The park abounds with a wide variety of fauna like large mammals including tigers, elephants, leopards, dhols, sloth bears, gaur, sambhar chital, munt jac and langurs and about 250 species of birds. The dominant flora is moist, mixed and dry deciduous forests and a few pockets of semi-evergreen forests are found along the western boundary and scrub forests exist in low rain forest regions on the eastern edge. About 15 per cent or 102 sq kms of the park is under teak plantation.

The park also supports 1550 tribal (inhabitant) families spread in and around it, among these families about 6145 *adivasis* (tribals) live in 54 *haadies* (tribal settlements) inside the park and about 25,855 *adivasis* reside on the periphery of the National Park. The prominent resident tribes are the Jenukurubas (honey tappers), Bettakurubas (hunters and gatherers), Yeravas and Soligas (small cultivators). The park confronts numerous conflicts centred between conservation priorities on the one hand and bona fide livelihood needs of local people on the other. The conflicts tantamount to illegal and indiscriminate tree felling, hunting of animals, frequent forest fires and encroachment. In order to mitigate human induced conflict, the

World Bank aided IEDP is under implementation since 1996 in the park with a view to achieve integrated conservation and development (WB, 1996).

Environmenental Pressures in Nagarhole National Park

Since its formation, NNP has been afflicted with many significant pressures on its biodiversity. The important pressures on the park area are identified as frequent forest fires, illegal poaching and logging by timber mafia, encroachment on peripheries of the park, livestock grazing, collection of NTFPs, man-animal conflicts, conflicts between local stakeholders and park authorities. Frequent forest fires are the major threats to biodiversity of the NNP. "Forest fires are set intentionally for timber harvesting, land conversion or shifting agriculture and also in the course of disputes over property and land rights" (WRI, 2000-01). Forest fires in NNP have become a regular feature during the summer period and the major forest fires have caused catastrophes to both flora and fauna. The controversy over the killing of a tribal youth led to destruction of over 35 sq kms of forests in 1990. However, the Indian Remote Sensing (IRS) satellite pictures have revealed that about 18,000 ha or 180 sq kms of forests, shrubs, herbs, undergrowth grass and unknown number of animals and birds were worst affected in 1990 (*The Hindu Survey on Environment*, 1992). In 1992, about 2000 ha or 20 sq kms of the forest area was burnt to ashes. Relentlessly in 1996 forest fires once again destroyed almost 1000 ha or 100 sq kms of forests. In 1997, 250 ha or 2.5 sq kms of forests went up in flames. In 1999 according to the IRS picture, an area of 90.08 ha or 90.08 sq kms of forest area was affected due to the forest fire (Madhav, *The New Indian Express*, August 5, 1999 and Sharma, *Frontline*, June 4, 1999).

Apart from wildfire, timber smuggling by timber mafia and illegal poaching by wildlife traders are on the rise in recent years. Recently a wildlife group has discovered large-scale tree felling inside the National Park in which over 500 stumps of sandalwood and teak have been found (Jayasri, 2002). Poaching of wild animals is, however, flourishing in the National Park. 'Jaw trap' poaching of tigers and other wild animals by interstate poachers was unearthed in May 2002. This incident shows that the park is amenable to poaching activity in spite of Rs. 2 crores spent every year by FD for the protection and management of the park. Wild Life First (WLF), a voluntary organisation reported deaths of 77 elephants in NNP. The report further stated that around 44 tuskers were killed by poachers (*The New Indian Express*, February 21, 2003). Apart from the above pressures on the park, planters have encroached forest areas around the National Park to grow agricultural and plantation crops. Further, planters are given the right to own guns to protect themselves from the animal menace and other risks and animals frequently become victims whenever they stray into the plantation areas. Large tracts of forestlands were submerged around Nagarhole due to construction of major irrigation dams like Kabini and Taraka further; as many as 500 tribal families were displaced.

Animal grazing within and around the park is said to be another threat to the biodiversity of the park. According to the World Bank's Eco-Development Report (1996), grazing inside the park has threatened wildlife as swamps are drained and converted into fields. About 5000 heads of cattle graze inside the park, mostly in outer buffer zones, lead to habitat degradation (WB, 1996). The collection of food, fuelwood, MFP and other NTFPs by the local community is viewed as another important pressure on the peaceful existence of wild animals and also on biodiversity at large (WB, 1996). Local communities are strongly opposing the eco-development project and they are agitating to protect themselves from displacement. The basic rights over forests for eking out their livelihood in a sustainable way is denied by the park authorities. This has, however, resulted in the deteriorating relationship between the park managers and local community over conservation versus livelihood realisation. All these intricate pressures on the park have spurred uncontrolled destruction of biodiversity as well as livelihood needs of forest dwellers.

Objectives

1. To estimate the extent of dependence of the local community on Nagarhole National Park for collection

of non-timber and timber forest products towards their livelihood needs.
2. To study the extent of annual employment and income creation from collection of non-timber and timber forest products.
3. Finally, to prepare a blueprint for unlocking sustainable livelihood opportunities by meeting conservation needs of the National Park with people's involvement.

Methodological Framework

The survey was carried out by giving equal representation to people living in and around Nagarhole National Park, which is under state management. A formal questionnaire was developed; a draft questionnaire was tested through a pilot survey. A random sampling technique is used for the selection of households from *hadis* of NNP. Four *hadis* from inside the national park (INP), viz. Gadde *hadi*, Gonigadde *hadi*, Siddapura *hadi* and Murkal *hadi* and three *hadi*s from outside the national park (ONP), viz. Bommadu *hadi*, Chandanakere *hadi* and Karekandi *hadi* were selected. A total number of 175 households were selected from the national park for the purpose of survey. The distribution of sample households is as follows: 100 households from INP, 75 households from ONP. The detailed information collected from the sample households was as follows: the socio-economic status, households' dependence on a wide range of NTFPs and TFPs for meeting livelihood needs and employment and income generation and conservation and management of the national park. The study estimates the direct use values or consumptive benefits of forest products such as NTFPs which is a market-based approach, the main methods commonly applied by scholars in the estimation of NTFP direct value. Methodology followed in assessing extent of reliance on forest produce includes direct pricing method, cost of collection method, and direct substitutes method. The research study is principally descriptive and analytical in nature. This data includes occupations of household heads, collection of NTFPs and their types, quantities consumed and marketed, time spent in gathering each commodity, duration of consumption, prices of NTFPs in local markets. The results were used to test hypotheses by adopting Chi-square test. In addition, standard deviation, co-efficient of variation, percentages and averages were used to analyse different issues that emerged in the course of the study.

A Profile of the Study Area and Sample Households

The Nagarhole National Park (NNP) consists of many aboriginal tribal settlements or *hadis*. In order to give due representation to households living inside and outside (fringe) the national park, four *hadis* from inside the national park (INP), viz. Gadde*hadi*, Siddapura, Gonigadde and Murkal were chosen and three *hadis*, viz. Chandanakere, Bommadu and Karekandi were selected from outside or on the periphery of the national park (ONP) for the study. The location of the study area, NNP of Virajpet taluk in Coorg district is given in Figure 1.

The geographic, socio-economic, demographic and basic characteristics of the tribal settlements living inside and the periphery of NNP are given in Table 1. The study area NNP is situated in Virajpet *taluka* of Kodagu district and covers a total area of 643.42 sq kms. Of the total area, Core Zone and Tourism Zone consist of 192 sq kms (29.86 per cent) and 110 sq kms (17.09 per cent) respectively and non-core area or buffer zone covers an area of 341 sq kms (53.03 per cent). There are 51 tribal settlements within the park comprising about 1974 households with a total population of 7389. The forest area is sparsely populated with a very low density of population. The average size of households is 3.74 and the density of population in INP is 11.49 per sq km, which is less than the district's mean density of 118 per sq km. The park provides shelter to diverse ethnic tribal groups, viz. Jenu Kurubas, Betta Kurubas, Paniyas, Yeravas, Soligas, and Hakki Pikkis etc. The study area comprises four *hadis* from INP and three *hadis* from ONP. There are 361 households and the total population size is 1293. Of the 361 households 175 (48 per cent) households were interviewed. The literacy rate in both the settlements is 42 per cent. Tribals living inside the park were using the forestland for a variety of agro-pastoral production until 1972. The establishment of the national

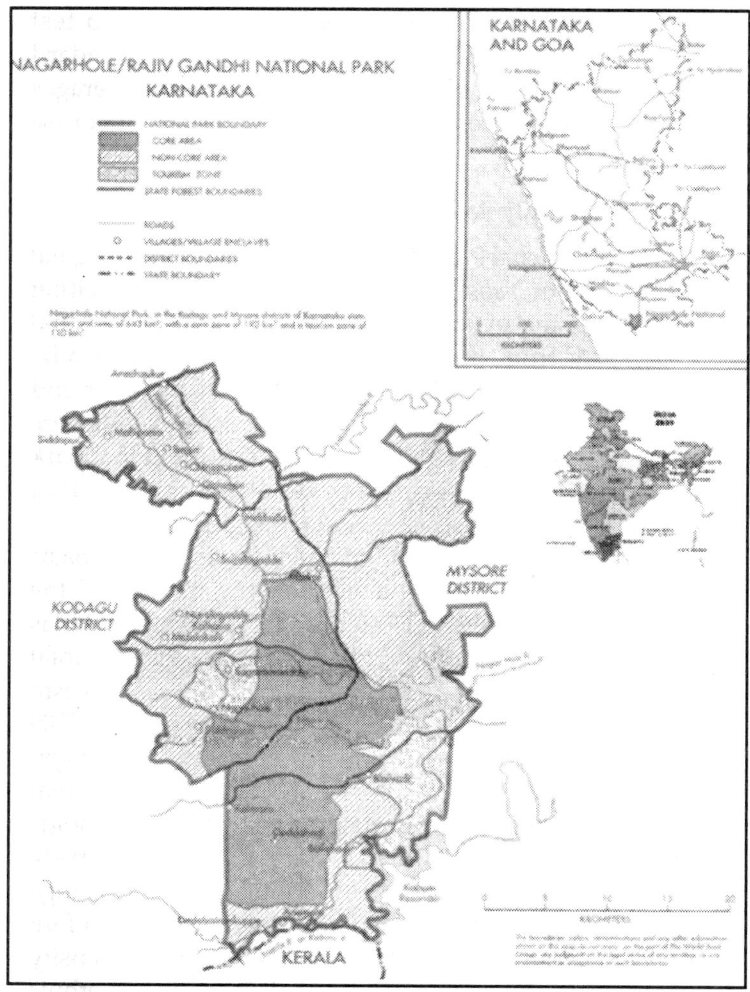

Figure 1: *The Location of the Study Area—Nagarhole National Park*

park with the implementation of Wildlife (Protection) Act 1972, by the government, excludes tribal communities from the land, which was traditionally supporting their bona fide livelihood needs. Consequently, small-scale agricultural operations have been prohibited and tribals are forced to abandon their agricultural activities as well as livestock rearing inside the park. Once the land for traditional cultivation and pastureland for

Table 1: A Profile of the Tribal Settlements in Nagarhole National Park

Total Geographical Area of the Park	643.42^	100 (%)
1. Core Zone	192	29.86
2. Buffer Zone	110	17.10
3. Tourism Zone	341	53.03
Total Number of Tribal Settlements	51	–
1. Total Population	7389	–
2. Number of Households	1974	–
3. Average Size of the Household	3.74	–
4. Density of Population	11.49^	–

	INP					*ONP*				
Particulars	*Gadde hadi*	*Goni gadde*	*Murkal*	*Sidda-pura*	*Total*	*Bommadu*	*Chandana-kere*	*Kare-kandi*	*Total*	*Grand Total*
Total Population	312	201	86	89	688	326	112	167	605	1293
Total Number of Households	57	81	24	28	190	86	38	47	171	361
Average Size of Households	5.47	2.48	3.58	3.17	3.62	3.79	2.94	3.55	3.53	3.52
No. of Sample Households	30 (52)*	30(37)	20(83)	20(71)	100(52)	35(40)	25(65)	15(39)	75(43)	175(48)
Literacy Rate (%)	43	39	47	42	42	51	57	49	42	42
Total Agricultural Land (ha)	17	15	11	17	60	71	60	79	210	270
Per capita land holding (ha)′	0.29	0.18	0.45	0.60	0.31	0.82	1.57	1.68	1.22	0.74
Total livestock	No	No	No	No	No	28	35	25	88	88

EDP [ø]	Yes	Yes	No	No	Y-2	Yes	Yes	Yes	Y-3	Yes-5
Primary Health Centre (PHC)	Yes	-	-	-	01	-	-	-	00	01
Primary School	+	+	+	-	+03 -01	+	-	-	+01-02	+ 04-02
Drinking Water Source	HP	Sm	HP	Sm	HP-2 Sm 2	HP	Stream	HP	HP-2 Sm 1	HP-4 Sm-3
Electricity Supply	-	-	-	-	- 4	+	+	+	+ 3	+ 3 - 4
Type of House	TH	TH	TH	TH	TH: 4	Tiles	Tiles	Tiles	T-3	TH- 4 Tile-3

^ Sq. Km. [ø] EDP= Eco-Development Programme.
[*] Percentage of sample households,
ʹ Land holding including kitchen garden in INP
[+] Present, [-] Absent, HP= Hand Pump, Sm= Stream.
TH: Thatched houses, Tiles: Tile houses
Source: Compiled from Various Sources

animal grazing has been lost they are forced to seek jobs in plantation areas where they are forced to work as bonded labourers on adjoining coffee estates. Tribal communities however, continue to lead a sustainable livelihood by gathering NTFPs and occasionally hunting small games. Being a hunter-gatherer, tribal people possess a rich traditional environmental knowledge (TEK) pertaining to spatial and temporal distribution of forest resources. Apart from collection of MFP, they offer their labour on coffee estates in order to supplement their livelihood. Only a few households have undertaken agricultural operations and kitchen garden activities on the fringes of NNP in spite of prohibition. Agricultural operations have been carried out in INP in a restricted way, for instance, in Gaddehaadi 17 ha of land are under agricultural activities including kitchen garden, Gonigadde has 15 ha, Siddapura 11 ha, and Murkal 17 ha of agricultural land. The tribal settlements on the periphery of the park command a large area of agricultural land compared to tribal settlements in INP. For instance, Bommadu has 71 ha, Chandanakere 60 ha and Karekandi 79 ha of agricultural land. The total land under cultivation constitutes about 270 ha, of which, 60 ha of land area is in INP and 210 ha of land area in ONP. The per capita land holding in INP is 0.31 ha and in ONP it is 1.22 ha. Livestock rearing is strictly not put into practice in the park and no household owns livestock for the last two decades. However, it is practised in *hadi*s located on the periphery of the park. The park is under severe pressure on account of relentless encroachment on its periphery. This is particularly due to encroachment for alternative uses of forestland for instance, plantation crops, agricultural needs and grazing of livestock. The Eco-Development Programme (EDP) has been implemented in *hadi*s of ONP; however, many *hadi*s of INP have rejected the EDP apprehending displacement and losing livelihood security. Local communities depend on forests for a variety of needs. Tribal people have specialised in hut construction which is usually made up of a timber and good quality bamboo with clay paste. Houses in INP are more or less thatched with mud walls. Thatching of roof is done with bamboo and local grass. Houses in ONP are largely built with bricks and tiles. The basic amenities such as primary health centre, primary school, drinking water and electricity supply are not made available even till date in these tribal settlements. However, all *hadis* of ONP have these basic facilities. Primary health centre is a distant dream for the local communities except in Nagarahole. Chandanakere, Karekandi and Siddapura *hadis* do not have primary schools.

The occupational status of the sample households of NNP indicates that 67 per cent and 52 per cent of households from INP and ONP respectively are plantation labourers working in coffee estates as evident from Table 2 and Figure 2.

Table 2: Occupational Status of the Sample Households in NNP

The Study Area	*Cultivators*	*Agricultural Labourers* Coffee Plantation	*Agricultural Labourers* Other Crops	*Labourers in Forest Department* Salaried	*Labourers in Forest Department* Daily Wagers	*Others*	*Total*
INP	04	67	07	11	07	04	100
	(04)	(67)	(07)	(11)	(07)	(04)	(100)
ONP	19	39	04	07	03	03	75
	(25.33)	(52.00)	(5.33)	(9.33)	(4.00)	(4.00)	(100)
Grand	23	106	11	18	10	07	175
Total	(13.14)	(60.57)	(6.28)	(10.28)	(5.71)	(4.00)	(100)

Note: (Figures in parentheses represent percentages)

The cultivators constitute 13 per cent of the total households. The proportion of households engaged as agricultural labourers other than plantation crops is 7 per cent and 5.33 per cent in INP and ONP accordingly. The majority of workers living inside the park are working as salaried class (11 per cent) and daily wagers (7 per cent), however, the proportion of labourers engaged in FD is less in case of ONP. Barely 7 per cent of households from both areas are engaged in other works.

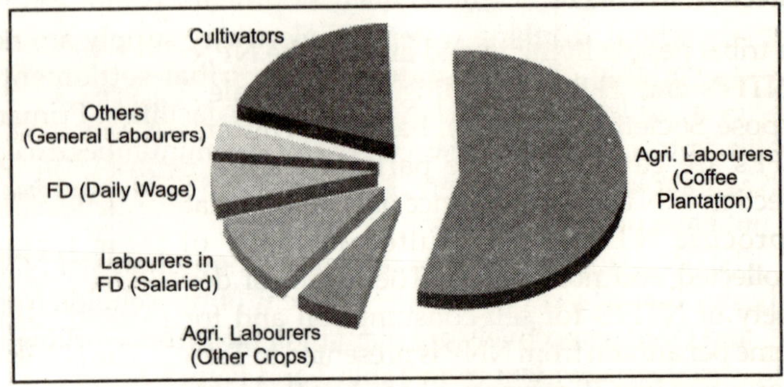

Figure: 2. *Occupational Status of Sample Households (%)*

Dependence of Local Communities on Forest Resources

Local communities inhabiting in NNP have depended on forest resources for eking out their livelihood for ages. An attempt is made in this section to quantify the extent of dependence on forest resources for a variety of direct and indirect benefits. NTFPs are defined as "biological materials other than timber that are extracted from natural forests for human use" (Gakou et al., 1996). NTFPs play an important role in sustaining livelihood of forest dwellers. As rightly pointed out by the FAO, "NTFPs contribute significantly to household food security and nutrition, generate additional employment and income, offer opportunities for processing enterprises, contribute to foreign exchange earnings and support biodiversity conservation and other environmental objectives" (Mallik, 2000). The collection of NTFPs and TFPs not only creates employment opportunities but also generates income to the tribal households. Self-consumption of NTFPs is considered to be more significant for fetching non-cash income than for marketing them for earning cash (Mallik, 2000). However, in recent years, tribal people are harvesting a variety of forest products for commercial purposes in order to supplement their livelihood. The average money value derived from the collection of a range of NTFPs is estimated, since many of the NTFPs do not have any market value, the prices of close substitutes are taken for estimating the money value of NTFPs.

Collection of NTFPs

The tribal people living in and around the NP, collect an array of NTFPs and TFPs. According to large-scale *Adivasis* Multi-purpose Societies (LAMPS), based at Thithimathi, about 41 NTFPs are gathered in the park. However, prohibition of collection of NTFPs and absence of an appropriate organisation to procure NTFPs has resulted in many of them being uncollected and not utilised. The extent of dependence on a variety of NTFPs for self-consumption and for earning cash income per annum from NNP is presented in Table 3. The NTFPs are grouped into 10 categories based on their nature and utility. They are – 1. Food, 2. Honey, 3. Wild fruits, 4. Medicinal plants, 5. Fuelwood, 6. Wild spices, 7. Wild nuts and seeds, 8. Bee wax and gum, 9. Wild meat and fish, and 10. Green fodder.

1. Food: The most important source of food for the tribals right through the year is a variety of roots and tubers. They gather seven to eight different varieties of roots, viz. *akki genasu, noore genasu, naarae genasu, utthari genasu, pulla genasu,* young bamboo shoots and greens from NNP. Some roots are eaten raw, while others are boiled or roasted and used with sweet honey. The right time for collection of food products is during April and June. Out of 100 sample households, 91 per cent of them are from INP and 93.33 (out of 75 HH) per cent of them from ONP rely on regular food gathering activity. The average quantity of food gathered per annum works out to 103.66 kgs in INP and 42.10 kgs in ONP. The composition of annual non-cash income of the food products per household is placed at Rs. 518.30 (8.34 per cent) in INP and Rs. 210.01 (4.65 per cent) in ONP with the average market price of food at Rs. 5 per kg. It accounts for 4.28 and 1.91 per cent of total non-cash income derived from the collection of a variety of NTFPs both in INP and in ONP respectively.

2. Honey: Honey collection is one of the major and also traditional activities of *jenu kurubas* (honey gatherers). It is collected from great heights of trees and rocks and *jenu kurubas* are skilled in climbing big trees for collecting honey. Honey is collected both for self-consumption and sale and is considered as medicine for curing common ailments and also used as

Table 3: The Extent of Annual Dependence of Households on Forests for Collection of NTFPs in NNP

Sl. No	NTFPs	INP					ONP				
		% of families collecting the product (1)	Quantity per house-hold (Kg) (2)	Cash income (From sale) (3)	Non-cash Income (from Self-consumption) (4)	Total value (Rs) (3+4) (5)	% of families collecting the product (1)	Quantity per house-hold (Kg) (2)	Cash Income (From sale) (3)	Non-cash income (Self-con-sumption) (4)	Total value (Rs) (3+4) (5)
1	Food: Roots & Tubers	91	103.66	-	518.30 (8.34)	518.30 (4.28)	93.33	42.10	-	210.01 (4.65)	210.01 (1.91)
2	Honey	93	43.09	1677.27 (28.51)	261.77 (4.21)	1939.05 (16.03)	92	42.97	1618.66 (25.03)	314.99 (6.98)	1933.65 (17.62)
3	Wild fruits	76	72.56	203.74 (3.46)	884.65 (14.21)	1088.40 (9.00)	88	52.71	245.10 (3.79)	545.54 (12.09)	790.65 (7.20)
4	Medicinal Plants	62	13.77	-	96.39 (1.55)	96.39 (0.79)	30.66	9.45	-	66.15 (1.46)	66.15 (0.60)
5	Fuelwood	100	43.19*	-	3671.15 (59.12)	3671.15 (30.36)	100	27.40	486.52 (7.52)	1842.47 (40.86)	2329.00 (21.22)
6	Wild Spices	67	37.23	1294.41 (22.00)	194.78 (3.13)	1489.20 (12.31)	73.33	23.47	818.91 (12.66)	119.88 (2.65)	938.80 (8.55)
7	Wild Nuts and Seeds	84	167.77	1405.90 (23.90)	104.03 (1.67)	1509.93 (12.48)	64	197.66	1668.82 (25.81)	110.11 (2.44)	1778.94 (16.21)
8	Bees Wax and Gum	87	17.33	1299.75 (22.10)	-	1299.75 (10.75)	72	21.69	1626.75 (25.16)	-	1626.75 (14.82)
9	Wild Meat and Fish	33	4.78	-	478.00 (7.69)	478.00 (3.95)	37.33	5.53	-	553.00 (12.26)	553.00 (5.03)
10	Green fodder	00	-	-	-	-	48	149.33**	-	746.65 (16.55)	746.65 (6.80)
	Grand Total	77 (100)	-	5881.07 (100.00)	6209.07 (100.00)	12090.14 (100.00)	69 (100)	-	6464.76 (100.00)	4508.80 (100.00)	10973.56 (100.00)

Note: *(Fuelwood in quintals) ** (Bundle comprising 25 to 30 kgs of green fodder)

nutrition supplement. The peak period for collecting honey is during the months of April and May and September and October. About 93 per cent of households collect honey per annum on an average of 43.09 kgs in INP and 92 per cent of households collect the same on an average of 42.97 kgs in ONP. While the total income derived from the collection of honey is Rs. 1,939.05 in INP and it is Rs. 1,933.65 in ONP. Of the total income derived from the collection of all NTFPs, income from honey constitutes (about 16.03 and 17.62 per cent in INP and ONP respectively) the second highest income for the tribal households. The market price of one kg of honey is Rs. 45. Honey fetches 28.51 per cent of cash income and 4.21 per cent of non-cash income to the tribal of INP. Tribal of ONP, whereas, obtains 25.03 per cent of cash and 6.98 per cent of non-cash income for sale and self-consumption of honey respectively. Tribals sell honey generally to LAMPS at Thithimathi and to the local shops in nearby towns.

3. Wild Fruits: Another important category of NTFP collected by the local communities of NNP, is wild fruit. A variety of wild fruits are collected in the forest area and these provide essential nutrition to tribals. The most important wild fruits collected are; tamarind, jackfruit, wood apple, gooseberry (nelli), legi, mango, nerale etc. The average price for all these fruits is fixed at Rs. 15 per kg. More than 76 per cent of tribals in INP gather a variety of wild fruits available seasonally with an average of 72.56 kgs per family per annum. In case of ONP about 88 per cent of households collect with an average of 52.71 kgs per households per annum. The composition of annual total income from wild fruits stands at 9.00 per cent in INP and 7.20 in ONP. Both cash and non-cash income derived from fruits has been estimated at Rs. 203.74 (3.46 per cent) and Rs. 884.65 (14.24 per cent) representing households of INP and Rs. 245.10 (3.79) and Rs. 545.54 (12.09 per cent) representing households of ONP.

4. Medicinal Plants: The extent of dependence on medicinal plants, roots, tubers and herbs clearly demonstrates that, local communities even today cure common ailments themselves in the village itself and rarely demand the services of professional doctors. In INP more than 62 per cent of households depend on medicinal plants and each household earns Rs. 96.39 (1.55 per cent) per annum from medicinal plants in the way of self-consumption. The dependence of local communities on medicinal plants for marketing or earning cash income is not found in the study area. In case of ONP only 30.66 per cent of households collect medicinal plants for own use and earn Rs. 66.15 (1.46 per cent) income per year. The share of income from medicinal plants accounts for 0.79 and 0.60 per cent in INP and ONP respectively.

5. Fuelwood: Fuelwood collection is the most important and customary activity that fetches the highest and regular income to local communities. Although the collection of fuel wood from NP is prohibited according to the Wildlife Act 1972, local communities have limited access to fuelwood collection for meeting the essential needs. All sample households from INP and ONP frequently collect fuel wood. On an average, 25 to 30 kgs of fuelwood are collected in one trip per head. Local communities on an average make two trips to forest per week for gathering fuelwood. Local communities disclose that they collect usually fallen and dead or dry wood and observe that it would not affect the forest ecosystem. The dependence of local communities of INP on fuelwood is only for domestic use. However, local communities of ONP even collect fuelwood for sale apart from domestic use. The collection of fuelwood brings in Rs. 3671.15 non-cash income to households of INP. The estimated value of fuelwood collected stands at Rs. 2329 from the households of ONP for both purposes. All households living in INP and ONP collect fuelwood with an average of 43.19 and 27.40 quintals per annum respectively. The households of INP earn 59.12 per cent of non-cash income from collection of fuelwood, whereas households of ONP earn 40.86 per cent of non-cash income and 7.52 per cent of cash income from the collection of fuelwood. Of the total income from the collection of NTFPs, households of INP earn about 30.36 per cent of income and households of ONP earn 21.22 per cent of income. These figures clearly show the extent of dependence of local communities on collection of fuelwood.

6. Wild Spices: Local communities collect a variety of wild spices both for domestic use and also for marketing such as wild pepper, marati moggu and chakke, etc, from the forest area. About 67 per cent of households from INP and 73.33 per cent from ONP collect these products on an average quantity of 37.23 and 23.47 kgs respectively per year for both self-consumption and for sale. The cash income earned from wild spices has been estimated at Rs. 1,294.41 (22.00 per cent) and Rs. 818.91 (12.66) per annum respectively in INP and ONP. The non-cash income earned stands at Rs. 194.78 (3.13 per cent) and Rs. 818.91 (12.66 per cent) for INP and ONP respectively. Of the total income from the collection of NTFPs, the share of income from wild spices accounts for 12.31 per cent and 8.55 per cent for INP and ONP respectively.

7. Wild Nuts and Seeds: Extraction of a variety of wild nuts and seeds from the park for one's own use as well as for sale has prevailed for years. Households of NNP gather soap nut, jai kai, vate huli, alale kai, medichilad beeja, wild castor seed, gul nut, lin seed etc and harvesting of these items is seasonal and occasional. The traditional knowledge of extraction of NTFPs is passed on to the younger generation by the experienced and older generations. The percentage of households extracting these products is estimated at 84 and 64 per cent in INP and ONP respectively. An average quantity collected per annum per household is 167.77 kgs and 197.66 kgs respectively. The share of cash income and non-cash income for own use and marketing accounts for Rs. 1,405.90 (23.90 per cent) and Rs. 1,668.82 (25.81 per cent) and Rs. 104.03 (1.67 per cent) and Rs. 110.11 (2.44) in both areas respectively. The share of income from the wild nuts and seeds, compared to total income derived from other NTFPs, accounts for 12.48 per cent in case of INP and 16.21 per cent in case of ONP.

8. Bees Wax and Gum: Households of NNP gather bee wax and gum mainly for sale and they are mainly sold to middlemen or private traders. The extent of dependence on these products by the households of NNP stands at 87 per cent and 72 per cent in INP and ONP respectively. The composition of cash income from these products is Rs. 1,299.75 (22.10 per cent) and

Rs. 1,626.75 (25.16 per cent) in INP and ONP. The total money value derived by the households of INP and ONP from the sale of bee wax and gum is estimated at 10.75 per cent and 14.82 per cent respectively of the total value of all NTFPs.

9. Wild Meat and Fish: Hunting of wild animals in NNP invites severe punishment to poachers and it is strictly prohibited. However, occasionally local communities admit hunting of small games and collection of meat of dead wild animals. They catch fish seasonally from streams and ponds. Both the items are gathered mainly for own consumption. Only 33 and 36 per cent of households of INP and ONP admit that they collect 4.78 and 5.53 kgs of these items respectively. The non-cash income derived from the collection of wild meat and fish from the both settlements is estimated at Rs. 478.00 (7.69 per cent) and Rs 553.00 (12.26 per cent) respectively.

10. Green Fodder: Livestock rearing in INP is prohibited and only the households of ONP collect green fodder. Locally, the value of a bundle of green fodder is fixed at Rs. 5. About 48 per cent of households of ONP gather annually 149.33 bundles of green fodder for stall-feeding. The non-cash income derived from the gathering of green fodder accounts for Rs. 746.65 (16.55 per cent). Households of ONP derive about 6.80 per cent of total income from the collection of green fodder.

The households of INP and ONP derive income worth Rs. 12,090.14 and Rs. 10,973.56 per annum from the collection of a variety of NTFPs respectively. Of the total income, the share of cash income in the two settlements from the sale of NTFPs accounts for 48.64 per cent and 58.91 per cent respectively. The composition of non-cash income for self-consumption of forest products is estimated at 51.35 per cent in INP and 41.08 per cent in ONP accordingly.

Of the nine important categories of NTFPs collected from households of INP, four are gathered exclusively for self-consumption or domestic use and one product is solely for sale. The rest of the four products are collected for both self-consumption as well as for sale. Of the total income derived from the collection of NTFPs, fuelwood alone fetches more than 30.36 per cent of income, followed by honey (16.03 per cent);

both products fetch about 46.39 per cent of income and the rest of the NTFPs bring about 53.61 per cent of income to the households of INP.

By and large all tribal people, including women, are involved in collection of forest products. The households of ONP collect 10 categories of NTFPs, of which, four are gathered for domestic or self-consumption and five are collected for both sale and own use and the remaining one item is collected solely for sale. Of the total income generated from the collection of NTFPs, fuelwood, honey, wild nuts and seeds fetch 55.05 per cent of income and the rest of NTFPs bring about 44.05 per cent of income. The dependence on NTFPs by the households of INP is largely for self-consumption (51.35 per cent) while the dependence of the ONP households is largely for earning cash income from sale (58.91 %). The extent of dependence of tribal on various NTFPs is shown in Figure 3.

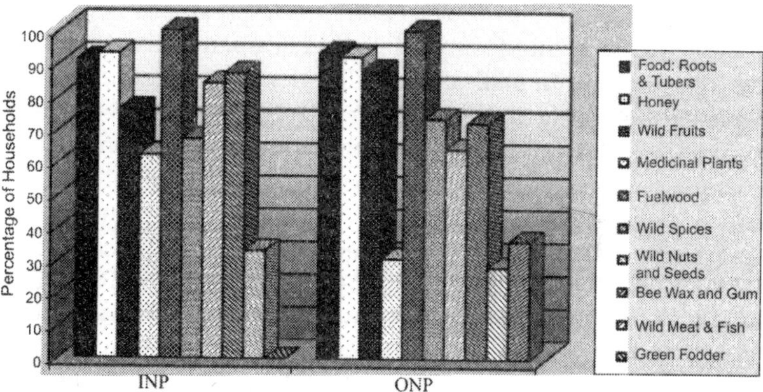

Fig 3: *Extent of Households' Dependence on Various NTFPs per Annum (%)*

Thus, from the foregoing analysis, it is evident that the households' dependency levels are varied depending upon the availability, requirement, marketability and more importantly free access to various NTFPs in the study area.

Collection of Timber Forest Products (TFPs)

Local communities collect different types of TFPs with the permission of FD for meeting their basic domestic requirements in a limited way and not for sale. The households living inside the park gather only three categories of TFPs while households of ONP collect four categories of TFPs for the purpose of domestic use. The extent of dependence of local communities for the collection of a variety of TFPs is given in Table 4. The dependence of households on TFPs of INP and ONP is about 87 per cent and 64 per cent respectively and they collect, on an average, 10.71 and 23.50 poles per annum. Timber used for domestic requirements alone fetches about 23.49 and 47.92 per cent of non-cash income to the households of INP and ONP respectively. The dependence of households on bamboo accounts for 91 per cent (INP) and 50.66 per cent (ONP) annually. Incomes earned from bamboo are estimated at 40.57 per cent and 29 per cent of the total income from TFPs. Collection of cane and fiber is accounted for 73 per cent in case of INP and 36 per cent in case of ONP. The income generated from cane and fibre is estimated at 35.94 per cent and 19 per cent respectively

Table 4: The Extent of Annual Dependence of Households on TFPs in NNP

Sl No	*Timber Forest Products (TFPs)*	INP *% of families collecting the product*	*Quantity per annum (Poles)*	*Total value (Rs)*	ONP *% of families collecting the product*	*Quantity per annum (Poles)*	*Total value (Rs)*
		(1)	*(2)*	*(3)*	*(1)*	*(2)*	*(3)*
1	Timber	87	10.71*	535.50 (23.49)	64	23.50	1175.00 (47.92)
2	Bamboos	91	18.50*	925.00 (40.57)	50.66	14.22	711.00 (29.00)
3	Cane and Fibre	73	32.77*	819.25 (35.94)	36	18.63	465.75 (19.00)
4	Mulch and Green manure	00	-	-	45.33	01**	100 (4.08)
	Total	83 (100)	-	2279.75 (100.00)	49 (100)	-	2451.75 (100.00)

Note: (Figures in parentheses represent percentages to the column total)
* Quantity (Poles) in numbers
** Quantity (Mulch and green manure) in bundles average 25-30 kgs

in INP and ONP. Only the households of ONP collect mulch and manure. About 45.33 per cent of households depend on mulch and green manure and they earn an income of 4.08 per cent to the total income from TFPs. The dependence on TFPs is high in case of ONP households (Rs. 2,451.75) compared to INP households (Rs. 2,279.75).

Local communities gather TFPs for various purposes like agricultural implements, house construction, wooden utensils, green manure, and fencing materials (Table 5). Households were requested to give their first priority for collection of TFPs. Accordingly only their first choice is taken for analysis. Out of the total collection of TFPs, 63 per cent of INP households collect mainly for house construction and 23 per cent for fencing of houses and backyards to protect them from the menace of wild animals and 10 per cent of households collect timber for wooden utensils and only 2 per cent households for preparing agricultural implements.

Table: 5: Households' Dependence on TFPs by Purpose

Purpose	*Nagarhole National Park*		*Grand Total*
	INP	*ONP*	
Agricultural tools	04 (04.00)	29 (38.66)	33 (18.85)
Fencing material	23 (23.00)	09 (12.00)	32 (18.28)
House construction	61 (61.00)	18 (24.00)	79 (45.14)
Wooden utensils	10 (10.00)	04 (05.33)	14 (08.00)
Green manure	02 (02.00)	15 (20.00)	17 (09.71)
Total	100 (100.00)	75 (100.00)	175 (100)

Note: (Figures in parentheses represent percentages to their representative totals)

The demand for TFPs largely comes from households living in ONP as 38.66 per cent of them collect TFPs mainly for making agricultural tools. The percentage of households collecting TFPs for the construction of houses, green manure and fencing material accounts for 24 per cent, 20 per cent and 12 per cent respectively. The graphical illustration of collection of TFPs for various purposes by the households of INP and ONP is given in Figure 4. It is evident that the majority of households from

INP and ONP gather a variety of TFPs principally for house construction compared to other purposes.

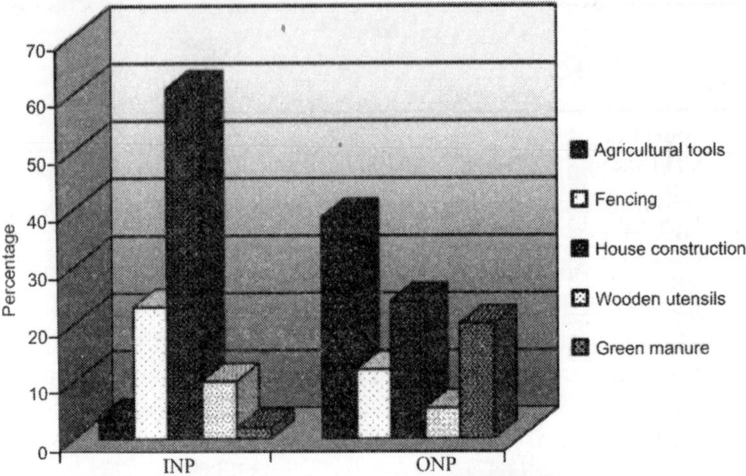

Figure 4: *Collection of TFPs by Households for Various Purposes (%)*

Employment Generation from Forest Resources

Forest activities like collection of NTFPs and TFPs generate direct, indirect and self-employment opportunities for the forest-dependent communities right through the year. Collection of forest products is considered a major economic activity for local communities of NNP since they spend most of their time in extracting forest products as detailed in the preceding sections. The employment generated by forest resources has been estimated by evaluating the working days (man-days) spent by a household in collection of a range of forest products with respect to other economic activities (Table 6).

It is found that annually about 294.78 (52.78 per cent) of mean man-days of employment are generated for each household of INP from collection of NTFPs and TFPs, out of the total annual employment of 558.49 man-days per household. The collection of NTFPs and TFPs generate 233.44 (40.19 per cent) of mean man-days of employment for the households of ONP, out of the total annual employment of 580.76 man-days per household. This indicates the importance of forest economy

Table 6: Composition of Annual Employment of Households in Man-Days

Sl. No.	Activities	INP Mean Man-days	INP S.D.[1]	INP C.V.[2] (%)	ONP Mean Man-days	ONP S.D.	ONP C.V. (%)
1	Collection of NTFPs and TFPs	294.78 (52.78)	273.87	92.90	233.44 (40.19)	230.23	98.62
2	Agriculture and allied activities	61.32 (10.97)	156.26	254.84	90.67 (15.61)	189.37	208.87
3	Forest Department work	73.65 (13.18)	41.75	56.69	47.33 (8.14)	61.21	129.32
4	Plantation work	120.51 (21.57)	117.14	97.20	187.87 (32.34)	261.47	139.16
5	Others	8.23 (1.47)	22.95	278.89	21.45 (3.69)	42.94	200.16
	Total	558.49 (100.00)	100.63	82.22	580.76 (100.00)	99.38	63.28

Note: [[1] S.D.= Standard deviation. [2] C.V.= Co-efficient of variation (%)]
[Figures in parentheses are percentages to the total]

in providing employment opportunities to forest dwellers. The generation of employment from forest-based activities is around 57.6 per cent of total man-days in other parts of the country as per the evidence of some studies (Mallik, 2000 and Prakash, 1999). Employment generated by agriculture and allied activities amounts for only 61.32 (10.97 per cent) mean man-days in INP and 90.17 (15.61 per cent) mean man-days in ONP. FD has provided seasonal and occasional employment opportunities to the households of INP and ONP. Employment generated from FD is estimated around 73.65 (13.18 per cent) and 47.33 (8.14 per cent) man-days per annum respectively. Another main source of employment is plantation work, which provides 120.51 (21.57 per cent) and 187.87 (32.34 per cent) man-days annually for households of INP and ONP respectively.

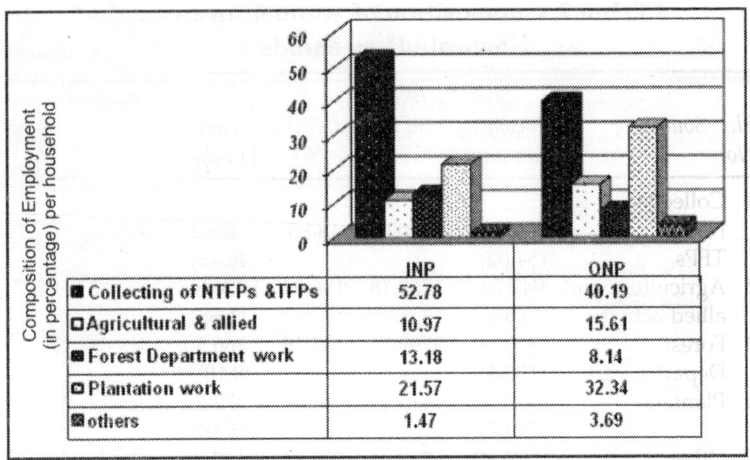

	INP	ONP
Collecting of NTFPs &TFPs	52.78	40.19
Agricultural & allied	10.97	15.61
Forest Department work	13.18	8.14
Plantation work	21.57	32.34
others	1.47	3.69

Figure: 5: *Annual Employment Generation Per Household (%)*

The graphical presentation of annual employment generation is presented in Figure 5. It is apparent from the foregoing analysis that employment generation from both NTFPs and TFPs is more stable (with variability of 92.90 in INP and 98.62 in ONP) than from other activities. Therefore, collection of NTFPs and TFPs is the major source of economic activity not only in generating employment opportunities but also income to the forest dwellers of NNP.

Composition of Income from Forest Resources

Local communities of NNP are largely dependent on forest products for their livelihood and they derive annual income to the tune of Rs 26,601.29 (INP) and Rs 28,901.36 (ONP) per household from various sources (Table 7).

Out of the total annual income per household, income generated from collection of NTFPs and TFPs (for both own use and sale) in both the settlements of INP and ONP comprises of Rs 14369.89 (54.02 per cent) and Rs 13425.31 (46.45 per cent) correspondingly. While agriculture and allied activities contribute to the income to the tune of Rs 947.78 (3.56 per cent) in INP, it is Rs 3376.88 (11.68 per cent) in the case of ONP. The income derived by working in the FD constitutes Rs 3682.50 (13.81 per cent) to the total income for households of INP and

Table 7: Composition of Annual Income of Sample Households

Sl. No.	Sources	INP Income Man-days	INP S.D.[1]	INP C.V.[2] (%)	ONP Income Man-days	ONP S.D.	ONP C.V. (%)
1	Collection of NTFPs and TFPs	14,369.89 (54.02)	2710.10	18.85	13,425.31 (46.45)	6335.17	47.18
2	Agriculture and allied activities	947.78 (3.56)	1765.18	186.24	3,376.88 (11.68)	3335.38	98.77
3	Forest Department	3,682.50 (13.84)	3799.14	103.16	2,366.50 (8.18)	1548.66	65.44
4	Plantation	6,025.50 (22.65)	4475.41	74.27	7,272.22 (25.16)	4016.27	55.22
5	Others	1,575.62 (5.92)	1745.98	110.81	2,460.45 (8.51)	2279.46	92.64
6	All sources	26,601.29 (100.00)	1219.22	42.05	28,901.36 (100.00)	1845.88	52.69

Note: [[1] S.D. = Standard Deviation. [2] C.V. = Co-efficient of Variation (%)] (Figures in parentheses signify percentages to the total)

Rs. 2,366.50 (8.18 per cent) for households of ONP. The second important contributor to income is plantation work and tribal people earn money from this activity mainly for meeting the household requirements. The income generated from plantation is estimated at Rs. 6,025.50 (22.65 per cent) in INP and Rs. 7,272.22 (25.16 per cent) in ONP. After the income derived from the collection of forest products, the income from plantation is considered the second highest source of income for households. Income received from other sources stands at Rs. 1,575.62 (5.92 per cent) and Rs. 2,460.45 (8.51 per cent) in both the settlements of INP and ONP respectively. The significant contribution to income from forest products is revealed by many studies also, for example, income from the collection of NTFPs in Kalahandi district in Orissa state stands at 52.2 per cent (Mallik, 2000) and 51.44 per cent in the study area of Uttara Kannada district in the Western Ghats region in Karnataka (Prakash, 1999). The graphical presentation of the composition of annual income from NTFPs and TFPs from both settlements as compared to other sources is given in Figure 6.

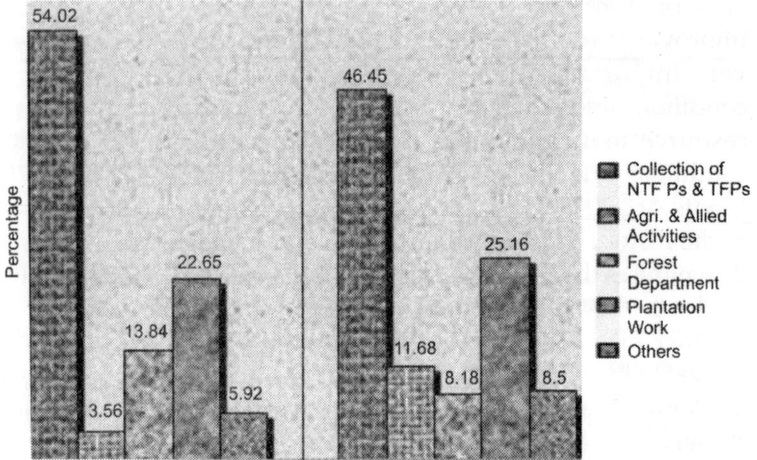

Figure 6: *Composition of Annual Income from Various Sources*

The above analysis clearly reveals that the collection of NTFPs and TFPs fetches the largest composition of income compared to other sources of income to the households of both INP and ONP. It can also be observed from the interpretation of co-efficient of variation analysis that income generated from the collection of forest products is more stable compared to plantation and agriculture and allied activities with a variability of 18.85 per cent and 47.18 per cent in both the settlements. This clearly shows that collection of forest products continues to play a pivotal role in the tribal economy by contributing a substantial and steady income.

The role of the local community in forest management has been well recognised all over the world. The academicians, policy makers, and practitioners all over the world have proposed many alternative systems of forest management (Singh, 1996). They include privatisation, nationalisation or centralised public management, and cooperative or collective management by local communities, etc. As observed by Singh et al. (1996), "there is no single best system of management that could be commended for all situations and for all times to come. The management of forest in a particular region is influenced by a variety of factors such as the characteristics of the resource, attributes of the resource users, the decision-making environment and the goals of resource management. For improving the management of natural resources it is therefore, very important for resource managers to understand the conditions under which each of the three alternative systems of resource management is likely to succeed as well as the conditions under which a system is likely to fail". The Forest Rights Act, 2006 (FRA), is considered as an important landmark in the history of forest resource use and management because it recognises the traditional rights of the local communities. This act for the first time in the history of forest acts intertwines two distinct ideas such as "people's science" and "science" in conserving and managing of forest resources. However, the implementation of this act requires proper institutional and conservation mechanism which takes care of both conservation and also livelihood needs of local community. In this regard a blueprint for meeting both the goals is envisaged in the following section.

A Blueprint for Unlocking Sustainable Livelihood Opportunities

Conservation of India's rich and mega biodiversity is absolutely essential for its immense contribution not only to India's long-term economic development but also to the entire world because, India's biodiversity is valued and recognised as one of the 12 Mega Biodiversity countries in the world. India's forests are also a homeland for millions of forest dwellers and other rural communities for eking out their livelihood and very subsistence and forests cannot be conserved without people's participation. Unlocking of sustainable livelihood opportunities along with sustainable conservation of forest resources with peoples' participation provides win-win situation for national park conservation.

Historically, forests in India, have been conserved and managed by local communities by applying their age-old traditional environmental knowledge, which were considered the best strategy evolved by local communities respecting the harmony of nature to lead a sustainable way of life. Local communities have traditionally managed forests in a sustainable way through self-restrained and regulated use of forest resources and also through practice and enforcement of social norms. Local communities of Coorg district, historically, are nature lovers and strong conservationists as they have been practicing worshiping of trees or SGs for centuries by leaving the entire stretch of habitat in its serenity. Their lifestyles are also incredibly fine tuned with nature. It is also evident from the present study that majority of local communities of the study areas have expressed their willingness to participate in forest conservation.

However, the successive authoritarian forest and wildlife policies have refused to accept the 'people's science' in management of forests and alienated local communities from the management of forests. The appropriation of forests by the forest department has uprooted the traditional livelihood structures and socio-economic and cultural fabric of local communities. This has resulted in conflict between people and forests / wildlife. The creation of national parks has had negative impact on local communities and their traditional forest based economy, especially where no provision has been made to accommodate their livelihood needs.

The Government Forest Act, 1865, passed by the then British government was meant to empower the government to declare any land under tree as forests and punish those who violated the act. The Indian Forest Act (IFA), 1878, was designed to empower the state to protect and control forests throughout India by overlooking community control. The IFA, 1927, was in no way different from earlier laws, in fact it imposed more stringent punishments to violators of the Act. The first Forest Policy (1952) after independence had showed apathy towards local communities for using and conserving forests at the cost of national interest while it permitted industrial exploitation. The Wildlife (Protection) Act, 1972, which aimed at protection of Protected Areas or National Parks, had no provisions for joint management of PA with local communities. However, the paradigm shift in policies took place with passing of the National Forest Policy, 1988 and Wildlife (Protection)

Amendment Act, 2002, emphasising the need for conservation of forests and environment simultaneously by meeting subsistence requirements of local communities. However, JFM is restricted only to degraded forests and JPAM has not yet materialised on the ground. These lopsided polices have adversely affected environment and impoverished livelihoods of millions of local communities.

It is evident that the present forest and wildlife policies empower only the state to conserve and manage forests and there is little scope for people's participation. However, Dey, MoFE (Kothari et al., 1996 and 1998), observes that without changing the present Wildlife (Protection) Act 1972, adequate opportunities for people's bonafide requirements cna be met from PA. He further points out that section 24(2)(C) allows local communities to enjoy their rights within sanctuaries at the discretion of the chief wildlife warden (CWLW) and Section 29 allows human activities in specified zones of PA if they are not destructive to wildlife (Kothari et al., 1996). Yet, the main bottleneck in allowing local communities to enjoy their bonafide rights is invoking of Section 29, which says that any human intervention, which destroys PA, will not be encouraged. Further these policies have alienated local communities from their homeland and violated fundamental rights to their livelihood needs besides resulting in increasing conflicts between conservation priorities and livelihood priorities.

Therefore, if JPAM and JFM were to succeed, several changes in forest and wildlife policies are required to accommodate livelihood needs of stakeholders. Displacement of local communities from forestlands has affected their livelihood and destroyed their socio-cultural ethos. Therefore, displacement is impractical. The need of the hour is to accept the historically neglected TEK of local communities in forest conservation by reforming our attitudes or mindset in order to make reconciliation towards JPAM. Reconciliation can aim at substituting authoritarian, top-down and elitist forest policy with democratic, down-to-earth and community driven forest policy for ensuring both forest conservation and livelihood security of the local communities.

The existing experiences of JPAM have shown the way for implementing JPAM in NNP. Community based conservation (CBC) is successfully being implemented in BRT Wildlife Sanctuary in Karnataka. Bhimashankar Wildlife Sanctuary (BWS), in Western Ghat of Maharashtra, is well managed with peoples' participation by forming Sanctuary Protection Committee (SPC). Kialadevi Wildlife Sanctuary in Rajasthan and Dalma Wildlife Sanctuary in Bihar are being successfully managed by the local communities by forming forest protection committees. The lessons of JPAM from abroad are also guiding principles for implementing community-based conservation of NNP. Annapurna Conservation Area in Nepal, Kakadu National Park in Australia, Khunjerab National Park in Pakistan are being successfully managed with people's participation.

It is evident from the above examples that formation of JPAM along with people's participation in NNP is the need of the hour. The feasible conservation strategies for NNP including the zoning pattern of the park area, the nature and extent of control over park, management options, areas to be managed by local communities, institutional arrangements, local communities' rights over resources for meeting their bonafide needs and the role of the Forest Department are proposed and presented in Figure 7.

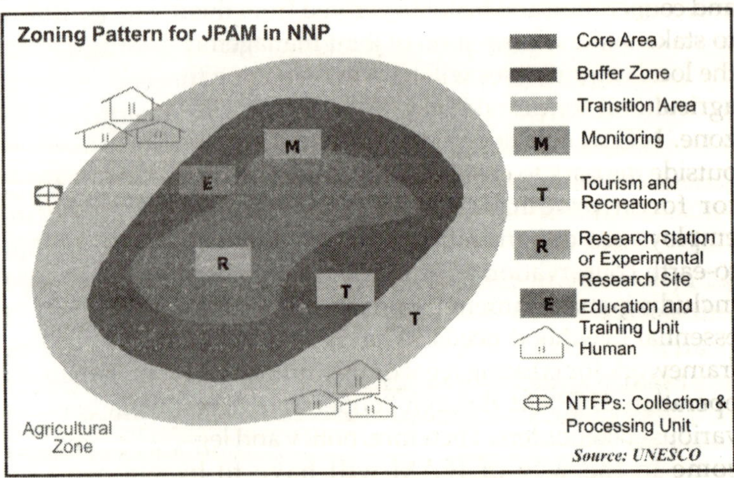

Figure 7: The Proposed Joint Protected Area Management for NNP

The United Nations Educational, Scientific and Cultural Organisation (UNESCO) launched the "Man and Biosphere" (MAB) programme in 1971 for conservation of Protected Areas (Batisse, 1997). It advocated conservation strategies for the involvement of local communities in conservation and management of national parks. The same model with necessary modifications to suit local conditions is recommended for conservation and management of NNP, as local communities are willing to participate in JPAM (along the outer layer of the park by retaining stake over forest products).

The total geographical area of NNP (643 sq kms) should be legally categorised into three territorial components comprising core zone (192 sq kms), buffer zone (110 sq kms) and transition area (341 sq kms). The core zone should be devoted to the sole purpose of biodiversity conservation for meeting long-term environmental objectives. The second territory, buffer zone surrounding the core zone, can be used for activities compatible with the conservation objectives, such as research, education, nondestructive resource use, recreation and eco-tourism. The third territory, a flexible outer transition area, constitutes the region where sustainable resource management practices are promoted and developed. JPAM should be effective in managing the park along with local communities' participation and cooperation and benefits derived from this area may accrue to stakeholders. Formation of joint management committee by the local communities will help in managing the transition and agricultural zones and Forest Department will focus on the core zone. NTFPs collection and processing unit has to be set up outside the park to ensure reasonable prices and value addition for forest products. The unit can also create sustained employment opportunities to local communities. This down-to-earth conservation approach incorporates all the objectives including environmental conservation along with meeting essential livelihood needs. What is urgently required is policy framework for creating legal or institutional mechanism for the operation of JPAM through cooperative agreements between various stakeholders. Therefore, policy and legal constraint that come in the way of JPAM will have to be removed for enlightened conservation approach.

Conclusion

Forest resources have direct bearing on the life-support system of local communities. They lose significant source of their livelihood (due to non-availability of an array of forest products) as a consequence of deforestation. Local communities also place high value on forest resources and their environmental role and they are also aware of detrimental effects of deforestation. This implies that local communities' willingness to participate in forest conservation depends on their access to forest resources for meeting their livelihood needs. Therefore, livelihood needs of local community must be integrated with forest conservation. However, search for alternative and sustainable strategies to protect forests and thereby the environment through active involvement of local community is the feasible solution.

References

Agarwal, A. (ed.) (1999), *The State of India's Environment: The Citizens' Fifth Report*, 2 parts, Centre for Science and Environment, New Delhi.

Brown, G. (1997), Management of Wildlife and Habitat in Developing Countries in Partha Dasgupta and Karl-Goran Maler. (ed) 1997. *The Environment and Emerging Development Issues*, 2 Vols. Clarendon Press, Oxford, UK.

Chopra, K., Kadekodi, G.K. and Murthy, M.N. (1990), *Participatory Development: People and Common Property Resources*, Sage Publications, New Delhi.

Chopra, K. and Kadekodi, G.K. (1999), *Operationalising Sustainable Development: Economic-Ecological Modelling for Developing Countries*, Sage Publications, New Delhi.

Dasgupta, P. and Maler, K. G. (1997), The Resource-Basis of Production and Consumption: An Economic Analysis in Partha Dasgupta, and Karl-Goran Maler. (ed) 1997. *The Environment and Emerging Development Issues*, 2 Vols. Clarendon Press, Oxford.

Forest Survey of India, (FSI) (1988), *State of India's Forest*, 1987, Dehradun.

Gadgil, M. (1987), Depleting Renewable Resources: A Case Study from Karnataka Western Ghats, *Indian Journal of Agricultural Economics*, Vol. 42, No. 3, July-September, pp. 376-87.

Gadgil, M. (2007), Empowering Gramsabhas to Manage Biodiversity: The Science Agenda, *Economic and Political Weekly*, 17, 2067-2071.

Gakou, M. and Force, J. E. (1996), Learning with Farmers for Policy

Changes in Natural Resource Management, Forests, Trees and People, *Newsletter* No. 31, 1996.

Jayasri, A. (2002), Tree Felling in Nagarahole Riles Wildlife Group, *The Hindu*, August 29, 2002, p. 5.

Kothari, A., Singh N. and Suri, S. (1996), *People and Protected Areas: Towards Participatory Conservation in India*, Sage Publications, New Delhi.

Kothari, A., Suri, S. and Singh, N. (1995), People and Protected Areas: Rethinking Conservation in India, *The Ecologist*, Vol. 25, No. 5 September-October 1995, pp. 188-94.

Madhav, V. (1999), Forest Fires: Satellite Picture Nails Government lie, *The New Indian Express*, August 5, 1999.

Mallik, R.M. (2000), Sustainable Management of Non-timber Forest Products in Orissa: Some Issues and Options, *Indian Journal of Agricultural Economics*, Vol. 55, No. 3, July-September 2000, pp. 384-97.

Nathan, D. and Kelkar, G. (2001), Case for Local Forest Management: Environmental Services, Internalisation of Costs and Markets, *Economic and Political Weekly*, Vol. 36, No. 30, July 28-August 3.

Nadkarni, M.V. et al. (1989), *Political Economy of Forest Use and Management*, Sage Publications, New Delhi.

Nadkarni, M.V. (1996), Forests, people and Economics, *Indian Journal for Agricultural Economics*, Vol. 51, No. 1 and 2 January-June.

Nadkarni, M.V. (2001), Poverty, Environment and Development in India, (Chapter 2), in Adrian Hayes and M.V. Nadkarni, *Poverty, Environment and Development in India*, UNESCO Principal Regional Office for Asia and the Pacific, Thailand, pp. 25-89.

Nayak, B. (2001), Economic-Ecologic Values of an Indian Forest: A Case Study, *Indian Journal of Agricultural Economics*, Vol. 56, No. 3, July-September, 2001, pp. 325-34.

Prakash, S. (1999), An Economic Analysis of Non-Timber Forest Products (NTFP) in the Tribal Economy in the Western Ghats Region of Karnataka, *My Forest* Vol. 35 (3), pp. 173-83.

Proffenberger, M. and Mcgean, B. (ed) (1996), *Village Voices, Forest Choices: Joint Forest Management in India*, Oxford University Press, New Delhi.

Sharma, R. (1999), Devastation in the Nagarhole Park, *Frontline*, June 4, 1999.

Singh, K. and Vishwa, B. (ed) (1996), *Cooperative Management of Natural Resources*, Sage Publications, New Delhi.

Reddy, Y. et al. (1996), Western Ghats in Karnataka: Its Ecological Decline and Steps for Revival in Nair et. al. (ed) *Eco-development of Western Ghats*, Kerala Forest Research Institute, Peachy.

World Bank (1996), India: Eco-Development Project, Project Document, Global Environmental Facility, South Asia. Report No. 14914-IN.

9

Natural Resource Management Goal: Role of Community Based Organisation

A. Mazumdar and S. Das

Abstract: Crop, plants, forests, animals together with land, water, air, and light are the tangible elements of nature that provide most of the requirements of livelihood for the rural poor, particularly the tribal people who had developed the art of living on nature without depleting the resource base. Thus, to uplift rural economy and to ensure general well-being of the rural people the most logical option would be to engage the rural poor for productive utilisation and scientific collection of these resources, abundantly available around them, by utilising their capacity for labour, their only wealth and employing sound and appropriate technology duly strengthened by their traditional knowledge, perfected through generations of experience This should perhaps be the core approach of Natural Resource Management (NRM) and for obvious reasons, planning, implementation and monitoring has to be made participatory.

Ideally, the government effort should aim at –

(a) Generating immediate wage income by creating productive assets,

(b) Improving their skill and capacity through training and guidance,

(c) Securing their health by providing essential healthcare services.

Besides, there should be adequate support for infrastructure development, input supply and effective product disposal mechanism (Processing Storage and Marketing) with necessary insurance cover, to make the practice affordable, profitable and risk-free. Besides, for sustained supply of resources it is necessary to exercise restraint in lifestyle and recycling in resource utilisation. It is often debated that on-farm initiatives are not profitable. This notion itself is debatable because government machinery appears to be quite indifferent to this sector and their initiatives are hardly sincere and meaningful and are far from being ideal. Therefore, the fault is perhaps not in the system but actually is in the attitude and approach. It is also often debated that, converting villages to town is development. In this context it is important to understand that a village will somehow survive without a town but a town will certainly perish without the support of villages.

In the light of the prevailing over population in towns, the signal is very clear, that, unless agriculture and allied farm activities are made profitable by providing specified support and basic amenities like health, education, communication, power, etc. are extended in the villages, influx to town can not be prevented and in that event, urban life will become unbearable in spite of glittering development and rural resources will remain unused and become degraded in spite of having immense prospect. This is particularly true in case of the Indian subcontinent which is endowed with valuable natural resources of enviable abundance and brilliant human resource of immense potential.

The discussion may be concluded with a famous saying, meaning that,

> *'when the leaves become dry and the soil without a drop of water, then only, man will realise that one can not survive chewing a rupee'*

Introduction

Biodiversity is a complex matter that has been defined very simply and explicitly by Sir Ghillean Prance, the eminent Botanist as, "All life forms that hold the earth together." The biodiversity and the ecosystem in which it perpetrates; provide directly or indirectly all the requirements of every life form including human beings. The tangible components of biodiversity, in general terms, are the land, harbouring crops, plants including forests and the animals (domestic and wild). These, together with air, light and water constitute the principle ingredients of Natural Resource. These are the assets that can be managed to enhance the growth and create income opportunities sustainably for the rural poor, which they desperately need to alleviate their poverty and improve their livelihood status.

Context

On account of the geophysical and climatic condition, India is a mega diversity zone, representing almost all the bio-geographic regions and harbouring about 45,000 species of plants. There are over 2500 species of woody trees in India as against 40 in Great Britain and 200 in America. 'The flora of India is perhaps the richest and certainly the most varied on the surface of the globe' (Sir Joseph Hooker). In this context it may be mentioned that no other product of nature can perhaps replace wood in variety, utility, and indispensability. It can be seen in our everyday life in every direction be it in the villages, in towns and or the industries of all sorts. Besides there are innumerable varieties of non-wood species of plants in India that are used as food, medicines and commercial products which even under the present degraded condition generate sizable employment for the poor forest fringe dwellers. "NTFP help in generating 2 million person years of employment in India. In the South Eastern part of West Bengal, tribal people collect 27 commercial products, 39 food plant products and 47 medicinal plants for human or domestic animal use" (World Bank, 1991).

In this background it is perhaps logical to advocate that effort is to be made to replace as many life sustaining products as possible with wood and other NTFPs such as bamboo, cane, trailing shrubs, climbers, fibres, grass, etc. Keeping in mind the potential productivity of the unique forest resource of India to be harnessed by the duly developed brilliant human resource, the task is perhaps not insurmountable.

Ground Truth

The "Ajodhya Hills" in the District of Purulia is lovingly called the Pearl of Purulia for its soothing climate and scenic beauty. However, the life on the hill top is very difficult and the people there are extremely poor. There are many villages where water is scarce, cultivable lands are few and far, terrain is tough, and communication is difficult. On account of the inconvenience of location, government and other development agencies (except Forest Department), are seldom inspired to make their services available to them and people generally fall upon forests for their livelihood. Seasonal collection of NTFPs like sal leaves, mahua flowers, mushroom, medicinal plants, etc and making utility goods like Khejur (dates) leaves mats, brooms, etc and artifacts, are the only alternate source of their meager income. Lac cultivation was once practised with profit but that too has been abandoned on account of the lack of market and inability of accessing the once available. This paper attempts to provide some relief to these downtrodden poor families through appropriate and replicable management of natural resources available around them.

Objective

The objective of the paper is –

- To manage natural resources sustainably for ecological amelioration by preserving and increasing forest cover, harvesting rain water, conserving soil and moisture etc.
- To enhance economic status of forest fringe people by providing immediate wage income through creation of productive assets judiciously to meet human as well as environmental needs.
- To generate sustained income for them through management of created assets and available rural resources.

Methodology

This is an Operational Research paper and is the result of close association with the people of forest fringe villages particularly the Joint Forest Management Committee (JFMC) members for over half a decade, meeting with them and feeling for them. The method and approaches adopted for the purpose are narrated below.

1. Identify well functioning JFMCs.
2. Select Forest Dependent Villages (FDVs) adjacent to the above JFMCs.
3. Prepare PRA based Microplan* to develop alternate livelihood system for these JFMCs and FDVs and strengthen these managerially** through training, entrusting responsibility and guidance.
4. Establish links between JFMCs and FDVs by organising meetings, resolving conflicts and solving problems.
5. Develop a relation of mutual trust and respect by
   (a) Honouring the sentiment and suggestions of villagers,
   (b) Undertaking frequent visits and providing moral support and guidance to the villagers even when financial assistance is not available
   (c) Maintain transparency in action and discussion between FD personnel, JFMC Executive body, and JFMC & FDV members.
6. Adopt "Reach the Mothers through the Children" programme to involve mothers in eco development activities and to develop the budding children to form a vibrant society in future.

Participatory Rural Appraisal (PRA) Based Microplan

PRA with villagers to –

(a) Understand the present status of the village–map, demography, literacy and wealth status, social amenities, e.g. drinking water, health, education, communication, power, shops, market, bank, etc.
(b) Assess availability of skill, raw materials and resources.
(c) Identify strengths, weaknesses and aspirations of the community.
(These will form the bench mark information to be recorded and preserved) and
(d) To prepare the microplan on the basis of above.

Strengthening FPCs and FDVs

1. Involve all members in different activities aptitude and capability wise.
2. Form Working Groups-
   (a) Forest Protection Sub Group.
   (b) Fund Management Sub Group (Female members only).
   (c) Economic Sub Group – producer/collector, processor, marketer etc.
   (d) Infrastructure Sub Group – earthen dam, community hall, etc.
   (e) Social Sub Group – drinking water, education, health, sanitation, family planning
3. Contribution norms to be finalised and
4. Equitable benefit sharing to be determined during Microplan preparation.
5. Ensure female participation.
6. Promote community based organisation.

Discussion

Communities, mostly tribal families, living in and around forests had depended on nature for fulfilment of their basic needs (Malhotra and Proffenberer, 1989). By virtue of their conservation-oriented living system, perfected through generations of experience, they have in them, valuable indigenous knowledge in this regard. This knowledge and their capacity for labour, their only wealth, may be effectively utilised to manage the diverse natural resources abundantly available around them. Thus the most logical and justifiable Natural Resource Management (NRM) option would be to provide immediate wage income to these rural poor by engaging them for utilisation of these resources within their hold to create productive assets, employing sound and appropriate technology, duly strengthened by their traditional knowledge. At the same time, government effort should be directed towards improving their skill and capacity through training and education and secure their health by encouraging nutritive food habits and sanitation practices. Besides, there should be adequate support for infrastructure development particularly with regard to creation of economic plantations, formation of water bodies through rain water harvesting structures like Puddle Bundhs, Earthen Dams, Check Dams, etc, construction of motorable roads connecting villages to bus/train heads, input supply and product disposal mechanism (marketing) to make the practice affordable, profitable and acceptable. It is therefore apparent that NRM can not be taken up in isolation without considering the issue of development of human resource and the infrastructure in particular.

Under the prevailing acute economic constraints, the villagers in the area may not have the means nor the confidence to opt for vocation based income generation. Therefore, in the initial stage, wage generation by undertaking productive asset building activities is presumed to be the most appropriate and perhaps the only means for providing immediate income for them. At the same time there has to be a built in mechanism to create a fund, individually or on community basis or both, as may be determined by the villagers, from the wages earned, so that the villagers become capable to adopt suitable vocation for income at a later date, by utilising the assets, created by them. However there has to be a suitable mechanism to generate adequate funds to manage these assets. Besides, since the assets are linked with their livelihood, they will, in all likelihood, take care of proper maintenance of these assets.

The following disbursement mechanism is suggested to generate fund from wage earnings for subsequent vocation practice: a) Hand out wage – 70 per cent and b) Family/ Community Fund – 30 per cent (credited in Bank/Post Office). However, this will be possible only through the involvement of a reliable and dedicated, local Community Based Organisation (CBO).

Action Programme

A. The following activities are suggested for immediate wage income

1) Family oriented activities: Land treatment for irrigated cultivation, water recharging and short term fishery.

i. Dug up pools (Puddle Bundh – 5 per cent) at the middle and bottom of individual farmland.
ii. Scraping 'V' ditch in contour at suitable interval and planted with short duration crop.
iii. Boundary planting with Kudlung (*Hibiscus subderiffa*) for Bankura and Purulia districts.
iv. Dressing embankment for planting suitably with crop and grass.

2) Community oriented activities –

a. Soil and water conservation with emphasis on rain water harvesting –

   i. Re-excavation of all silted ponds and excavation of new ones, if possible.
   ii. Jhora training with Live Palisades supported with green posts of Sajina (Moringa), Rhizomes of Bamboo/Sproutable Bamboo posts (green), etc and filled with Brushwood and stones and planted with Slips of Amliso (*Thysonalaena agrostis*), etc on the uphill side of the palisades.
   iii. Extension of Amliso plantation by planting slips along jhoras during rains.
   iv. Making earthen dam on an efficient site (a small dam, creating a big water-body), particularly in the forest fringe areas, having sizeable cultivation nearby and where short term fishery can also be practised.
   v. Connecting big ponds/tanks with the existing irrigation canals with link trench and digging catchment-enlarging channels for inadequately filled Ponds and EDs.
   vi. Contour trench, boundary trench, cattle proof trench, etc.
   (Embankments should be dressed and planted with soil binding grass/crop of economic value)

b. Infrastructure development –

   i. Building Approach road (motorway), connecting village with main road.

ii. Stream/River training with Check dams, having cultivable land in the vicinity
iii. Space for storage and processing

B. Activities under immediate non wage income

Scientific collection of Medicinal plants, edibles and ornamental NTFPs such as, Mohua, Mushroom, Kend-Peal fruits, etc, Kudlung (*Hibiscus subderiffa- Malvaceae*) for fibre, oil, pickle/ jam and fire sticks.

C. Income Options requiring gestation period (deferred income)

1) Animal Husbandry-
   i. Breed Improvement of poultry birds/goats by introducing better breed (RIR) males at 5:1 proportion, (Tola-wise) and sterilising the remaining local males, for increased meat.
   ii. Practicing Goatery, Duckery, Piggery, Poultry (?) etc.
   iii. Training Rural Veterinary Assistants (Prani-Bandhu).

2) Pisciculture – Fishery + Beautification ('Mudiali Nature Park' model)

3) Agriculture –
   i. SRI (System of Rice Intensification) method of paddy cultivation (PRADAN).
   ii. Organic Farming (vegetable gardening) – Prerequisites are –
      a. Cow dung and compost manure
      b. Vermi compost (with proportionate mixture of neem leaf in the feed).
      c. Organic insect repellent, to be coupled with remodelling of cowshed-floor
      (this item may be taken up commercially after necessary field trials).
   iii. Orchard (NABARD) and Agro-forestry with bamboo in the periphery – to be introduced appropriately.

4) NTFP Management
   i. Manufacturing herbal products – Preparing mouth freshening tablets and dusts (having stomach/lungs relieving and mouth refreshing property)

ii. Judicious Cultivation Medicinal plant
iii. Commercial/Ornamental NTFP –
   a. Commercial-Lac/Tassar, Sal leaf, Sabaigrass, Phooljharu, Khejur mat, Abeern(*Gulal* or powder colour) from Palash flower, Kendu leaves and Sal seeds (under embargo), etc.
   b. Artifacts – Bamboo, Sabai grass, Khejur leaves, Drift wood, Dry leaves/fruits/seed, tree fungus.

5) Cottage industry – Muri, Biri, Paperbag and Carry bag

D. Rain water harvesting

This is an area which demands utmost and immediate attention and all efforts have to be made by all development agencies to arrest every single drop of rain water as has been suggested in the earlier paragraphs. Two simple designs for direct harvesting of rain water is given below –

i. Low cost structure with bamboo and plastic sheets, for drinking water.
ii. Roof water harvesting- collected with Ridge Piece and stored in plastic tank or plastic lined ditch for potable water

Justification for Selecting the Activities

The technologies required for executing the proposed activities are simple, do not require complicated equipments and can be easily done with equipments the villagers are familiar with. Thus, the programme can be launched easily and immediately. With regard to the impact of implementing the programme, it may be stated with conviction that apart from generating immediate income from wage earning and subsequent sustained income from asset management for the poor forest fringe dwellers, the aforesaid activities are likely to ameliorate the ecology of the area by harvesting rain water, by making the jhoras stable and productive, by preventing soil erosion and most importantly, by reviving the dry streams perennially.

Mandatory Requirement for Success

JFMC Meeting – It needs to be mentioned in this regard that

routine meetings with sincere participation of the FPC members may be an effective means to motivate them to carry out development planning, conflict resolution, forest protection, etc and solving problems related to individuals or community. Besides, the exercise is likely to enhance capacity, increase efficiency and build up confidence, ensuring sustenance of the system. Therefore, the necessity for organising frequent meetings can never be over emphasised. However there must be suitable incentive for the organisers to convene such meetings and a small investment in this regard by the agency will certainly give worthwhile dividend in the long run.

Thus, although it may appear that implementation of the suggested action programme is utopian and impracticable, yet it may convincingly be argued that by conducting frequent and fruitful meetings as mentioned above, it may not be insurmountable, particularly because the proposed activities are simple and with which the villagers are used to.

Infrastructure requirement to create income opportunities–

A. Structures

(i) Brick/Ring Well with recharging pits, mainly for drinking water.
(ii) Re-excavation/Replenishment of water storage structures (pond, ED, well etc.).
(iii) Earthen Dam (ED), iia. Check Dam, iib. Puddle Bundh, for irrigation.
(iv) Compost Pit/Vermicompost platform (covered).
(v) Irrigation channel
(vi) Constructing/repairing of motorable approach road with causeways and culverts as required and suitable for plying of, at least van rickshaws.
(vii) Environ-matched rural housing with sanitation and roof-water harvesting provision.

B. Equipments

Pump set and pipe, spray pump, sewing machine, sal leaf plate machine, secateur, chopper, grinder, tarpaulin, weighing balance, van-rickshaw etc.

C. Covered Space

(i) Store house and marketing outlets linked with Cold Chain.

(ii) Processing Centre.

(iii) Community Hall – For conducting meeting, training, health camp, child/adult education, *pathachakra*, etc.

D. Power

Importance of Agriculture: The Mainstay of the Indian Economy

It is often argued, that agricultural income is too low and the risks in the practice are rather too high, compared to other sources of income. This is true because of the present management scenario in the sector where practically no useful support is provided to the agriculturists to augment their income or to mitigate the risks. Our country is fortunate to be endowed with bountiful natural resources in terms of favourable soil (land), moisture (rainfall) and energy (sunny days), the like of which is not found in many other countries. Therefore, there is no reason why agriculture and allied farm activities, particularly in our country, should not flourish and compete with other income options, provided appropriate and adequate support, as highlighted in the previous paragraph, is provided. Besides, agriculture provides the basic needs of survival and what is more, it is an independent profession which can be practised with the head held high. However it need be mentioned that agricultural practice demands hard labour, exposure to elements, traditional know-how and perseverance. On the other hand job/service once secured, is perhaps the easiest form of income opportunity which is moderately risk free and does not require hard labour and application, at least under the present circumstances. This lures the young generation to towns and cities howling for jobs, abandoning their treasures in the villages.

A Note on Other Farm Activities

It must be realised that, for meaningful and sustainable management of natural resources rural economy has to be improved and when the goal really is to uplift economy and ensure general wellbeing, of the rural poor, on-farm activities have to be given the top most priority and should be managed with knowledge, efficiency and sincerity. The essential prerequisites of any resource management practice, agriculture being no exception, are,

1. Identification/selection – type and availability
2. Utilisation – technology, training, monitoring and infrastructure
3. Conservation – sustainability of resource base

1. Identification

Many rural resources remain unseen and unutilised because their importance and usage are not known, the glaring example being waste land which nobody reckons as wealth. Therefore it is important that all natural resources like land, water, trees, animals, etc. are identified, understood, quantified and documented. This is necessary to assess their status and explore possibilities of their utilisation and conservation. This may be done by entrusting responsibility on rural institutions after making them capable through training and practice.

2. Utilisation

Natural resources are used for various purposes, e.g. production, habitation, industrialisation, recreation, etc. In the present discussion only production, i.e. production of food and other essential requirements of man, for instance land, water, plants, animals and forests are considered. For obvious reasons this is the most vital part of NRM which covers all types of production practices that may be grouped into two categories.

(i) *Cultivation* – This includes production practices like agriculture, horticulture, floriculture, sericulture, pisciculture, animal husbandry, etc.

(ii) *Collection* – This includes collection of livelihood items from resources of natural origin. For example, forests, waste-land, water bodies, etc.

Most of the essential needs of human beings are met through these production practices which are looked after by qualified managers in their specific fields and are therefore beyond the scope of this discussion. Nevertheless, the salient point to be made in this regard is that the character and quality of all the used resources particularly soil and water have to be improved progressively to provide profitable production sustainably and more importantly to retain the status of the resource base undamaged as far as possible even after use. This can be attained only if the management system is guided by the principles of optimisation and recycling.

However innovative technology should be evolved to compete with the apparently lucrative but highly destructive current production system.

For income generation and also to make production really meaningful, the following areas are to be considered with due care,

1. *Processing* – This is necessary to make the product suitable for use or for sale. The processed product should have value added quality, safe for consumer use, attractive and durable enough to provide bargaining space. For instance simple cleaning, sorting and drying of Andrographis spp. (Kalmegh), a widely used medicinal plant, makes it acceptable, provides better prices and increases its shelf life to play with market forces profitably.
2. *Marketing* – It is essential that thorough market study is made before undertaking production and processing. It is because production is not income till the product is profitably marketed. (The tragic case of the potato cultivators of Chandrakona in Midnapore District is a case in point.)
3. *Diversification* – Market study and research for diversification of products is necessary to meet the demand and interest of the market.

3. Conservation

In the context of extreme poverty in rural areas and the easy accessibility of forest resources, sustainable management of forest covers is often difficult. Besides, under the compelling influence of brute market force, the expectation and lifestyle, even in rural areas have changed drastically and natural resources have lost their traditional values and significance. Thus the root cause of resource degradation may be attributed to need, greed and population pressure and also to the total lack of love or attachment coupled with utter indifference. Under this background the conservation initiatives should primarily aim at generating adequate immediate income both alternate and additional, and appealing to the emotion, sentiment and perception of human beings. The following options may be considered.

(i) Infusing love, respect and interest through proper education, nature study, rural excursions (know your root – your land, your people) etc. from an early age.
(ii) Exercising restraint over market-driven lifestyle and developing nature-based habits.
(iii) Creating a sense of belonging by bestowing ownership.
(iv) Developing appropriate technology and infrastructure to make NRM profitable and attractive.
(v) Generating a state of caution and fear by legislating implementable rules and regulations and more importantly by developing effective enforcement mechanism.
(vi) Expanding resource base artificially.
(vii) Determined approach to control population.

However, the most effective means of conservation, presumably, is to involve resource with living and livelihood. With regard to forest conservation the following options may be explored.

Food security – Sustainable collection of fruits, seeds, leaves, tubers, herbs, etc. for food.

Local economy – (a) Lac and Tassar cultivation to protect species like, Schleichera, Zyziphus, Beutea, Shorea, Terminalia spp. etc.

(b) Pristine tourism – to conserve habitat and facilitate Nature Study.

(c) Heritage Tourism – to depict the cultural heritage of a village in tranquil surroundings.

Local trade – (a) Scientific and sustainable collection and marketing of herbal products to protect medicinal herbs, shrubs and trees.

(b) Small scale cottage industry of utility goods and art pieces, e.g. Sal leaf plate, articles made of grasses like sabai, gonda, etc. Ornamental seeds, ferns, grasses, etc.

Health – Backyard herbal garden for common diseases.

Religion – Sacred grooves. Parts of plants for puja and other religious festivals,

Culture – Parts of specific plants for festivals, social ceremonies, etc (these are a few indicative ideas only and not exhaustive).

Economical and Ecological Management of Land

1. Individual Approach – Generally sizeable land is available in and around village homesteads which may be utilized with intensive cultivation for producing utility products of considerable magnitude vide Farmyard Management Plan – An Individual Effort Annexure-I

2. Group Approach – a. To undertake plantation works on vested waste lands, community lands, fallow lands belonging to the Government Departments, canal bank, flood embankment, river/jhora banks, roadside fallows, tank fore-shores, wastelands of individuals etc., FPC-wise or SHG-wise, for multi purpose products as per design vide Development of Upland Waste on a Community Basis (Annexure II)

b. To develop SMFE involving clusters of conveniently located FPCs.

3. Departmental Approach – The Forest Department together with other Government Departments should endeavour to strengthen FPCs and undertake forest and other rural resource development activities to bring production to optimum level. It is obvious that in the next few years, sizeable quantities of wood are to be produced from the country's forest resources to meet the industrial wood requirement of the country. If our bountiful natural resources are harnessed

efficiently and the rural human resources are engaged and guided properly, per capita share of wood can perhaps be increased manifold. However, this can be done by meaningful adoption of suitable management practice, judicious utilisation of resources and appropriate application of production techniques. It is to this end that the departmental approach should aim at.

NRM Management Principles

Following the ideologies of the great Savant, Swami Vivekananda, the NRM management strategy is primarily based on the principles mentioned below –

- Beggary can never lead to prosperity
- The essentials of self-reliance are self-respect and determination
- Power should be acquired through capacity enhancement
- Joint effort is strong, sustainable and meaningful
- Our nature is bountiful – if we could make use of what we have

Necessity of Small and Micro Forest Enterprise (SMFE)

It has long been established that economic stability of the forest fringe dwellers is obligatory for preservation of forests and amelioration of ecosystem. Various agencies, including the Department of Forests have been focusing their initiatives largely in this direction by utilising forests and other natural resources. Thus sizeable numbers of varieties of income generating activities are being practised individually and or in groups in many areas sponsored by a sizeable number of agencies. However, in many cases, these endeavours are seasonal and are fraught with the risk of discontinuation.

The objective of establishing Small and Micro Forest Enterprise (SMFE) is to coordinate all these activities into vocation-based small rural enterprises, organised, managed and monitored by the FPC/SHG members and the appropriate option will be, to bring all these enterprises in a given operationally convenient locality (say a Forest Beat), under one umbrella to form a slightly bigger and consolidated enterprise (SMFE) which will be mutually supportive and hopefully will function sustainably throughout the year and will fulfil other social commitments like child education, rural environment amelioration, family planning etc, along with the primary goal of sustainable income generation to ensure forest preservation. The beat level cluster committee/monitoring group may be groomed to form the SMFE through appropriate training and guidance.

Organisational requirements –

- A thoroughly motivated key person, with vision and dedication to guide, conduct and pursue the programme, supported by a group of sincere followers.
- Capacity building of human resource through training for, manager/production expert, accountant/store-keeper and market/liaison expert, which has to be followed up by entrusting responsibility and providing guidance.

  Training for skill development of artists/artisans, has to be followed up by input-support and monitoring up to the production stage.
- Developing infrastructure for –

  a. Production (assets, equipment, rural transport, etc)

  b. Administration (space for office, processing, storage, etc).
- Monitoring – Importance of monitoring can never be overemphasised. Actually there has to be a separate body with sincere members from within the group who are interested and can spare time, e.g., group leaders of SHGs.
- Building up institution, with identity, address and status.
- Fulfilling legal requirements for establishing the enterprise.

Operational Strategy –

- Segmentation of the area into operationally suitable Clusters.

- Selection of manageable number of conveniently located JFMC/FPCs in each cluster.
- Activity wise SHG formation in each JFMC/FPC, based on aptitude and availability of resources.
- Establishing monitoring group (*Tadaraki Dal*), cluster wise, for monitoring and marketing.
- Development of enterprise by inducting capable members from the monitoring group and coordinating and managing all the activities in the cluster.

Key components of SMFE establishment are –

- Formation and capacity building of *Ban 'O' Jibika Suraksha Tadaraki Dal* (BJSTD)
- Identification of commercially viable resources/services
- Conducting market research
- Selection of marketable items for production/Collection
- Infrastructure development
- Organisation (formation and functioning of SHGs)
- Fund support
- Training
- Monitoring of activities (production/processing, etc) through BJSTD
- Establishing SMFE - *Banaja Silpa Banijya Pratisthan* (BSBP).

By inducting members from BJSTD –

- Fulfilling legal requirements
- Packaging, labelling, storage and marketing by the *Pratisthan* (organisation).

Consolidation

Although income is necessary for comfortable living yet man does not live by bread alone. Generally, apart from comfort, most human beings aspire for peace, happiness and harmony in life. In light of the above, to ensure general well-being of the individual/family and to develop a vibrant and harmonious society in a clean green environment, the following activities may be considered for implementation after ensuring appropriate income opportunities for the forest fringe dwellers.

1. Forming a socially active women's group, namely *Samaj 'O' Paribesh Sachetak Mahila Bahini* from amongst the capable female members of the FPC/SHGs, who will endeavour to improve environment and eradicate social evils like unrestricted drinking habits, child abuse, female harassment, etc.

2. Establishing *Shishu Diksha Kendra* (child education centres) in each or a cluster of a few villages, for healthy upbringing of the budding children (between >2 and <6 years of age), by educating them tenderly and persuasively, to teach them to remain clean and tidy, to respect elders, to help the weak and disabled and to have the courage to protest against any evil intent. *Mahila Bahini* (women's force) may be made responsible for achieving this.

However it needs to be pointed out that,

Successful functioning of SMFE will perhaps require years of hard training, monitoring and guidance and even more years of continuous persuasion.

Besides, it has to be kept in mind that the ultimate goal of developing SMFE is Forest Preservation. Therefore, the primary responsibility of the *Banaja Silpa Banijya Pratisthan* (organisation) will be to pursue the following activities, i.e. conducting motivational meetings, facilitating organised patrolling, forming and activating woman protection group, organising route-monitoring (*Dharna*), etc. In effect, the *Pratisthan* will not only be a 'Commercial Enterprise' but also a 'Social Organisation', which will look after the general well-being of the forest fringe dwellers in a clean, green and fresh environment.

Findings

1. The essence of sustainability is self-reliance, which is attained only when the spirit of self-respect is inculcated and confidence is built up.
2. Without contribution participation is incomplete and without participation development is unsustainable.
3. Equitable benefit sharing is mandatory for sustenance of production-oriented development programmes.
4. Sustainable and meaningful rural resource management

lies in creating capable rural institution with legal status, supported by formation of vocation based SHGs.

5. Participation of women with necessary empowerment is mandatory for success and sustenance of any development initiative.
6. Key elements of empowerment are, identifying worthwhile stake, providing appropriate training, entrusting responsibility and most importantly, ensuring meaningful monitoring.
7. Community fund building and non-formal child and adult education should be included as an essential component in any rural development programme.
8. Production is not income, till the produce is marketed profitably and establishment of SMFE is necessary to provide sustained income to many.
9. Non-economic activities like sports, cultural programmes, etc are important development components to infuse zeal, efficiency and sense of solidarity.
10. In arid/semi-arid zones (Purulia, Bankura, West Midnapore, etc) priority should be given to rain water harvesting (roof and surface) for economic development and ecological amelioration.
11. To ensure social justice, decisions should be taken from the heart and implemented through the brain and not vice versa.
12. Voluntary effort does not last long.

Conclusion

To sum up, it may be stated that the essence of viable economy is the sympathetic understanding and efficient management of resources, both human and natural. Besides, under the Indian scenario, where too many people are too dependent on limited forests, the concept of the Joint Forest Management System should perhaps be considered as the ideal and the only tool for development of human resources for efficient management of natural resources.

Moreover it is often debated that converting villages to town is development. In this context it is perhaps necessary to understand that a village can perhaps survive without a town but a town without the support of a few villages will certainly perish in no time. In the light of the prevailing over population in towns, the signal is very clear that, unless agriculture and allied farm practices, by using rural resources including forests, are made profitable by providing necessary support as specified, and basic amenities like health, education, communication, etc. are extended to the villages, the influx to towns cannot be prevented and in that event urban life will become unbearable in spite of glittering development and rural resources will remain unused and become degraded in spite of enormous prospects, particularly in the context of the Indian sub-continent which is endowed with valuable natural resources of enviable abundance and brilliant human resource of immense potential.

The discussion may finally be closed with a famous saying,

> *"when the leaves become dry and the soil without a drop of water, then and then only, it will be realised that man can not survive chewing a rupee."*

References

Basu, J.P. (2008), *Joint Forest Management, Deforestation and Local People's Participation.*

Chatterjee, M. (1995), *Gender Role in JFM.*

Ghosal, S. (2011), Importance of non-timber forest products in native household economy, *Journal of Geography and Regional Planning,* Vol. 4 (3).

Malhotra, K.C. and Proffenberger, M. (1989), *Forest Regeneration Through Community Participation.*

Pattnaik, B. K. and Dutta, S. (2006), *JFM in South-West Bengal: A Study in Participatory Development.*

Sarin, M. (1995), *Joint Forest Management: Achievement and Unaddressed Challenges.*

ANNEXURE 1

FARMYARD MANAGEMENT PLAN – A Family Initiative

Trees in the villages are fast diminishing. Homestead lands and farmyards remain either fallow or planted in an unplanned manner. Thus most of the land resources continue to remain untapped or partially tapped. Generally sizeable extent of land is available in and around homesteads in the villages, which may be effectively utilised for producing resources of considerable magnitude by adopting intensive land resource management technique. This scheme is designed to bring these lands under use for resource production, income generation and ecological amelioration. Most of the land use practices have been incorporated in this scheme – silviculture, horticulture, agriculture, floriculture, apiculture, etc.

THEME

The theme of the scheme is based on the following principles

1. Identification of resources
2. Optimum utilisation of resources
3. Recycling of resources.

Keeping the above in view, attempt has been made to utilize every available space and resources and also to maintain soil balance perpetually. The tier system has been introduced to use both air space and soil depth to the maximum. Different planting patterns have been incorporated to accommodate available land of various shapes and sizes.

METHOD

The following planning techniques and patterns have been adopted, which have been demonstrated in the perspective plan. Annex- I

1. High Density Fuel Bed

Bed of size 2.4mx1.2m/3.6mx1.2m/4.8mx1.2m/6mx1.2m (as per available space) are to be dug up to 0.3m deep, cleaned of all roots, grasses, etc. and mixed with cow dung manure in the proportion of 3:1, Fast growing coppiceable species, e.g. Subabul, Eucalyptus etc. are to be planted at a spacing of 0.6mx0.3m in a staggered manner. Watering in the dry season is advisable. This will be worked at 3 years rotation and hence 3 or multiple of 3 nos. of beds are to be made.

2. *Alley Cropping*

This technique is to be applied in vegetable gardens which should be located near the water source (tube well, dug well etc.) so that waste water may be channelled to the vegetable garden through a non-concrete drain for automatic irrigation. The 0.3 m wide line is to be thoroughly dug up and mixed with cow dung in the vegetable garden 3.6m apart in the east-west direction. Duly treated seeds of Subabul, Eucalyptus, Gamar, Ghoraneem, etc. are to be thinly sown in two lines 20cm apart in the above 0.3m wide dug up line. The sown line is to be covered with straw and occasionally watered. The sowing is to be done in April. In the months of February-March next year the plants will be about 1.5 to 1.8m high when these are to be cut at the base, flush to the ground, with a sharp cutting instrument. Leaves may be used as fodder or green manure and the twigs as firewood. Fresh shoots will come up again from the stumps which are to be again cut next year in the months of February-March. Periodical manuring in subsequent years will give better production.

3. *Agro Forestry*

The areas which are unsuitable for vegetable production but suitable for dry cultivation, e.g. Cajanus, Mustard, Pulses, etc. may be used through this technique. The area should be thoroughly ploughed and planting pits are dug 0.6m apart in lines spaced at 3.6m interval. These lines should be in East-West direction. Timber species, e.g. Teak, Sissoo, Gamar, Mahogony, Setisal, etc. are to be planted in the tree lines 3.6m apart. The rest of the pits in the tree lines are to be planted with fast growing fuel and fodder species. The space in between tree lines is to be utilised for dry agricultural crops like Cajanas, Mustard, Pulses, Ginger, Turmeric, etc.

4. Close Plantation

The areas which are thoroughly unsuitable for any agri-crop may be brought to use under this technique. Planting pits are to be dug all over the area at a spacing of 0.6mx0.6m. Timber species, e.g. Teak, Sissoo, Satisal, Gamar, etc. and Fruit species e.g. Jack fruit, Mango, etc. are to be planted at a spacing of 3.6mx1.8m in a staggered manner. The remaining pits are to be planted with fast growing fuel and fodder species. From the second year thinning is to be undertaken to free the timber and fruit trees from suppression. Thus considerable quantity of fuel and or fodder will be available from the second year onwards.

Fruit gardens and flower gardens have been incorporated in the scheme:

Fruit garden near the home is an attractive proposition. Two combinations (1) coconut, banana, papaya and (2) tall fruit (e.g. jack fruit), dwarf fruit (e.g. guava, cashew nut, lemon etc.) and ground fruit, e.g. pineapple have been suggested to be maintained in three tier system of management. Under-planting of elephant yam is likely to give attractive dividends and turmeric, ginger and medicinal herbs may be inter-planted to cover the remaining ground. Areca nut with black pepper at the base is suggested around the home and along the boundary of the house.

A flower garden in front will add colour to the homestead and perhaps some money to the purse of the real enterprising owner. A pair of composite pits (to be used alternately), near the cowshed, connected with a drains from the kitchen, will ensure continuous supply of organic manure, provided all vegetable waste including leaves and grasses are dumped in the pit.

With so many trees around, the apiary will be a reasonably economic proposition. Besides, introduction of smokeless chulla, solar light/pump and low cost latrine will perhaps further the end of environmental, ecological and sanitation issues.

A water body of size (to the extent of 5 per cent of the area), at the downward end of the plot will harvest rainwater to provide life saving irrigation to plants, potable water for the family and undertake fishery to enhance family income.

A perspective design of an ideally developed village home as suggested above is enclosed, as Annex I.

Target Group

It is assumed that about 1 *bigha* (36m x 36m) of land is generally available in a village homestead. Small and marginal farmers having such homestead should be identified for the scheme. Besides, landless farmers with *patta* land may also be brought very effectively within the purview of the scheme. However, the planting models mentioned above are illustrative and selective models may be adopted according to the availability of land.

Conclusion

It is evident that through a planned and intensive management practice, considerable income can be generated and the ecological aspect also can be properly safeguarded by treating a meagre 1 *bigha* (36m x 36m) of fallow land. It demands only motivation, will to work and perseverance and neither high-tech methodology nor huge financial investment.

N.B.: The species suggested in the perspective plan are indicative to be selected as per requirement of the family and demand of soil and climate.

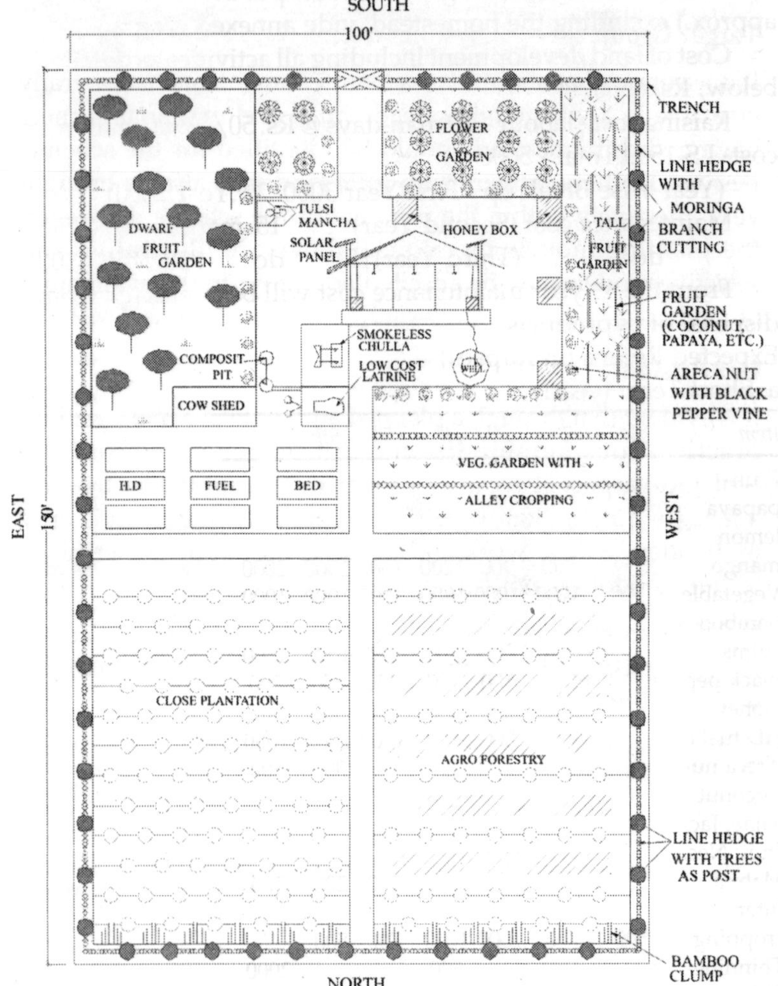
PERSPECTIVE PLAN
FARMYARD MANAGEMENT THROUGH INDIVIDUAL EFFORT
SOUTH
100'
TRENCH
FLOWER GARDEN
LINE HEDGE WITH
MORINGA BRANCH CUTTING
TULSI MANCHA
HONEY BOX
TALL FRUIT GARDEN
DWARF FRUIT GARDEN
SOLAR PANEL
FRUIT GARDEN (COCONUT, PAPAYA, ETC.)
SMOKELESS CHULLA
COMPOSIT PIT
LOW COST LATRINE
WELL
ARECA NUT WITH BLACK PEPPER VINE
COW SHED
H.D
FUEL
BED
VEG. GARDEN WITH
ALLEY CROPPING
EAST
150'
WEST
CLOSE PLANTATION
AGRO FORESTRY
LINE HEDGE WITH TREES AS POST
BAMBOO CLUMP
NORTH

Homestead Land Development Plan

Cost Benefit Analysis (Bengali Method.) per *Bigha* (100' x 150' approx.) excluding the homestead, vide annexed diagram.

Cost of land development including all activities as detailed below, Rs. 6500/-*

Raising cost - labour – 70 man-days @ Rs. 50/- 3500, material cost- LS 1500 Total - 5000

(Year-wise Break up - First Year 3000. 2nd.Year 2000)

Maintenance cost (Second Year) 15 man-days750 750

do (Third Year)15 do 750 750 6500

From the 4th year maintenance cost will be generated from disposal of byproducts.

Expected Return (in Rupees) –

a. Short Term (yearly)

Item	*1st.*	*2nd.*	*3rd.*	*4th.*	*5th.*	*6th*	*7th.*	*8th.*	*9th.*	*10th.*
Fruit- papaya lemon mango		700	900	1200	1500	1500	2000	2000	2500	2500
Vegetable	700	1000	1000	1000	1000	1000	1000	1000	1000	1000
Bamboo culms			200	500	1000	1000	1500	2000	2500	2500
Black pepper			100	100	150	150	200	200	200	200
Honey		100	100	200	200	500	500	700	1000	1000
HD fuel bed			500	700	1000	1000	1000	1000	1000	1000
Areca nut						300	500	1000	1000	1000
Coconut								500	600	1000
Sajne, Jack fruit, Neem, Mahua					100	200	500	500	700	1000
Inter-cropping	500	700	1000	1000	700	500				
Thinning				500			2000			5000
Fishery			500	500	500	1000	1000	3000	3000	5000
Product Income	1200	2500	4300	5700	6150	7150	10200	11900	13500	21200
Cost (Wage Income)	3000	2750	750							
NET INCOME	4200	5250	5050	5750	6150	7150	10200	11900	13500	21200

Sizeable quantity of fuel, form twigs and branches will be available from yearly pruning of branches (crown manipulation) which is mandatory for better plant-growth and return from inter-cropping. The financial equivalent of the same has not been taken into account in the calculation.

b. Long Term –
At 15th Year- Price of fast growing Timber Trees
1. Approximate cost of homestead development

(i) Homestead-	50000	
(ii) Well	20000	
(iii) Solar Installation	40000	
(iv) Tulu Pump	1000	
(v) Cattle	30000	141000

2. Cost of Homestead Land development- 6500*
3. Contingent Expenditure 2500
Total cost of the Project = 141000 + 6500 + 2500 = 150000 (one lakh fifty thousand only)
(Calculated costs of inputs and outputs are old (late 1990s) and approximate, requiring updating and market adjustment)

ANNEXURE 2

Development of Upland Waste on Community Basis

About 7 per cent of total land resources of West Bengal is uncultivable waste. These lands, even when distributed to the landless, remain unused for the obvious reasons – these are neither fit for profitable agriculture nor even for habitation due to scarcity of water, nature of soil and other hazards. Thus a sizeable extent of such land remains unused for ages although there is immense possibility of creating, assets as well as income opportunities, by adopting suitable afforestation technique or tree farming on these lands provided appropriate rain water harvesting structures like Puddle-Bundh, Earthen Dam, Check Dam etc are built up in the area. Having thus developed, this scheme envisages fruitful utilisation of these lands through afforestation and intercropping.

In this connection it need be maintained that delayed return is a major constraint for any afforestation scheme making the same unattractive and unacceptable to farmers, particularly the small and marginal farmers. The scheme has been designed to overcome this constraint by introducing early producing fruit and economic species, resorting to close planting with yearly pruning and intercropping with crops like pulses, mustard, ginger, turmeric, sweet potato, pineapple, elephant yam, etc, between the tree lines.

Besides, it has been seen that protection is the major problem for any afforestation scheme which may however be eliminated in the instant case, by involving local people (the target group) thoroughly and intimately in the programme and allowing them to undertake inter-cropping with usufruct right.

The key features of the scheme are:

1. Utilisation of unfertile wasteland.
2. Production of resources of local demand as well as of national need.
3. Income generation.

4. Economic rehabilitation of landless, small and marginal farmers.
5. Optimum utilisation of resources.
6. Soil and water conservation.

Target area –

1. Vested waste lands.
2. Community lands.
3. Fallow lands belonging to the Government Department i.e.
   a. L & L R Department land
   b. Canal bank, flood embankment
   c. River/Jhora banks
   d. Roadside fallows
   e. Tank foreshores

(2) Wastelands belonging to private individuals

Method

(a) Administrative

Vested wasteland or fallow land belonging to Government Departments in large blocks or in small isolated patches are to be identified. Suitable participants – preferably landless, small or marginal farmers having interest in land and cultivation – are to be selected from the villages situated near the areas of operation. They will be allotted a portion of area to be afforested, for inter-cropping and may also be engaged for afforestation works during lean season to provide subsidiary income.

The participants will be allowed the usufruct of the fruits and agricultural crops and a percentage of the tree crops which will be the property of the *panchayat* or the department as the case may be. In lieu, they will protect the tree crops which will they will have to do in any case for protection of their inter crop. Thus the major problem of protection – even of areas of small isolated and scattered nature – can be eliminated. Besides, they may be allowed to practise short rotation pisciculture in the pool formed due to earthen bund which will add to their income. The same methodology may be adopted in respect of uncultivable wastes belonging to private individuals.

(b) Technical

Raising Agro-forestry Plantation

Planting technique for tree crops is furnished below. For agricultural crop between tree lines selection of crop is to be made on the basis of soil type, season and requirement.

A. **Selection of species:** Species are to be selected as per soil type and choice of the participants and nursery is to be raised accordingly by the participants themselves.

B. **Soil work**

(i) Boundary Trench of size (90cm + 60cm)/2 x 60 cm are to be dug along the boundary of the plantation.

(ii) V-type demarcation/contour ditches 15cm deep are to be made by scrapping and filling the debris along the boundaries of the individual beneficiaries.

(iii) 60 cm *dia thalis*, 30 cm deep and cleaned of all roots and grass are to be made 4 m apart in line in east-west direction. The lines will be 4 m apart in north-south direction.

(iv) 3 m^3 cow dung/ha (600 *thalis*) are to be mixed in all the *thalis*.

C. **Planting Technique and Pattern**

1. It is important to remember that tree lines should be in east-west direction, so that the agri-crops get maximum sunlight. The details are furnished in the diagram enclosed in Annex II.
2. Water harvesting reservoir

   A linear earthen bund will be dug at the lower fringe of the operational area along the contour to harvest excess rain water, which may be used for short rotation pisciculture by the beneficiaries and also for small irrigation during the dry season.

D. **Sequence of Work**

Nursery work is to be started from January.

Earthwork for digging planting pits, making earthen bunds and V ditches are to be completed by the end of March.

Pit filling and manuring is to be done immediately after pre-monsoon shower, i.e. April/May.

Seed sowing is to be done after pit filling and completed by the end of May.

Planting of seedlings of timber, oilseed and fruit trees in planting pits is to be started by the end of June or as soon as the monsoon starts.

Hardy and fast growing fuelwood seedlings are to be planted by 'dig and plant' methods between two *thalis* all over the area and are to be completed by the end of July, together with planting of seedlings of palm, date palm and custard apple seedlings.

N.B. – There may be slight monsoonal variation in the time schedule but the sequence of work should be adhered to.

First weeding, forking and application of manure (200 gms of organic manure mixed with bacterial fertiliser/plant) is to be completed by mid-August.

Second weeding, forking and application of manure (200 gms of organic manure/plant) is to be completed by mid-September

Third weeding, forking is to be completed by mid-October

Intercropping of dry land agri-crop is to be undertaken as per season.

Mandatory-pruning of branches to be done every year during December/January.

Details of Work

1. Interrupted boundary trench (90 cm + 60 cm). Line sowing of babla on the outer edge and of Cajanus (Pigeon pea) on the inner edge of the boundary trench berm.

Palm and Datepalm are to be planted alternately 3 m apart with custard apple seed/seedlings in between on the ridge of this boundary trench berm.

2. V type contour/demarcation ditch 15 cms deep. This is to be made along the boundary of the individual beneficiaries and sown with subabul/Cajanus seeds as alley cropping.

3. Selection of species is to be made through PRA exercise with the villagers. Species mentioned under the planting pattern below are only illustrative.

4. **Planting Pattern**

Oil seed/economic trees

Neem, Karanja, Kusum and Mohua plants are to be planted in the planting pits 8 m apart in alternate lines.

Timber tree

Sisoo, Gamar, Teak, Mehagoni plants are to be planted in between oilseed plants as above.

Tall fruit plants

Bel, Bahera, Haritaki, Amlaki plants are to be planted 8 m apart in the remaining lines.

Dwarf fruit plants

Citrus, Musambi, Amrapali, Guava, Kaju as above.

Hardy fast-growing fuelwood trees

Trema, Dumur, Seuli, Subabul, Sidha plants along with Akasmoni, Eucalyptus are to be planted in between all the thalis by 'dig and plant' method.

5. **Water Harvesting Bund**

The technique and pattern is clearly indicated in the model diagram Annexure II

This is to be made at the lower edge of the operation area to arrest and store excess rain water.

Conclusion

This scheme opens up a new vista of activities aiming at environmental amelioration, production of assets of immense magnitude and creation of income opportunity of sizeable dimension to landless, marginal and small farmers by tackling the so far neglected but potentially productive uncultivable land resources of the State.

N.B.: The species suggested in the perspective plan are indicative to be finally selected as per requirement of people and the demands of soil and climate.

Suggested Spp -

Overall Spacing-1.5Mx4M
Planting Pit-4Mx4.5M

(NOT TO SCALE)

F - Tall Fruit - Bel, Behera, Haritaki, Amlaki
f - Dwarf Fruit - Lebu, Musambi, Amtapali, Guava, Kaju
T - Timber - Sisoo, Gamar, Segun, Mehogini
○ - Oil Seed - Neem, Karanj, Mahua, Kusum
⊛ - Fuel Wood - Subabul, Akasmoni, Eucalyptus
(Sidha, Seuli, Trema, Dumur - local spp)

Acknowledgement goes to –

Directorate of Forests, Government of West Bengal.
Lokasiksha Parishad, Ramakrishna Mission Ashram, Narendrapur.
Ford Foundation, USA.

German Agro Action, Bonn.
Department of Anthropology, Calcutta University.
Regional Centre NAEB (Ministry of Environment & Forests, Government of India), Jadavpur University, Kolkata.
National Bank for Agriculture & Rural Development (NABARD), Kolkata.
PRADAN, Purulia.
Jan Sikshan Sangsthan (JSS), Purulia, under the Ministry of HRD, Government of India.
Grameen Bikash Trust (GBT), Purulia.
Hensla Haraparbati Club, Hensla, Purulia.
Dr. Ajit Kumar Banerjee, Former Sr. Forestry Specialist, World Bank.
And in particular the JFMC members of Purulia Forest Division.

10

Custodians of Culture Sustain Forest Biodiversity Through Participatory Planning and Management in the Himalayas

R. Nusrat

Abstract: In the Himalayas of Uttarakhand, indigenous and tribal communities are under considerable pressure and are in different phases of cultural assimilation and change. These indigenous communities reside in fragile environments yet they have time-tested experience and valuable cultural knowledge that could be used for adaptations and mitigation of issues related to forest biodiversity. The present paper studies the ecological mode of cultural adaptations of the most spectacular semi-nomadic tribes of the Himalayas. Surviving on Transhumance herding, they represent the initial mode of human adjustment with nature. Himalayan tribal communities have expressed growing concern in international forums that most development planning aims at maximising economic development and rarely takes into account the reciprocal culture-land/resource relationships that are fundamental to tribal social institutions and sustainability of the forest biodiversity. Sustainability has become an institution owing to local cultural influences on resource use patterns and management for sustainable living. Eventually, the cultural identity and tribal institutions are being maintained due to the resilience that these communities portray in the Himalayas. Henceforth, this paper tries to explore as to how the biodiversity of the Himalayas is retained through their indigenous knowledge and it could further be enhanced through their participation and management techniques

Introduction

The forest resources are rapidly being degraded and depleted so the conservation of biodiversity becomes one of the prime concerns. Innovative forest management practices, based on traditional knowledge and developed by rural communities over the centuries, have contributed significantly to the world's natural and cultural heritage by creating and maintaining landscapes of outstanding beauty while helping to sustain production of multiple goods and services that enhance livelihood security and quality of life. Therefore, in order to have an in-depth knowledge of sustainable forest management, there is a need to understand how human cultures interact with landscapes and shape them into cultural landscapes. Traditional societies have co-evolved with their environment, modifying nature but actively maintaining it in a diverse and productive state based on their indigenous knowledge, socio-cultural practices and religious beliefs since antiquity (Ramakrishnan, 2000).

Traditional knowledge is a combination of ancient ingenious practices and techniques which are linked to the natural forest ecosystem and the human managed ecosystem through biodiversity driven traditional ecological knowledge and dependent on land use activities for their livelihood concerns. Traditional societies living in the forested areas view the forested landscape (inclusive of natural and human-managed ecosystem) around them as an integrated whole, and therefore, as indicative of their own cultural identity, with implication for sustainable forest conservation and management (Ramakrishnan, 2000). Natural resource management systems in the Himalayan region are strongly linked to the indigenous knowledge systems. The cultural landscapes provide a mechanism to understand how multiple objectives(timber production, non-timber forest products, protected areas, tourism) are central to sustainable forest management in landscapes that conserve heritage values and support the livelihood needs of local people (Ramakrisnan, 2000).

Forest land is strictly controlled and kept out of bounds of human activities. In the 2002 strategic plan document, the central government envisaged that by the end of 11th Plan in 2012, India will have restored its forest cover at least 33 per cent (India Together, 2005). For this purpose the 11th Plan emphasises on the planting of trees in areas that are traditional grazing lands. Apart from National Parks, pastoralists elsewhere had the right to graze their animals in parts of the forest against a fixed grazing fee. But now some forests are being closed by the implementation of Joint Forest Management Programmes. Others are being declared as wildlife sanctuaries and National Parks. Apart from this, forests are increasingly being diverted for purposes such as industry, road building and mining. During the years 1981 to 2001, a total of 23156 hectares of land have been diverted for various developmental activities in Uttarakhand of which a major part has been diverted for the hydropower projects (5086 hectares) and mining projects (8359 hectares).This has led to problems such as enhanced soil erosion and landslides. Due to which the eroded sediments in the area are filling reservoirs and choking the streams. Springs in many parts of the state have dried up or have become seasonal. In the areas east of Nainital, 40-45 per cent springs have met their fate (Valdiya, 1987).

In the local setting, the strategies which people apply in order to survive where the local people of course, are subject to changes and processes in the society around them over which they have no power, but where they build up strategies to react to these changes. An example can be seen in the alternating shift between nomadism, defined as "movement of the household during the annual round of productive activities" and sedentarisation defined as "a change from nomadism towards a settled life". For example, some Gujjar groups from the state of Uttar Pradesh in their winter quarters all year because of an ongoing conflict with the hill peasants in their summer quarters but as the conflicts got partly resolved, they returned to nomadism.

Study Area

The winter camps of the Van Gujars is in the Siwalik forest division which lies west of the Delhi Dehradun highway and outside the Rajaji National Park, lying between 20°25′N and 30°25′N latitude and 72°35′E to 78°15′E longitude. While the Rajaji National Park area lies in the east of the highway and includes Rajaji, Motichur and Chila lying between 29°50′N to 30°15′N latitude and 77°55′E to 78°30′E longitude. The Table below shows the distribution of Gujjar families in Rajaji National Park in various forest divisions.

S.No	*Forest Division*	*Number of Families*
1	Siwalik Forest Division	266
2	Eastern Forest Division	57
3	Western Forest Division	8
4	Lansdowne Forest Division	181
	Total	512

Source: Rajaji National Park Directorate, Dehradun.

The summer pastures comprise Govind National Park in Uttarkashi district covering an area of 472.08 sq kms was carved out from Govind Wildlife Sanctuary in 1990. The altitude of the

Map Showing Migratory Route of Van Gujars from Siwalik Foothill Forest to Alpines

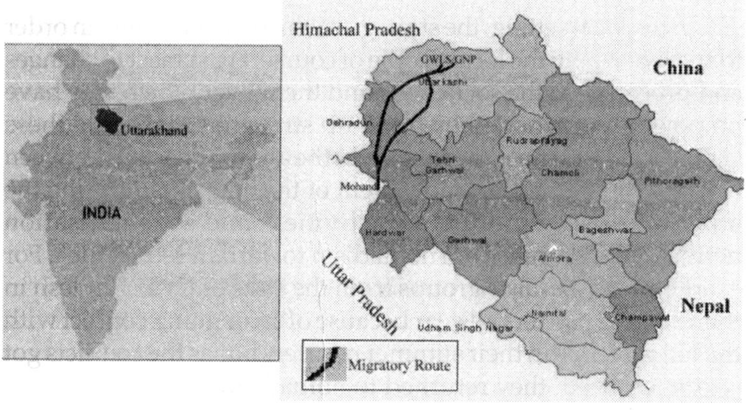

park varies from 2056 m to 6323 m above msl.The alpine meadows occupy approximately one-fifth area of the park which is used as summer grazing land for more than 30 migratory shepherd groups.

Methodology

The present article is an account of long participatory field survey and data collection about different stakeholders of forests and pastoralism in Uttarakhand. The focus has been given on Garhwal region in particular. Questionnaire survey and interviews were carried out among the Van Gujjars inside Govind Wildlife Sanctuary and National Park and of Rajaji National Park. The secondary data regarding Wildlife Sanctuaries and National Parks were collected from the Office of the Deputy Director of Govind National Park and State Forest Statistics of Uttarakhand Forest Department. Different acts regarding forest and conservation were analysed relating to the present scenarios of pastoralism in the region. Pastoral migratory routes were mapped by taking part in the seasonal migration with pastoralists through different forests and alpine pastures.

Culture Based Lopping Sustenance Techniques

While Park authorities emphasise that Van Gujjars are the root cause of forest destruction however, Van Gujjars' use of trees includes lopping for fodder and use of deadwood for firewood and *dera* (house) construction. Various studies indicate that in general, Dholkhand, Mohand and Chillawalli have high numbers of Vangujjar buffaloes and the better forest. Henceforth, there is no pattern of high number of Vangujjar buffaloes being associated with poor forests (RLEK, 1997). Van Gujjars enjoy the distinction of being the most destructive of the forests (Kumar, 1995). An extensive evaluation presents a reverse situation.

The buffaloes forage mainly on leaf fodder during the winter months and on the rich grass of the Himalayan pastureland during the summer. In winter, the Gujjars lop off branches from selected fodder trees making sure that enough nodal branches and leaves are left so that the tree may regenerate during the remaining period of the year. Also, they lop the branches just before the time of leaf fall of the particular species and in this way they ensure that the tree gets the full benefit of the foliage for growth. Buffaloes manure provides a very rich fertiliser for the forests.

When the Gujjars speak about the quality of tree fodder, they speak not of trees but of leaves. It is the leaves that are used, not the trees. Lopping is traditionally done only once every second year and the Gujjars claimed that to be the preferred practice.

Van Gujjars have been asserted as the main culprits causing major forest destruction as is evident from the various reports of the government. The lopping rules were not enforced as the allotment of areas changed from year to year, the Gujjars did not know the areas to which they would return next time and so felt no sense of responsibility and the damage continued unabated (Gupta's Plan, 1949-1963). As the reports suggest that Van Gujjars ignore all lopping regulations and lopping is viewed destructive to the forest. Heavy and concentrated lopping results in trees drying and dying (Kumar, 1995). However, there are studies that compared two adjacent and similar sections of the forests of Siwaliks, one with moderate lopping and other with no lopping. The study found that the lopped area had more growing seedlings and fewer weeds (Edgaonkar, 1995).

To all these restrictions, the cultural strategy of the Van Gujjars is that Gujjars lop trees in sequence. They start with trees on the ridges where there is less water and which therefore dry out and shed their leaves earlier. As winter proceeds they move their lopping down hill and the trees lopped last are the trees close to the *rao* which keeps water for the longest time. The very last tree to be lopped is the one nearest to the *dera* before they begin their migration up to the alpine *bugyals*. Clark et al. (1986) conducted the only other lopping study in the Rajaji National Park and suggested that Van Gujjars lop trees in a sequence parallel to leaf fall. Thus, they lop each species just prior to its leaf fall in the winter season. Within species, they lop trees first at higher altitudes which have less water and earlier leaf fall than to trees in lower and wetter locales. This has been supported by studies (Sharma and Gupta, 1988) that the time of year of lopping is critical in determining the amount of impact on the tree. Trees lopped in the winter season before leaf fall grew more and produced more fodder than trees lopped in other seasons. Henceforth, validating Van Gujjars' adaptive strategy with scientific evidences.

Another cultural strategy pertaining to lopping followed by Van Gujjars is that the top main branches of the trees must be left with some leaves throughout as according to them, lopping is akin to pruning and that one shapes the tree according to light and growth patterns. Thus, one should thin out the branches to encourage growth while leaving select branches in strategic locations. Moreover, Van Gujjars prefer to lop only every other year unless there were excellent soil conditions. They judge carrying capacity of an area in relation to the number of fodder trees available so as to only lop every other year. They pointed out that lopping opens up the tree canopy, and allows more light to penetrate to the forest floor, which in turn promotes more undergrowth. Clark et al. (1986) supports the Van Gujjars' strategy by emphasising that crown cover was relatively unaffected by lopping and that there was an increase in ground vegetation in an area with lopped trees which would decrease the possibility of erosion.

Legally, the Gujjars are not allowed to plant fodder trees or even to uproot weeds within their areas but they have habitually protected small saplings of useful trees and as they herd their animals, they also pull out weeds to provide space for trees. Furthermore, the Van Gujjars suggest that buffaloes presence in the lopped area return to the soil through manure and disperses seeds. Moreover, Van Gujjars clear weeds beneath trees when they lop.

It is a known fact that economical, indirect and quick benefits from forests are much higher than the direct and sustained benefits. The forest authorities have laid down rules for lopping which includes which kind of trees are allowed as fodder trees. The ones that are forbidden are the trees estimated as economically valuable as Sal (*Shorea robusta*) which makes good timber. The Van Gujjars do not consider Sal as a good source of fodder as in the Siwaliks, Sal is mainly reckoned as a good source in summer when Deer survives on their fruits and flowers; but at that time, the Van Gujjars are leaving for the mountains. So the Van Gujjars help in indirectly enhancing the valuable economical tree variety. To add to this, there are areas of natural grasses in the Siwalik forests growing on the steep ridges; especially the economically valuable *Bhabbar* grass which is traditionally used as a fibre for rope making (*baan* making) in the nearby villages. Gujjars do not consider this grass of economic importance as a poor source of fodder instead they use other grass *Ghorilla* grass as fodder which is available in minor patches. Henceforth, Van Gujjars adapted to a strategy of involving the use of less commercially viable forest sources in their consumption patterns, yielding minimum damage to the forests resources. The Van Gujjars realise it fully well that it is essential to preserve the forests and manage them substantially to ensure livelihood security of the forest-dependent communities and also provide ecosystem services to a large population.

Furthermore, Van Gujjars require wood as fuel for cooking and heating. The Park authorities state that a Van Gujjar family recklessly consumes on an average about one quintal (100 kgs) per day of fallen fuel in the lopping areas on the pretence of protecting their cattle from carnivores and their self-protection from cold (Kumar, 1995). While on the other hand, Clark et al. (1986) give an approximate figure of around 40 kgs per day of fuel wood consumption which is supported by an extensive study made by RLEK (RLEK, 1997).The study emphasised the fact that there is no shortage of dead wood within one hundred metres of *deras* and most common reason cited for such availability of dead wood is owing to tree damage caused by elephants. Another use of the forest wood is for construction of *deras*. Here the Van Gujjars adapt to the situation by using only dead and fallen wood for *dera* poles without felling the trees and normally the construction of *dera* is after a span of four to five years. In fact, if the Van Gujjars leave the *dera* empty through the summer migration, the wood of their respective *deras* of winter encampments are either stolen or sold by the forest authorities. As a consequence, the Van Gujjars have increasingly adopted the strategy of leaving at least one family member behind to protect the *dera* from destruction, eventually leading to an enhanced sedentarisation.

Culture Based Grazing Sustenance Techniques

Grazing rights and concessions which are mostly recorded in local codes, are based on practical economic considerations, because cattle rearing have become an essential part of our rural economy.

In India, the total available grazing resource comprise 14.63 million ha of cultivable assets, 11.3 million ha of permanent pastures, 14.63 million ha of cultivable wastes, 11.3 million ha permanent pastures, 23.5 million ha fallows and 3.66 million ha of miscellaneous tree crops and groves (Dept of Economics and Statistics, Ministry of Agriculture, Government of India). Besides 55 per cent of the 77 million ha of recorded forest area, i.e. about 38.5 million ha are also available for grazing. Thus, total areas of over 91 million ha are available for grazing.

It is a known fact that unlimited grazing is harmful to scientific forestry and therefore, restrictions need to be imposed in terms of the number and manner of grazing. While the forest policy of 1952 sought to bring it under the centre by discouraging continuous grazing and encouraging rotational grazing, levying fees for grazing, keeping grazing incidence to the minimum in protected forests and eliminating grazing from regeneration areas, it laid emphasis in improving the quality of both grazing and cattle themselves, advocated restrictions on sheep grazing and total ban on goat grazing in forests.

According to the Forest Department itself, about 80 per cent of the forests in Uttar Pradesh are open for grazing throughout the year. There is a constant pressure on Van Gujjars by the Park officials blaming them of increasing their animal and human population along with increasing grazing and biotic pressure in the park area. Furthermore, the increasing sedentarisation of the Gujjars families is adding on to the pressure. Park authorities blame for the increased number of the Van Gujjars' population, yet they have not even doubled assuming 512 families in 1937 with 6 persons a family and approximately 5500 Van Gujjars today in the recent census. Although their birth rates have been high, so has infant mortality (RLEK, 1997). So the increase in Van Gujjars' population in regards to Human has been much lower than the substantial human population increase in overall Dehradun District.

As regards the Rajaji National park, Villagers from a distance of up to 10 kms use the resources of the proposed park for grazing, fuelwood, *Bhabbar* grass and fodder, with heavier dependence by those closer to the boundary. The park statistics estimate that there are 105 villages with potential dependence comprising 1.65 lakh people.

Table 1. Number of People and Livestock in Villages Peripheral to the Rajaji National Park

Name of District	*No. of villages*	*Total Population*	*No. of Livestock*	*Park Grazing permits*
Dehradun	34	78,482	31,410	12,000
Haridwar	35	63,094	28,898	30,000
Pauri Garhwal	36	24,354	16,724	22,000
Total	**105**	**1,65,930**	**77,032**	**64,000**

Source: Table excerpted from Kumar (1995) - Management Plan of Rajaji National Park.

The worst part is that most of these cattle are directly or indirectly dependent for their fodder or food on the nearby forest (Satendra, 2002). One of the most noticeable facts have been that 1/3rd of the total animals grazing in the forests of Siwaliks are goats and sheep whose grazing is harmful to the forest. Average number of sheep and goats per family among the Van Gujjars families were only 0.04 and 0.51 respectively (Hasan, 1986). However, this could not be said of hill people and other local inhabitants whose goats and sheep are hundreds of time more than those of the Gujjars. The Van Gujjars cooperate with the forest officials in implementation of the forest policy as the Van Gujjars have a very small number of sheep and goats whose grazing in the forests is discouraged under the forest policy.

Despite park officials emphasis on the damage caused by the Van Gujjars' animals, villager animals clearly put dramatically more pressure on the areas that are utilised. Further on analysis shows that Gujjars have only 13,000 buffaloes against about 2,25,000 buffaloes grazing in Uttar Pradesh forests. Thus an important fact emerging out is that only 5.8 per cent of the buffaloes grazing in forests belong to the Gujjars (Hasan, 1986). There are up to 4 or 5 times as many villager cattle using approximately 25 per cent of the area (generally the periphery) as the number of Van Gujjar buffalo using roughly 75 per cent of the area (generally the core area). In addition the villager cattle are present throughout the year for grazing depending only on grass as they do not eat the lopped leaves of the trees, adding further on to the pressure.

As pertaining to the Van Gujjars' cattle grazing pressure, the point of emphasis is that an area can sustain a higher number of cattle in winter and monsoon months than in the summer season. In the winter months, the Van Gujjars' buffaloes mostly depend on tree fodder obtained through lopping so there is no option for the buffaloes to feed on the grass which is mostly auctioned out by the forest authorities to gain revenue and is not made available to the Van Gujjars. During the summer season, the Van Gujjars migrate along with buffaloes to higher *bugyals* allowing the grass crops to regenerate, increasing the carrying capacity of the forests. During the monsoon months when the forests is in the best position of 'giving' resources, Van Gujjars are not at the 'receiving' end as they have migrated to the alpines. After returning from Alpines in autumn, it is only for a small span of time that the Van Gujjars are permitted to harvest grass. At that time in September-October lopping of new leaves of the trees is forbidden and to cover the gap the Van Gujjars are allowed to gather grass for their animals and as a source of hay for the spring months when the forest dries up and the leaves fall. However, It has been observed by the National Commission on Agriculture that grazing per se is not always harmful to forest growth. As a matter of fact, a light grazing is beneficial for regeneration condition especially in moisture type of forest (Report of National Commission on Agriculture, Part IX, 1976).

The eventual adaptive strategy of the Gujjars with regard to grazing in order to improve the nutritional status with the limited resources has been scientifically approved. The nutritional status can be best improved through feeding green fodders/silages/hay with the provision of night feeding (Mudgal, 1970). Van Gujjars practise night feeding since time immemorial. They leave their buffaloes in the forests to feed in the night and in the morning; the buffaloes arrive at the determined time and place for milking. It has been evident that the strategies followed by the Van Gujjars have helped in sustaining the forests.

Culture Based Sustenance Strategy Related to Implications of Development on the Migratory Routes:

Various developmental activities like irrigation and hydropower stations, road building, mining, etc have also adversely affected the forest cover. As per the State Forest Department Report, during last two decades around 26,000 ha. Forest land has legally been transferred for various development schemes in Uttarakhand. Increased influx of tourists almost in every corner of mountains has not only increased the number of newly constructed hotels and lodges but also increased the resource dependency and encroachment on the resources and habitats of pastoral herders inside the forests. Average annual increase in official number of tourists arrived in different protected areas of the state is 20.7 per cent during 2000-2009 (Figure-1). Different tourism agencies are taking tourists into forests and alpines for trekking and camping in the name of adventure tourism and experience the wilderness. Interestingly, they are even allowed to enter the core zone of national parks. Tourists entering nearly every curve of forests throw away plastics, glass bottles and other camping wastes which are sometimes consumed by the grazing livestock causing diseases and deaths.

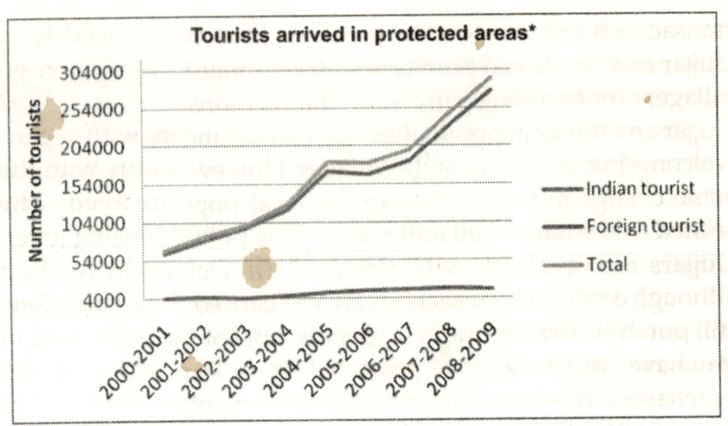

Fig. 1: *Tourists arrived in different protected areas in the State*

Data for Askot Wildlife Sanctuary were not available.
Data Source: Uttarakhand Forest Department, 2009.

With the advent of the State of Uttarakhand in 2000 and growing emphasis on infrastructure development, the Himalayan states have gone through dramatic development in the last few decades and besides infrastructure development these states have seen tremendous tourism development, extensive road building, hydropower plants, hotels, etc across the length and breadth of the Himalayas. Alongside the construction of roads in Uttarakhand accelerated after 1962 Chinese and 1965 Pakistan aggression in India. For defense purposes, many new roads even up to the most of interior places were constructed. Total 16,654 kms of metalled and 2593 kms of non-metalled roads have been constructed or developed in the region (Satendra, 2002). As a result, the Van Gujjars have had to alter their migratory routes and face problems of livestock being killed on roads, thefts and a constant pressure to move. There are instances where animals die due to eating noxious weeds growing close to the roads on degraded land.

Besides, the herds pass through a number of villages through the middle altitudes where fodder and water are available. Earlier the movement was during the day and the herds were halted in agricultural fields where substantial quantities of dung were left when the herd moved. Thus the villagers got manure without any expenditure. There were other transactions also, such as the purchase of *pural* (fodder) by the Gujjar and occasional purchase of *jhotas* (male buffaloes) by the villagers for breeding purposes. The relationship between the Gujjar and the local population was cordial and the Gujjar were welcome in the vicinity of the villages. However, there has been some change in the attitude of the local population which is related to resource availability as well as political reasons. The Gujjars are no longer welcomed in the vicinity of villages although economic transactions are still carried through. Gujjars still purchase fodder from villagers as most of the areas on their trail have been declared as protected areas. Today a Van Gujjar purchases a head load of 2 quintals at a rate of Rs 800 which is consumed by 10-12 number of buffaloes a day. Along with this, the villagers charge them for the halting spaces that they provide to Van Gujjars for camping of their buffaloes to graze on. Approximately, the Van Gujjars pay Rs 1000 per night for halting and grazing at a villagers' field. These mounting expenses have compelled poor Gujjars to adapt to situation by making camps at secluded places away from villages, at times along the highway itself. The halting places are also merged together with a constant decrease in the number of *paraos* (halts) on the migratory routes. The adaptive strategy of the Van Gujjars to overcome the developmental issues pertaining to their migratory routes has been to pursue the upward movement during the night. During migration, women endure the most by leading the *qafilas* and strategically negotiating with forest officials, simultaneously taking care of *maal* (caravan with loaded packed animals) moving faster than the *baas* (herd of buffaloes) who move slowly, herded by manfolk. Here the resultant adaptation has yielded a strategy whereby the menfolk start early with slow moving *baas* for the next halt while the womenfolk rest till dawn and reach with the *maal* faster to the destined *parao*.

With the road network in the interior of the Himalayas, the Gujjars can now use public motorised transport to carry their equipment as well as other necessary provisions up to the points from where the trek up mountainous trails to the *bugyals* (grasslands) begins. For example, in the Tons valley, public transport reaches up to Sankri, some 200 kms from Dehradun. The Gujjars migrating to Fateh Parbat, Kedarkantha, Harkidoon, Posthara, etc can use it to transport their equipment and advance parties upto Mori, Naitwad or Sankri in just one day as against about ten days taken previously. This adaptive strategy has although frictioned and attacked the very process of transhumance taking away its essence. The objective left for the Van Gujjars today is to reach the *bugyals* the shortest possible time so that the herds can graze the healthy and nutritious grasses.

Culture Based Sustenance Strategy Related to Agriculture

The growing population trend in the Himalayan hills has forced the people to convert forest and common lands into crop or horticulture production. Expansion and intensification of crop farming and increasing horticulture (apple orchards in

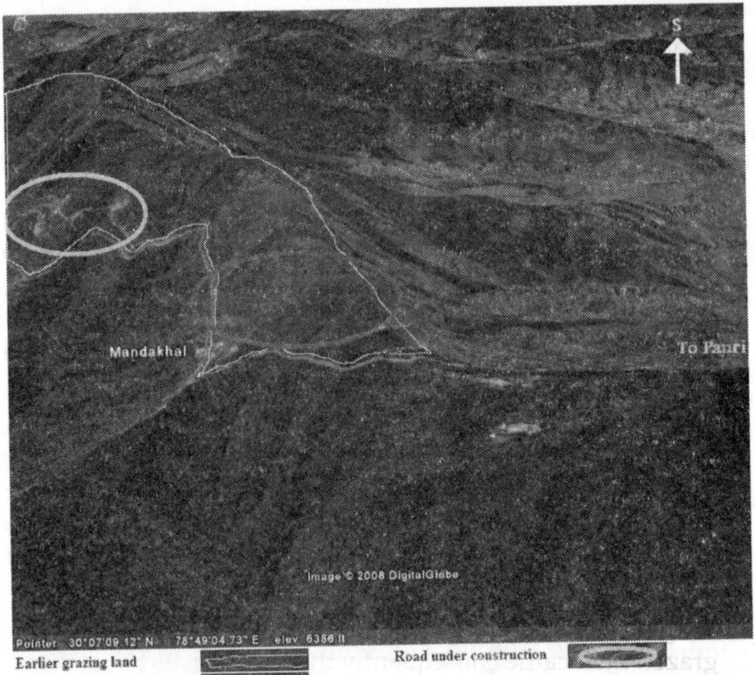

particular) have affected the pastoral migratory routes. Common lands in many villages have been converted for cultivation of cash crops such as potatoes and beans. Net sown area has increased from 13.38 per cent in 2002-03 to 13.5 per cent in 2006-07. This has caused the shrinkage of grazing lands around the pastoral villages and puts extra pressure on the alpines and forests for grazing. Apple orchards are increasing in number on open hill slopes and fenced with stone walls. Some of these open slopes had been used by the migratory pastoral herders for camping owing to ample sunshine to cope with cold weather. Now the pastoralists are compelled to camp inside nearby forests. The colder forest microclimate is harmful for the livestock. Apart from that the distance between two consecutive camping sites has been increased two to three times at some places due to the deletion of one camping site (Figure 2)

Culture Based Sustenance Strategy Related to Reduced Pastures

Across all the Himalayan states, the biggest threat to the pastoral livelihoods is the problem of shrunken pasturage. This decreasing availability of pasture resources has been due to misinformed conservation policies of these states, and encroachments on the pasture resources.

It seems that a combination of confrontation and convergence of interests works in an ongoing manner to strike a symbiosis between the agricultural and pastoral population. While the mode of land use becomes the point for contention or confrontation, the mutuality in the economic advantage brings both the groups to the bargaining platform that decides the nature of interaction between agricultural and pastoral population. The existence of such an ideal symbiotic relationship is hardly noticed anywhere (Swayam, 2001). In the high altitude too a conflict situation is creeping up. Earlier the agro-pastoralists in the high altitudes only raised goats and sheep which used to go to pastures at higher elevations where heavy cattle like buffaloes could not climb. Now they keep cattle which are grazed at the pastures of lower altitudes where Van Gujjars grazed their cattle consequently the Van Gujjars are compelled to take their buffaloes to high pastures. The presence of Gujjar's herds in the higher *bugyals* creates a conflict situation with the highland shepherds who do not want the Van Gujjars to migrate to the *bugyals* as they fall within the jurisdiction of their villages and the presence of two type of animals in the *bugyals* results in competition for resources. Sheep do not touch the grass browsed by other cattle so have to be taken further up beyond the reach of buffaloes causing hardship for the shepherds. If shepherds have the backing of traditional rights as inhabitants of the region then Van Gujjars are equipped with the official permits issued by the forest department along with a receipt of payment for the grazing in the areas. However, the Van Gujjars have devised strategies of amicably dividing the areas to be grazed with shepherds and further on the economic gains through barter of milk products and other things with the other communities with whom they share the eco-niche. The transhumant communities in Himalayas are the societies where animals have helped in adapting humans to the extreme inhospitable condition s of high altitudes, through various production processes (Farooquee et al., 1994).

The Table below shows the barter system prevalent in the alpines between the Van Gujjars and the villagers in approximate values based on observations:

Gujjars give	*Value (market value)*	*Gujjars take*	*Value (market value)*
1litre milk	Rs 22	4 kg potatoes	Rs 32 (8 per kg)
1 goat	Rs 3000	1 night field grazing	Rs 2000
1 kg butter	Rs 200	25 kg potatoes	Rs 200 (8 per kg)
1 *Khais* (woollen sheet)	Rs 450	1 *Goondh* (horse cover)	Rs 400
Total	**Rs 3672**		**Rs 2632**

Source: Based on field study

The findings clearly show that the Van Gujjars lose out in economic terms from the barter system but since they live in such inaccessible areas that easy access to availability of things of utility plays an important role in their pursuance of barter system.

In the hill districts, the Gujjars have to compete for pasture with the hill peasants. The buffaloes are heavy animals and they cannot climb up high enough to reach the rich grass pastures in the high altitudes. The buffaloes are restricted to stay in areas, already populated by sedentary peasants, the Rajput and Brahmin agriculturists mentioned creating strong friction over the limited resources. Wherever the coexistence between pastoralists and agriculturists is noticed, the balancing of confrontation and convergence of interests is a continuing process. The principles of social and economic interaction are often slandered and realigned in accordance to the group dynamics .In the context of marginal ecologies, such a situation is the most natural outcome wherever both pastoralists and agriculturists share the eco-niche (Swayam, 2001). Gujjars feel that the forest officials are much more receptive to the demands of the local settled inhabitants than to those of the Gujjars. It is the buffaloes of the Gujjars alone which are being blamed for causing landslides and deforestation. It is also the buffaloes of the Gujjars alone which are to be regulated in the forest. The villagers feel that the nomads are intruding on their traditional rights in the commons, causing overgrazing of the forest range.

Culture-based sustenance strategy related to asset capital base:

The five components that basically form the asset base in the Gujjar community have been represented with the extent of accessibility of Gujjars to the asset base. According to the Gujjars the asset base with maximum accessiblility is natural asset along with human asset while social (extent of social participation in formal social and political organisations), physical (accessibility to metalled roads, schools, PHC, etc) and financial assets (credit availability, bank facility, etc) are meagerly accessible to them.

Representation of Perceptual Accessibility of the Gujjars to the Asset Base

Despite all the allegations against them, the Van Gujjars are known for their indigenous knowledge of resource management through the strategy of rotational grazing. Rotational grazing is defined as alternating periods of grazing and rest or more

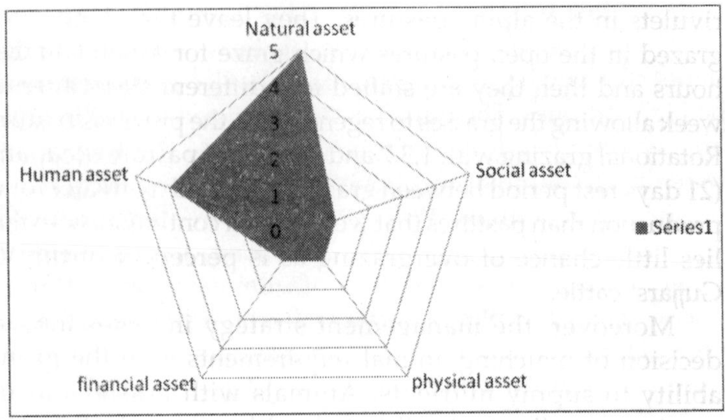

Source: Based on field study

paddocks in a grazing management unit throughout the grazing season. Production of new growth after grazing depends upon the amount of residual leaf and carbohydrate reserves because they will supply energy for plant growth. Rotational grazing with the correct stocking rate will maintain adequate stubble height and carbohydrate reserves after grazing to maximise forage regrowth. In addition to increased regrowth rates, Rotational grazing at the proper stocking rate also aids in pasture persistence by allowing better stubble height control. The Van Gujjars are well aware that rotational grazing has the potential to increase grazing efficiency, the percentage of forage produced that animals actually consume. The Van Gujjars believe that in continuously grazed pastures, the greater proportion of forage is trampled, soiled and rejected by the animals than in rotationally grazed pastures. Furthermore they add that grazing cattle retain approximately 20 per cent of the nutrients ingested from forages and the remaining 80 per cent is excreted through feces and urine. Feces and urine are important sources of nutrients for forages, mainly for grazing systems with low inputs; thereby rotational grazing followed by the Van Gujjars increases the uniformity of distribution of the excreta. The Van Gujjars in the literal practice of rotational grazing graze their animals in the creation of natural feed bunks of different slopes of pastures separated by the streams or rivulets in the alpine pastures. They leave their cattle to be grazed in the open pastures which graze for around 14 to 16 hours and then they are shifted to a different slope after one week allowing the grasses to regenerate in the previous pastures. Rotational grazing with 1,3.7 and 21 days of pasture occupation (21 days rest period between grazing) resulted in greater forage production than pastures that were grazed continuously so there lies little chance of overgrazing as is perceived of the Van Gujjars' cattle.

Moreover, the management strategy includes inherent decision of matching animal requirements with the pasture ability to supply nutrients. Animals with greater nutrient requirements (i.e. first calf buffaloes) have access to pastures first and graze the greater nutritive value forage. They can be followed by cattle with lower nutrient requirements(i.e. mature buffaloes).The young Van Gujjar males are designated the responsibility of periodic handling of the grazing cattle under a watchful inspection of a senior Van Gujjar male who makes timely management decisions pertaining to the strategy of Rotational grazing.

Culture Based Sustenance Strategy Related to Protected Areas

The Indian Himalayan Region (IHR) in terms of the uniqueness and richness of biodiversity elements is represented fairly well (15 National Parks and 59 Sanctuaries covering 9.6 per cent of the geographical area) within the PA network of India (Rawal and Dhar, 2001). The legally designated protected areas (PAs) and other conservation sites in India comprise 614 units, including National Park, Sanctuary and Biosphere Reserve, covering about 7.35 of the total geographical area. Stretches of grasslands and alpine meadows locally called Kharak or *bugyals* are often found intermixed with the forest vegetation in this region. Other grassy patches of rather recent origin are being developed due to deforestation, grazing and occasional fires. These grazing areas have been under moderate to high grazing pressure by sedentary as well as by migratory graziers.

In the Himalayas, comparable conflict developed as colonial governments appropriated forests from local communities to promote scientific forestry (Guha, 1990). Similarly, the creation of National parks and protected areas has led to the removal of local inhabitants and/or their exclusion from traditionally used natural resources (Maikhuri et al., 1999). The Van Gujjar families migrating to the Alpine pastures today face the same fate of being the 'victims of conservation' (Gooch, 2009). It started in the forest of foothills at the beginning of the 1990s with Rajaji National Park, but during the last decade most of the summer pastureland in the upper ranges has also been converted into national parks, global heritage sites or sanctuaries. The tree line forest of the park is grazed by the buffaloes of 13 Van Gujjar families who have the official grazing permits ever since the official permits were allotted from the Forest Department and not a single new permit was issued after that. The Forest Department restricted the entry of Van Gujjars into the Govind National Park. The situation worsened all the more after 2006.The migrating families were not issued the grazing permit and allowed to move only on humanitarian grounds. All the stakeholders dependent on the Park resources are displaced. As an effect there is a large pastoral population in the Himalayas which is affected by the formation of parks where their rights to access pasture have been denied for the purposes of biodiversity conservation (GOI, 2009).

Evidence is gradually accumulating that pastoralists livestock can benefit the conservation of wild animals, especially predators. Often there is a long history of co-evolution between wild species and livestock. Evicting the livestock from wildlife reserves may lead to an exodus of predators, or result in habitat changes that make it unattractive for wildlife, e.g. in the Bharatpur Bird Sanctuary in eastern Rajasthan, ban on grazing by buffaloes led to the disappearance of Siberian cranes that had frequented the sanctuary (Ramsar Forum, 1998). Similarly, the Van Gujjars do not see wild predators as essentially antagonistic to them and their herds and they do not seek vengeance when one of their animals is carried off. What they say is that also tigers and leopards belong in the natural order of the forest and that they—just as the Gujjars and their buffaloes—have rights to be there (Gooch, 1998).

When livestock is barred from entry to protected areas, there is often very high growth of grasses, regularly leading to forest fires. Local people know that grazing animals control the growth of grass, so preventing the spread of fires. This is supported by scientific observations in the southern United States that showed how livestock grazing measurably reduces the fire hazard by removing and breaking up potential fuel and by establishing trails through the forest (Campbell, 1954).

Local people also know that livestock browsing stimulates trees to branch, leading to denser and more luxuriant top growth. Research in the Sahara confirmed the stimulating effect of camel grazing on plant growth (Gauthier - Pilters and Dagg, 1981). Observations from the field study show that the Van Gujjars' buffaloes who are left for grazing for around 14-16 hours graze for 2 hours in an instance and then browse for one hour leading to an enhanced top growth. Further on, browsing leads to dispersal of seeds by being carriers through their skin. Henceforth, migratory Van Gujjars' livestock also play an important role in the dispersal and germination of seeds and in linking different ecosystems, thus contributing to plant biodiversity.

Culture Based Man-Animal Relationships

The diverse natural habitats all over the Himalayan region are a rich repository of plant diversity that are used for a variety of purposes, i.e. food, fibre, fodder, medicine, spices, dyes, etc. Forests represent a whole way of life for tribal peoples and as such their life and economy are, therefore, intimately interwoven with the forests and forest wealth. In the Indian Himalayan region, the use of medicinal herbs/plants is still a tradition continued by ethical/local communities. Even today, the traditional healthcare practices (household remedies) hold much potential or most of the people depend upon the common household remedies (Farooquee, 1994; Maikhuri et al., 2000).This is a fact that 1,748 medicinal plants, 675 wild edibles, 155 sacred plants, 118 essential oil-yielding medicinal plants and 279 fodder plants have been recorded from the Indian Himalayan region (Samant et al., 1998).

The Van Gujjar tribal communities have a wealth of knowledge on the use of medicinal plants in their locality. Collection of medicinal plants from the wild has been long conducted while grazing livestock in the forests and alpine pastures. The Gujjars have a fairly good knowledge of the various diseases their buffaloes suffer from. These diseases are not peculiar to Van Gujjars' buffaloes as the livestock of the region as a whole suffer from them, but what is of special interest is that the Gujjars over the generations have preserved the knowledge of a curative system which is traditional and indigenous. Earlier limited medical assistance was available as there were very few veterinary hospitals or dispensaries within easy reach of the Gujjars.

The Gujjars use their indigenous curative system when the characteristics of a disease gets evident like Khurpaka (foot and mouth disease), Galghontu(Haemorrhagic septicaemia), Nakada/thanela (mastitis),Taku(epifemoral fever), Rinderpest and Surra.They have indigenous prescriptions in which concoctions of roots and tubers as well as a mixture of ash and whey are administered to the afflicted animal. Apart from the knowledge of these diseases, the Gujjars are aware of the afflictions caused by various weeds including lantana and poisonous grasses or creepers.

The Gujjars likewise do diagnose some human diseases and have their own indigenous systems of curing them. In case of humans too the recourse to modern medicines was kept as a last resort. However, of late Van Gujjars while going to alpines carry a substantial amount of allopathic medicines as the pasture areas are inaccessible in case of emergencies, e.g. the Van Gujjars migrating to Govind National Park need to trail through at least 21 kms of dense forests in order to reach the nearest medical help at Sankri.

Discussion

With the decreasing pasture land, disturbed migratory routes, decline in Jajmani rights, restriction of access to forest resources, enclosure of forests, expansion of irrigated agriculture, breakdown of village institutions, deterioration of pasture and common property resources, etc, the Van Gujjars face severe problems and challenges for their livelihood security.

Uttarakhand has got a new name—the "Energy State" of India for its massive hydel power projects almost on every big and small river. Large areas of forests as well as settlements and agriculture land are diverted into dam sites or reservoir. Forest grazing lands on migratory routes of pastoral herders are also lost due to these dam constructions. However, the Van Gujjars have adapted to the situation by migrating at night and halting at secluded places yet at times owing to heavy traffic and construction sites they face difficulties, opting for the tougher terrains as migratory routes. Moreover, the growing population trend in the Himalayan hills has forced the people to convert forest and common lands into crop or horticulture production. Expansion and intensification of crop farming and increasing horticulture (apple orchards in particular) have affected the pastoral migratory routes. Common lands in many villages have been converted for cultivation of cash crops such as potatoes and beans. Net sown area has increased from 13.38 per cent in 2002-03 to 13.5 per cent in 2006-07. This has caused the shrinkage of grazing lands around the pastoral villages and puts extra pressure on the alpines and forests for grazing. The Van Gujjars adapt by merging the halting places.

The Van Gujjars rely heavily on an economic system based primarily on animal husbandry. The primary resource of the Van Gujjars is livestock and as their territorial rights are confined to marginal environments, it is imperative for the community to move seasonally in order to ensure adequate grazing and water for the livestock. They occupy marginal lands because the better favoured environments are almost occupied by settled permanent agriculturists. Henceforth, making use of the environments that other economic systems either do not want or cannot use. As regards their occupation, the Van Gujjars may be regarded as more of an exception than as a rule among pastoralists of the world, as they rely almost entirely on their herds for their livelihood (Gooch, 1998). The Van Gujjars form a monopoly in the organic milk market with their cattle feeding on nutritious grass resulting in high milk yield. The

Transhumant communities in Himalayas are the societies where animals have helped in adapting humans to the extreme inhospitable conditions of high altitudes, through various production processes (Farooquee et al., 1994). Due to non-existence of commercial markets in the high altitude alpines, the Gujjars adapt to converting the major part of milk production to butter and ghee to be sold to the dealers on the way back to the foothills. The latest adaptive strategy ensued by the youngsters is to work as labourers in the apple orchards or in forestry planting saplings or carrying timbers for supplementary income in the Alpines.

With the advent of 'Operation Flood', the Van Gujjars were suggested some form of change of animal stock either by crossbreeding or by getting rid of old herds and buying new high performance buffaloes. The Van Gujjars have outrightly rejected this adaptation as they stress that animals from outside will not be able to live in the forest. They emphasise that animals from outside would not be able to adapt in the climatic conditions of alpine, walking for miles in all possible harsh conditions of no water and no food. The animals from outside need to be stall-fed which is not the same for Van Gujjar buffaloes as they walk around and graze. As an alternative adaptive strategy, the Van Gujjars have accepted new ways of marketing milk and milk products. However, what is evident from an interaction with them is that this rejection of crossbreeding strategy is in fact another adaptive strategy of the Van Gujjars in order to pursue their transhumance because with the new animals it would no longer be possible to maintain traditional patterns of milk production from the roughage of marginal forests which would mean accepting a settled life outside forests and giving up nomadism.

The insecurity taking to land use pattern in the protected areas is seeping into their existence as the Van Gujjar families entering Govind National Park are allowed to enter the National Park after paying of the grazing taxes. Yet they are not issued any receipts for the paid taxes, depriving them of any evidence of their claim on the forest resources under the 'other traditional communities'. Earlier upon reaching the Alpines, the Van Gujjars constructed the roof of their *deras* which took almost

10-15 days to be prepared by leaves of *Kaandlu* trees. This roof was so solid that it lasted for almost 40 years and needed some repairing every year. But today the Van Gujjars with the increasing insecurity limit themselves to the usage of plastic sheets as the roof of their *deras* which is more instant to use. This adaptation strategy had moved them further from a natural organic environment to a more synthetic and artificial one. Ultimate survival strategy gets depicted in the amalgamation of various fragmented *deras* of the lower Siwaliks into one big *dera* at Alpines in order to conserve the limited resources; emphasising the fact that the greater the number, the greater would be the depletion of resources.

Participation in social networks has the potential to reduce vulnerability and strengthen resilience. Social assets can also reduce insecurity and vulnerability in the relationship of different actors. Gujjars survive on typical **indigenous social institutions** which have their unsaid codes of conduct. The *van panchayat*s formed within this community constitute the older members of both the genders and every matter is solved through intensive discussions voiced in the van panchayat meeting. All the males of the Gujjar community attend the meeting but it is an unsaid rule that a decision pertaining to any problem is never arrived on the first day. Males go back home, discuss the matter with the respective females of the family and then voice their concerns regarding the matter at the meeting the next day after which a final decision is taken. The latest trend in the Foothills is the membership of the Gujjar participation in civil society institutions (NGOs) like RLEK and SOPHIA who work tirelessly for their welfare. This association ensures individual affiliation to the immediate society outside their own community setting. **Barter exchange** forms an integral part of the local culture and weekly haats are a well established social and economic institution. Social time forms an integral component of social capital for in the Gujjars' daily time use follows seasonality and the Islamic calendar, while the daily time use pattern of both men and women varies immensely between foothills and Alpines. The Table below presents information on daily time use of women in the foothills and in the Alpines:

Daily Time Use of Women in the Foothills and in the Alpines

Activity	*Foothills*	*In the Alpines*
Strenous work	1 hr	2 hrs
Non-strenuous work	1 hr 30 mins	1 hrs
Household chores	7 hrs	3 hrs
Childcare	3 hrs	3 hrs
Total work day	12 hrs 30 mins	9 hrs
Time to one self	2 hrs 30 mins	5 hrs
Sleep	9 hrs	10 hrs

Source: Based on fieldwork

The Table enumerates that although women tend to do more strenuous work in the Alpines because of the daily task of churning of butter out of the larger milk yield but the rest of her day life is more comfortable with the water points in the Alpines being within proximity and leisure and resting hours being more. However, in the foothills, they work tirelessly between lopping, collection of water and in tending to domestic chores along with childcare. Nevertheless, the stay in Alpines is one of more leisure, pleasure and bountiful in terms of monetary gain.

Van Gujjar women enjoy the status equal to men. The Van Gujjar women adapt to the changing situations by a strategy of the eldest women leading the herd on the migratory route in order to negotiate with the forest officials. Further on, the women seem more willing and more adaptive to modern ways of family planning and they have shown a positive result during a project of family planning launched by the government.

Eventual adaptive strategy of Van Gujjars for the sustainability of their very identity survival has been adding of the prefix *Van* (forest) to the common Gujjar name in order to stand demarcated from the countless other Gujjar groups in Northern India. The strategy has sustained to an extent of getting referred to as Van Gujjar even in the official government documents.

Conclusion

As the eventual outcome of the paper, the need of the hour is inclusion of Van Gujjars in 'Socialised forestry where people are an inherent part of the process of management, sustainability and conservation of nature. Sustainable pastoralism would be the only answer to the unpredictable climate changes and ever changing landscapes of the Himalayas. Pastoralists are the best judges to ascertain the replenishment of depleting resources. The Van Gujjars are inevitable for maintaining the biodiversity in the alpine pastures through grazing and can best maintain the lower Siwaliks forest through plantation and conservation of local species of fodder trees. As long as forest resources are there and there is existence of local people who need them, nomadic pastoralists like the Van Gujjars will keep migrating as they are using the unutilised resources which otherwise would go waste. There ought to be a comprehensive plan for the Van Gujjars like socialised forestry leading to the propagation of scientific afforestation. This informal scientific knowledge can be amalgamated with a formal education system with special emphasis on the ethno veterinarian systems of livestock herd management along with stress on local breeds need to be recognised, protected and capitalised on. Therefore, the impeccable strategy of constructing a realistic development project with a maintained nomadic lifestyle, emphasising a life within the framework of 'normality' would be the ultimate sustainability measure for a sustainable development of nomadic people sharing symbiotic dependence on animals and nature.

References

Clark, Sevill and Watts, R. 1986, *Habitat Utilisation by Gujar Pastoralists in Rajaji Wildlife Sanctuary.* Dehradun: Wildlife Institute of India.

Edgaonkar, A. 1995, *Utilisation of Major Fodder Tree Species with Respect to the Food Habits of Domestic Buffaloes in Rajaji National Park, India.* Abstracts: Ninth Annual Research Seminar 25th-26th September, p. 14.

Farooquee, N.A., 1994, *Transhumance in the Central Himalaya: A Study of its Impact on Environment.* Ph.D. Thesis, HNB Garhwal University, Srinagar Garhwal, India.

Gauthier-Pilters, Anne Innis Dagg, 1981, *The Camel: Its Evolution, Ecology, Behaviour, and Relationship to Man,* University of Chicago Press

Gooch, Pernille, 1998, *At the Tail of the Buffalo,* Department of Sociology, Lund University.

Gooch, P., 2009, Victims of conservation or rights as forest dwellers: Van Gujjar pastoralists between contesting codes of law, *Conservation and Society* 7(4): 239-248

Government of India (2009), *State of Environment Report, India, 2009.* Ministry of Environment and Forests, Government of India 2009.

Hasan, Amir, 1986, *A Tribe in Turmoil: A Socioeconomic Study of Jammu Gujjars of Uttar Pradesh*, Uppal Publishing House, New Delhi.

Kumar, D., 1995, *Management Plan of Rajaji National Park.* Vol. I & II, Rajaji National Park, Dehradun.

Maikhuri, R.K., Nautiyal, S., Rao, K.S. and Saxena, K.G. (1998), Role of medicinal Plants in the Traditional Health Care System: A Case Study from Nanda Devi Biosphere Reserve. *Current Science* 75 (2): 152-157.

Poffenberger, Mark, 1995, The Resurgence of Community forest Management in the Jungle Mahals of West Bengal, in David Arnold and Ram Chandra Guha (eds.), *Nature, Culture, Imperialism: Essays on the Environmental History of South Asia.* Oxford University Press, New Delhi.

Rawal, R.S. and Dhar, U. (1997), Sensitivity of Timberline Flora in Kumaun Himalaya, India:Conservation Implications. *Arctic and Alpine Research* 29(1): 112-121.

Ramakrishna, P.S., Chandrashekara, U.M., Elouard, C., Guilmoto, C.Z., Maikhuri, R.K., Rao, K.S., Sankar, S. and Saxena, K.G. (eds.) 2000, *Mountain Biodiversity, Land Use Dynamics and Traditional Ecological Knowledge.* Oxford & IBH, New Delhi.

Ramsar Forum, 1998, "Buffalos and wetlands" – Grazing in wetland management. www.ramsar.org/forum/forum_buffalos.htm

RLEK (Rural Litigation and entitlement Kendra), 1997, *Community Forest Management in Protected Areas: Van Gujjar proposal for the Rajaji area*, Dehradun, Natraj Publishers.

Swayam, S., 2001, Sedentarization and Adaptation Strategies of Pastoral Communities in Gujarat: Some Reflections on the Change in Labour Management, *Journal of Indian Anthropological Society*, Vol 20(1).

Satendra, 2002, *Disaster Management in the Hills*, Concept Publishing Company, New Delhi.

Sharma, S.K. and Gupta, R.K., 1988, Effect of seasonal lopping on the top feed production and growth of *Prosopis cineraria. Indian J. For.* 44: 253–255.

Singh, K., 1994, *Managing Common Pool Resources*, Oxford University Press, New Delhi.

Samant, S.S., Dhar, U. and Rawal, R.S. (1998), Biodiversity Status of a Protected Area of West Himalaya-1. Askot Wildlife Sanctuary. *International Journal of Sustainable Development and World Ecology* 5: 193-203.

Report of the National Commission on Agriculture, Part IX, Forestry, Ministry of Agriculture, Government of India, New Delhi, 1976.

Valdiya, K.S. (1987), *Environmental Geology: The Indian Context.* Tata Mcgraw Hill, New Delhi, p. 83.